George Kaloudis

EUROPE: RETHINKING THE BOUNDARIES

To my parents, Ted and Phyllis, with love

-PM

To the mouth from the south

-LTH

Europe: Rethinking the Boundaries

Edited by
PHILOMENA MURRAY
University of Melbourne
and
LESLIE HOLMES
University of Melbourne

Ashgate

Aldershot • Brookfield USA • Singapore • Sydney

Published by
Ashgate Publishing Ltd
Gower House
Croft Road
Aldershot
Hants GU11 3HR
England

Ashgate Publishing Company
Old Post Road
Brookfield
Vermont 05036
USA

British Library Cataloguing in Publication Data
Europe : rethinking the boundaries
   1. Boundaries 2.Territory, National - Europe 3.Europe - Boundaries
   I.Murray, Philomena II.Holmes, Leslie, 1948-
   320.1'2'094

Library of Congress Cataloging-in-Publication Data
Europe : rethinking the boundaries / edited by Philomena Murray and
  Leslie Holmes.
     p.   cm.
  Based on a conference held in Melbourne in September 1995, and
organized by the Contemporary European Studies
Association of Australia (CESAA)
  Includes bibliographical references and index.
  ISBN 1-84014-003-8 (alk. paper)
   1. European federation. 2. European Union. I. Murray,
Philomena. II. Holmes, Leslie. III. Contemporary European Studies
Association of Australia.
D1060.E82 1998   98-19208
321'.04'094--dc21   CIP

ISBN 1 84014 003 8

Printed and bound in Great Britain by MPG Books Ltd, Bodmin, Cornwall

Contents

Preface

This book is basically the outcome of a conference that was held in Melbourne in September 1995 on a theme that has been adopted as the present volume's title. The conference was organised by the Contemporary European Studies Association of Australia (*CESAA*), and attracted participants from all over Australia.

The book has taken longer to produce than either the editors or the other contributors would have preferred, for two related reasons. First, one of the editors (Holmes) left Australia for almost a year of constant travel (work-related, of course!) just as the original version of the book was nearing completion. Unfortunately, and as the second reason, Murray was hit by a feral car shortly after Holmes' departure; a major outcome of this accident is that she has been unable to do more than a few minutes' work a day since November 1996. Only since Holmes' return has it been possible for the two editors to liaise closely with each other again on a day-to-day basis, and hence to reactivate and complete the project.

But the delay has in hindsight been advantageous. It has meant that all contributors have had an opportunity to reconsider and improve their original pieces; in one or two cases, the final version is considerably different from the original. In all events, all contributors updated their chapters in late 1997. Given that the various topics covered are at least as significant now as they were in 1995, and in light of the updating, we believe that the present volume has not suffered because of the delay.

We would like publicly to thank Iona Annett, Annmarie Elijah, Craig Lonsdale, Carolyn O'Brien, John Polesel and Tim Szlachetko for the hours and effort they contributed to the production of this book; each had an important role to play, and we are grateful to them. We also wish to acknowledge the considerable support of various kinds given to us by the Department of Political Science at the University of Melbourne.

Philomena Murray and Leslie Holmes
Melbourne, January 1998

About the Contributors

Christine Agius is completing her PhD in the Department of Political Science at the University of Melbourne, and is currently researching at the University of Manchester. Her research interests include European foreign policy, the politics of the European Union, enlargement issues, security structures in Europe, and neutrality. She has taught in undergraduate courses within the Department of Political Science at the University of Melbourne. Published works include articles on the enlargement debate in the EU; the backlash towards EU membership in Sweden, Austria and Finland; and the European response to French nuclear tests.

Christopher Barrett is a former research student in the Department of Political Science at the University of Melbourne. His interest is in the domestic politics and foreign policy of the Federal Republic of Germany. He is currently the National Security and Trade Adviser to the Australian Federal Leader of the Opposition.

Rémy Davison presently teaches in the Department of Political Science at the University of Melbourne. Previously, he has lectured in international business at Griffith University, and in European politics and International Relations at Monash, La Trobe and Deakin universities in Melbourne. He has published articles on international trade and the automotive industry in the *Melbourne Journal of Politics* and the *Flinders Journal of History and Politics*. His recent publications include *Euromoney: EMU and Integration* (Griffith University, 1995). He is joint editor of the *Australasian Journal of European Integration*. His research interests include EU economic integration, international relations and international political economy. He is presently completing a study on the political economy of the Single European Market.

Leslie Holmes has been Professor of Political Science at the University of Melbourne since 1988 and Director of its Contemporary Europe Research Centre since 1997. Among his numerous publications are *The Policy Process in Communist States* (Sage, 1981), *Politics in the Communist World* (Oxford University Press, 1986), *The End of Communist Power* (Polity and Oxford University Press, 1993) and *Post-Communism* (Polity and Duke University Press, 1997). He is a past President of the Australasian Political Studies Association, and is currently a member of the ICCEES (International Council for Central and East European Studies) Executive and editor of the *ICCEES Newsletter*. He was elected a Fellow of the Academy of the Social Sciences in Australia in September 1995, and was Jean Monnet Visiting Professor at the European University Institute in Florence in March 1997.

F. Damaso Marengo has studied at the universities of Genoa, London School of Economics, Chicago and Sydney. He is currently an officer in the Australian Department of Foreign Affairs and Trade with responsibility for European Union issues. Until 1989, he was an academic researching and lecturing in political science, history and international relations in various universities in the UK, USA, Italy, South Africa and Australia. Dr Marengo has published on Italian politics, industrial relations, management issues and political corruption. His major interests in international relations are perceptions and the manner in which they can affect international communication and bargaining perceptions.

Philomena Murray is a Senior Lecturer in the Department of Political Science at the University of Melbourne and founder President of the Contemporary European Studies Association of Australia (CESAA). She is co-editor of *Visions of European Unity* with Paul Rich (Westview, 1996) and co-editor of *Europe in the 1990s: Australia's Options* with Lilian Topic (CESAA, 1994). She was a diplomat from 1984 to 1989 in Dublin and Paris, and has worked in European Union institutions in Brussels. She has written on European integration, major actors in the European Union and the party groups in the European Parliament, and is currently completing a book on EU governance.

Jeremy Salt is an Associate Professor in the Department of Political Science, Bilkent University, Ankara. He formerly lectured in the Department of Political Science and the Department of Middle Eastern Studies at the University of Melbourne, where he took his PhD, and was a Visiting Professor at Bogaziçi (Bosporus) University in Istanbul. He has written numerous articles on late Ottoman history and Turkish, Arab, Palestinian and Islamic politics, for journals including *Middle Eastern Studies* and *Journal of Palestine Studies*. Other publications include *Imperialism, Evangelism and the Ottoman Armenians 1876-1896* (Frank Cass, London, 1993), 'An Islamic scholar activist: Mustafa al Siba`i and the Islamic movement in Syria 1945-1954' (*Journal of Arabic, Islamic and Middle Eastern Studies*, forthcoming) and 'Nationalism and the Rise of Muslim Sentiment in Turkey' (*Middle Eastern Studies*, 31 (1), 1995).

Glenda Sluga is Director of European Studies and lectures in modern European history at the University of Sydney. She has published articles on nationalism and identity in *Nations and Nationalism*, the *Journal of Contemporary History*, and *Gender and History*, among others. She is currently completing two books - *The Boundaries of Identity: the problem of Trieste in the twentieth century* and *Gendering European History* (with Professor Barbara Caine).

Acronyms and Abbreviations

ABB	Asea Brown Boveri
AMG	Allied Military Government
APEC	Asia Pacific Economic Cooperation
ARENA	Advanced Research on the Europeanisation of the Nation state
AWAC	Airborne Warning and Control
CAP	Common Agricultural Policy
CDU	Christian Democratic Union (Germany)
CEC	Commission of the European Communities
CEE	Central and Eastern European (states)
CEFTA	Central European Free Trade Area
CESAA	Contemporary European Studies Association of Australia
CET	Common External Tariff
CFSP	Common Foreign and Security Policy
CIS	Commonwealth of Independent States
CJTF	Combined Joint Task Force
CMEA	Council for Mutual Economic Assistance
Comecon	(same as CMEA)
Coreper	(Committee of Permanent Representatives)
CSCE	Conference on Security and Cooperation in Europe
CSU	Christian Social Union (Germany)
EC	European Community
ECE	East Central Europe
ECSC	European Coal and Steel Community
ECU	European Currency Unit
EDC	European Defence Community
EEA	European Economic Area
EEC	European Economic Community
EES	European Economic Space
EFTA	European Free Trade Area
EMI	European Monetary Institute
EMS	European Monetary System
EMU	Economic and Monetary Union
EP	European Parliament

EPC	European Political Cooperation
ERM	Exchange Rate Mechanism
ESDI	European Security and Defence Identity
EU	European Union
EUROFOR	Euro-Mediterranean Force
FDI	Foreign Direct Investment
FDP	Free Democratic Party (Germany)
FPÖ	(Freedom Party of Austria)
FRG	Federal Republic of Germany
FSU	Former Soviet Union
GATT	General Agreement on Tariffs and Trade
GDR	German Democratic Republic
GEMSU	(Treaty on) German Economic, Monetary and Social Union
GM	General Motors
GNP	Gross National Product
IFOR	Implementation Force
IGC	Intergovernmental Conference
JHA	Justice and Home Affairs
MAD	Mutually Assured Destruction
MEP	Member of European Parliament
NACC	North Atlantic Cooperation Council
NATO	North Atlantic Treaty Organisation
OECD	Organisation for Economic Cooperation and Development
OJ	Official Journal (of the European Communities)
OOPEC	Office for the Official Publications of the European Communities
OPEC	Organisation of Petroleum Exporting Countries
OSCE	Organisation for Security and Cooperation in Europe
ÖVP	(Austrian People's Party)
PARP	Planning and Review Process
PFP	Partnership for Peace
PHARE	Poland and Hungary: Aid for the Restructuring of Economies
PKK	(Kurdistan Workers' Party)
PLO	Palestine Liberation Organisation
PRC	People's Republic of China
SEA	Single European Act
SFOR	Stabilisation Force
SIM	Single Internal Market
SMEs	Small and medium-sized enterprises

SPD	(Social Democratic Party of Germany)
SPÖ	(Social Democratic Party of Austria)
TEMPUS	Trans-European Mobility Scheme for University Studies (for CEE countries)
TFCMA	Treaty of Friendship, Cooperation and Mutual Assistance
TEU	Treaty on European Union
TNCs	Transnational corporations
UEF	Union of European Federalists
UK	United Kingdom
UN	United Nations
UNICE	Union of Industrial and Employers' Confederations of Europe
UNPROFOR	United Nations Protection Force
USA	United States of America
USSR	Union of Soviet Socialist Republics
VAT	Value Added Tax
WEU	Western European Union
WTO	Warsaw Treaty Organisation (to 1991); World Trade Organisation (since 1995)

1 Introduction
Europe: Rethinking the Boundaries

PHILOMENA MURRAY

Since the 1980s, there has been a renewed surge of interest in the meaning of 'Europe' and a reconsideration of its boundaries. There are several reasons for this rekindled interest, and why it is on the European agenda. One is that the European Community (EC), known since 1993 as the European Union (EU), has both deepened and widened. Nine countries have joined the original six in the past two decades, including the newest members, Austria, Finland and Sweden in 1995. At the same time as this widening of the EU's boundaries, there has been a deepening of cooperation among its member states. The two major treaty reviews, the 1990–1 Intergovernmental Conference and Maastricht Treaty on European Union (TEU) and the 1996–7 Intergovernmental Conference and resultant Amsterdam Treaty, are symptomatic of moves towards further integration of these member states.

Secondly, the collapse of communism has been accompanied by the disintegration of the three federal communist states that existed until the early 1990s—Czechoslovakia, Yugoslavia and the USSR. For Claus Offe, this redrawing of boundaries—of which there could be yet more—is as much a part of what he calls the 'triple transition' in the post-communist world as are the more obvious transitions in the economy, and in the polity from a one-party state to a democracy.[1]

These first two factors—one centripetal, the other centrifugal—highlight the fact that both Western and Eastern Europeans are being pulled and are pulling in different directions simultaneously.

A third factor, like the second, derives from the collapse of communist power. For decades during the Cold War, the West encouraged anti-communist moves in Eastern Europe and the USSR, and argued that one of the salient features of the 'real democracy' it advocated for the communist bloc was freedom to travel and re-locate. But when the walls came tumbling down—literally in the case of Berlin—Western Europe soon discovered that there were problems in encouraging excessive freedom of movement. Germany, for instance, was inundated with asylum-seekers from the formerly communist

1

world, who placed severe strains on a system that was already finding it considerably more difficult and expensive to incorporate the former German Democratic Republic (GDR) than originally anticipated. As more and more East and Central Europeans were denied proper access to Western countries, so the accusations of hypocrisy and 'sell-out' increased. Now it seemed that in place of communist borders that kept people in were Western borders that kept people out—a 'Fortress Europe'.

However, the issue of boundaries in contemporary Europe is by no means confined to post-communist versus Western states. Another aspect is the highly controversial one of alleged civilisational boundaries, as elaborated by Samuel Huntington. But is this argument valid in the case of Europe? This is another question to consider in this volume.

There have been remarkable transformations of boundaries in Europe during the last half century—and particularly in the last decade of the twentieth century—and many of these are related to the creation of the European Community and the division of Europe into East and West with the Cold War and its implications. The transformations which have taken place are not simply those of territorial boundaries, although these have been considerable. In addition, there is an alteration of the boundaries of action of the nation state in the European and international arenas. There have been shifts in the concepts of citizenship, nationality and supranationality in Europe. A discussion of boundaries must encompass several strands and developments. These are explored in this Introduction and in the chapters of this volume.

It is the intention of this collection to reflect on, and rethink, the nature of boundaries in Europe, particularly since the end of the Cold War, the end of the Soviet Empire and the ratification of the TEU—a Europe that is deeply affected by the end of the division of Europe into East and West, and one that is in many ways deeply connected to Russia as well as to countries like Turkey, whose precise relationship with Europe is disputed.

The chapters analyse the implications for the nation state of the numerous centripetal and centrifugal forces currently operating, including the relevance of the Huntington thesis; the impact of European integration on the nation state, democracy and for the EU itself; the implications for Europe of a unified Germany; the interaction and alleged cultural clash of Islam and Europe; the impact of the Mediterranean countries on the EU; how ethnic and gender identity impact upon Balkan boundaries; and how the concept of neutrality is affected by changing boundaries.

The boundaries in flux

The boundaries of Europe are under scrutiny from a number of perspectives. Firstly, there is the controversial issue of the enlargement of the membership of the EU and hence an extension of the EU's border. Secondly, boundaries are questioned in terms of the re-examination of the boundaries of governance. What is at issue, and often contested, is a radical rethinking of the nature of economic, fiscal and monetary policy, particularly with Economic and Monetary Union and the single currency, the Euro.

Thirdly, and related to this new type of political and economic organisation, the EU has promoted the extension of the citizenship principle, in terms of rights, in the creation of a type of European citizenship in the TEU. Fourthly, there has been debate on the extension of membership of the North Atlantic Treaty Organisation (NATO) to include East European states and a rethinking of the dimensions of the European Security and Defence Identity. Fifthly, there is a re-examination of the civilisations of Europe and its states, and a wide-ranging discussion regarding the Huntington thesis on a 'clash of civilisations'. Finally, Europe is witnessing a rethinking of the boundaries of community and belonging, of inclusion and exclusion in terms of who is considered European, a national or citizen, and who is a migrant, often a non-citizen in terms of shared community myths, experiences and imaginations.

There is a clear challenge to rethink the boundaries of Europe itself—where does Europe end and begin? It has increasingly become apparent that the word 'Europe' is not synonymous with the EC, the EU or Western Europe, that it is no longer acceptable for politicians, analysts or policy makers to retain an Atlanticist or West European view of the continent.

The meaning of Europe: 'detaching geographical boundaries'

Europe has several meanings and interpretations. This century until the end of the Cold War saw the word Europe associated primarily with Western Europe and Atlanticism, and in particular with the EC. Joll referred to the Europe of the Treaty of Rome, which established the European Economic Community (EEC) as a 'provincial affair'.[2] Salgado refers to East European states asking (almost as outsiders) for support from 'Europe', or wishing to join 'Europe',[3] and correctly sees the EC as not being representative of whatever Europe may be. She sees the EC as a portion of the divided Europe as follows:

> Redefined in this narrow sense of a dominant political and cultural identity prevalent in one part of the continent, and later of the six (subsequently twelve) states

formally incorporated into the European Community, 'Europe' became rather *detached from its geographical boundaries*, closer to the USA and apart from its old European empires.[4] (my emphasis)

William Wallace suggests that the mental maps which guided West European leaders for three or four decades have been challenged by, firstly, the re-emergence of old maps of historical Europe and, secondly, by the imagery of the global market and Pacific as an alternative focus to the Atlantic.[5] Even Europe's geographical meaning is contested. For some, it refers to an area from the Atlantic to the Urals. For others, it refers primarily to Western Europe, while for a third group it extends from Finland to Malta and from Ireland to Turkey and stretching deep into Russia. This geographical term 'Europe' is also a cultural one and has ideological overtones, linked with Christendom and the Holy Roman Empire. The vision of a United States of Europe was one with boundaries which were more ideological than territorial, ideals which posited a pan-European United Nations—a system based on economic and political cooperation among states, with some recognition of the importance of cultural identity and cultural diversity. Whether there exists a European identity is still a matter for debate, and while the debate is in part linked with discussion of the EU's citizenship provisions, the context is broader, more complex[6] and pan-European. The thought-provoking discussion of 'what is Europe?' by William Wallace leads to the crucial debate on the 'clash of civilisations' promoted by Huntington, and discussed in this volume in some detail.

It has become clear that the West European use of the term 'Europe' referring to the EU alone, is no longer acceptable. The changing boundaries of the EU, which may soon enlarge to include countries of East and Central Europe, denotes a broader and less West-Eurocentric conception of Europe, though Europe is and will remain greater than even the expanded EU of the future. For now, however, let us concentrate on the most significant actor in Europe, the EU.

European boundaries since 1945

Europe, the principal site of the Cold War, was divided into two camps, separated in ideological terms by the Iron Curtain—a boundary that effectively rendered it difficult, for decades, to move from East to West and *vice versa*. There was, in effect, the creation of at least two Europes, one in the West allied with the US, and the other part of the Warsaw Pact dominated by the Soviet Union. Western Europe, with some of the wealthiest and most developed capitalist democracies in the world, witnessed a radical reconceptualisation by many intellectuals and resistance movements of the meaning and purpose of the nation state to encompass both federal and functionalist desires for interstate cooperation and undermining of national sovereignty.[7] In the late 1940s there were continued attempts to create a new type of political order after the devastation of the Second World War. This reassessment of options in the post-war era led to the creation of the EC, with the creation of a customs union, a common market for goods and services and a common agricultural policy, institutional structures and methods of decision making. By the 1990s, the EC, later the EU, was to be characterised by the creation of a single market, with a transparency of borders in terms of economic transactions in the largest frontier-free market in the world. There is free movement of the factors of production in the fifteen member states. The EU is also characterised by the gradual alteration to the boundaries of action by states, with the movement from independent economic policies to harmonised and even common ones, such as social policy, Common Agricultural Policy (CAP) and the cohesion policies, which entail an enormous transfer of common EU funds across borders of the member states.

These developments altered the nature of sovereignty and especially the scope of national competences, with a pooling of sovereignty in the EU over time. This change in sovereignty is the subject of intense debate. The main issue is whether the state has lost sovereignty and, if so, what this means. This in turn has led to a debate on the meaning of sovereignty, the state, government and the nation state. Is the EU beyond the nation state, the nation state writ large, a new type of polity, or a superstate? Is sovereignty divisible or indivisible? What does all this mean in the post-Cold War world? Since Maastricht, with the creation of the Common Foreign and Security Policy (CFSP), intensified cooperation in Justice and Home Affairs (JHA) and projected Economic and Monetary Union (EMU), an undermining—or at least change—of traditional notions and definitions of sovereignty has been taking place.

We are faced with a vocabulary and set of images that mean that even the terms we use can hinder attempts to analyse the EU. We are so familiar with terms and confines such as 'the state' and 'national government' that it is at times challenging then to evaluate the implications of terms such as globalisation and internationalism. In particular there are problems in determining what European supranationalism means for citizenship at a national level, and for social and regional movements.[8]

The EU has distinctive origins, institutions, and policies. Within it, there are conflicts between nationalism and supranationalism, and challenges to identity and definitions of boundary expressed in terms of region, gender, ethnicity, nationality and citizenship. It plays a world role in trade, is a major player in the global economy, and possesses a commitment to the creation of an EMU.

The breaking down of economic boundaries

By the beginning of the 1990s, with the creation of the Single Internal Market (SIM), the EC of Twelve members was the largest frontier free market in the world. With the increase of membership in 1995 to Fifteen, it became undisputed as a leading economic bloc and major trader. The EU member states substantially altered economic, fiscal and wage policies in working towards the achievement of the convergence criteria for entry into EMU. This has included restricting public spending and reducing public debt. Although there have been many doubts about the feasibility of EMU, including whether it could in fact be achieved in time for the deadline set in the Maastricht Treaty on European Union, the December 1996 Dublin Summit of the European Council firmly established the basic workings of the Euro, the new European currency, as the anchor for the EMU programme.

The increased transparency of economic frontiers in the shape of the SIM, with its free trading area and free movement of the factors of production, has not been a comprehensive success. Increasingly, doubts have been raised by analysts, regional representatives and trade unions about whether the SIM and EMU promise successful results for all, since, for example, poorer regions have suffered from the negative aspects of trading conformity.[9]

The EU has common external boundaries to the rest of Europe and the rest of the world. It has a common external tariff, an effective boundary to be crossed by non-EU states for the movement of goods into the trading area. The creation of the SIM is a type of inclusive trade bloc and its contours a readily distinguishable barrier to others—to the extent that it was even seen by some observers in the late 1980s as yet another 'Fortress Europe', in economic and especially trading terms, towards the rest of the world. The EC had also extended the Single Market with the European Economic Area (EEA) agreement, whereby trade and economic links were established with some members of the European Free Trade Association (EFTA) in the early 1990s.

Political boundaries

The member states of the EU's Intergovernmental Conference of 1996–7 carried out a reassessment of the EU's institutions and of the political power exercised by the states and the EU. This is regarded by analysts as part of the so-called 'deepening' debate, concerning whether or not the states of Western Europe should continue to integrate their economic systems and policies, and also their political processes, resulting in ever more decisions being made in and by the EU rather than exclusively by the nation states. This deepening issue is part of the reassessment of the nation state as it is transformed into a 'member state', with a re-examination of the notion of sovereignty and a debate on the implications of the interdependence of the member states. Is there now such a thing as an independent nation and an independent state? While physical or territorial borders are less important in the context of the SIM and hence in economic and trade transactions, identity still tends, with reason, to be linked with nationality, national territory and population—in short, membership of a nation.

There is another respect in which political boundaries are under review, with the evolution and increased relevance of sub-national movements and governments, known as the politics of the 'Third Level'.[10] While the nation state retains governance supremacy in many areas, in several European states the subnational demands for representation and increased powers of decision-making have led to the reassertion of regional boundaries and identities. Thus, it is apparent that there are centrifugal as well as centripetal forces at work, that is, below the nation state in the regions and above the nation state in the EU structure. Writers such as Scharpf and Marks refer to this dispersal of decision-making competences as multi-level governance.[11] These changes are taking place concurrently, so that federalising influences are evident both above and below the state. The creation at the EU level of the Committee of the Regions under the TEU has led to a reassessment of the meaning and impact of the term and actuality 'region'. Loughlin suggests that the Committee has now even gained official recognition of the sub-national territories, alongside the recognition of national territories as found in the Council of Ministers, and it is an important forum for the representation of regional and local issues within the EU,[12] although it is not involved in actual decision-making.

Boundaries for action are set not only at EU, nation state and regional levels. There is also increasing evidence of transnational representation in Brussels and elsewhere of social movements and pressure groups such as women's groups, environmental groups, peace movements, agricultural lobbies, business associations such as UNICE and ethnic minority groups, all contributing to a reassessment of democracy as traditionally associated with the nation state. Indeed, there is an increasingly relevant and vociferous debate on the need for cosmopolitan democracy, much of which is focused on the EU entity.[13] Held defines the cosmopolitan model of democracy as a 'system of governance which arises from and is adapted to the diverse conditions and interconnections of different peoples and nations'; it includes the creation or strengthening of regional parliaments, such as the European Parliament, and the possibility of general referenda (of groups) which cut across national boundaries on issues such as energy, transportation or other issues.[14] Indeed it is clear that many social movements have a transnational organisational base, in Europe and beyond. Kaldor suggests that the horizontal networks created by green, peace and human rights groups are part of a transnational political culture that can create a transnational public opinion, which could well develop into a consensual approach to international institutions.[15] Thus it is clear that transnationalism is not only determined in formal political terms but also in social terms and in civil society.

Security boundaries

Since the end of the Cold War in Europe, there has been a reassessment of the role of the North Atlantic Treaty Organisation (NATO), with altered American involvement and more demand by East European states to be actively involved. There has for some time been a perceived need for a European security organisation. There is also some questioning as to whether the EU's CFSP structures could form the nucleus of such an organisation, or even a pan-European Army. What will be the role of the Western European Union (WEU), NATO and the North Atlantic Cooperation Council (NACC)? Increasingly, there is a need to clarify the boundaries of the European Security and Defence Identity within Europe, as the nature of changes in international relations are reflected in the foreign policy stances of the post-Cold War states of Europe. Defence is a crucial issue here. Since the 1975 Helsinki Final Act of the Conference on Security and Cooperation in Europe (CSCE), defence and security have remained high on an agenda for pan-European cooperation on these issues. The renamed and revamped Organisation for Security and Cooperation in Europe (OSCE), some argue, is crucial to the outcome of security in the region.

The international strategic implications of an extension of NATO membership to include the countries of Eastern and Central Europe will be profound and have repercussions for Russia and the Commonwealth of Independent States (CIS), the US and the countries of the Pacific Rim. The changing roles of both NATO and the EU and their security agendas has led to changing security structures. In terms of defence, this is now an element, albeit a nascent one, of the Common Foreign and Security Policy of the EU. It is envisaged that US military equipment and personnel will play less of a role in tomorrow's Europe, while the EU will play more. The certainty of knowing who the enemy was in the Cold War theatre of Europe has also altered significantly. The former essentially unreflexive nature of identity and culture has been undergoing reassessment too with the 'new security agenda' of societal insecurity in the face of immigration, leading in some cases to a perception of the newcomer as undermining the culture of the nation and state.[16] This is often part of a perception of the 'Islamic threat' as undermining national security. Increasingly there is police and justice ministry cooperation on issues of terrorism and drug trafficking.

And there is a growing insecurity—in the sense of being increasingly uncertain about one's own role and functions—in seeing the transformation of the EC/EU from an agency that was primarily perceived as an economic and not a political entity, and that had no foreign policy-making powers or plans for significant monetary changes, to one that now seeks to be involved in so many overtly political, foreign policy-related and monetary areas. The EC and EU agendas have increased at an almost exponential rate, which has given rise to a fear of a superstate encroaching on national prerogatives. Indeed the project of monetary union has been referred to as 'the commanding enterprise of the 1990s'.[17]

Culture and civilisational boundaries

The Maastricht TEU gave rise in many countries to a sense of national 'cultures' being undermined or threatened, at the same time as changing boundaries of culture, media, communications and technology, as well as large population movements, were evident on a global scale. One of the reasons for distrust of the Treaty was concern about a provision in the TEU for European citizenship, although the fact remains that this citizenship is conferred by the nation state. This means that when one starts to define citizenship or a European culture, as is beginning to happen, there is always the risk of excluding by the process of including.

What this means, in the political context of the EU, is that the EU is West-European-centric and excludes most migrants from the benefits of free movement and citizenship. There is a perception that the EU states are seeing migrants as ethnically and culturally different to the extent that they are a threat to the security of the state's self perception, its national mores and conception of national culture, however erroneous that perception may be. So migrants are seen as the 'other' and are excluded in various ways. It could even be part of the clash of civilisations that William Wallace and Samuel Huntington refer to in their recent provocative work.

The conception of a citizenship that is both European and national shifts the boundaries of identity in various ways. There is increasing recognition of the multiple identity aspect of the citizenship debates in Europe and elsewhere, and it is now more and more acceptable to talk of multiple identity, overlapping identities, and loyalties to different and distinct groupings, regions, nations and states.[18] Meehan has pointed out that, like conceptions of citizenship, senses of identity are contextual.[19] This is particularly the case in multi-ethnic and multicultural Europe. However, Anthony Smith has contended that national identity cannot be replaced by an artificial European identity, as the latter lacks shared cultural identity, shared experiences, memories and myths.[20]

The enlargement of the European Union's boundaries

The accession of Austria, Sweden and Finland to the EU on 1 January 1995 marked the fourth increase in the membership of the original six-member European Community created in the 1950s.[21] The 1995 enlargement meant that the EU's area increased by more than one third to 3,235,000 square kilometres, the population increased by 6.2 per cent to 370 million from 349 million, and total GDP increased approximately 7 per cent.[22] The enlargements in 1973 to include the United Kingdom, Denmark and Ireland, in 1981 when Greece joined the EC and in 1986 when Spain and Portugal joined, each resulted in substantial changes to these nation states. They also marked substantial changes to the structure of the EC itself, in various ways. Goebel sees 'each enlargement [as] marking a new stage of constitutional, political and economic growth quite visible in a historical perspective' and regards the first enlargement as 'a comparably large augmentation of the Community's political authority, economic force and scope of practical operations'.[23]

Thus it can be seen that the enlargements of the EC/EU's boundaries are not simply geographical or territorial, but rather denote a developing and often unpredictable relationship between the member states and the EC/EU, in terms of national and supranational competences, authority and power. They also mark an increased politicisation of the EU's activities, which while not related to the enlargements exclusively, nevertheless coincided with the increase in the scope and nature of policies dealt with by the EU institutions, as well as the increase in the funding of the EU in the budget, known as 'Own Resources'. The boundaries of action of the nation states which make up the EU altered over time with an increased interdependence of the national European institutions, the latter based mostly in Brussels.

Later these boundaries were to be further developed and challenged as, by the 1980s, the interdependence was also characterised by a regional or subnational level of governance and decision making. This was best exemplified by the creation of the Committee of the Regions under the TEU (although this has had its problems), and also by the establishment of highly efficient transnational, cross-border cooperation of regions in business and other activities.[24]

With the alteration of the boundaries of the EU has come a diversification of the political and economic policies and processes of the member states— that is, there is, in a sense, more heterogeneity among the constituent states and, with further enlargements, that trend is likely to continue. For example, successive enlargements in the past have seen an alteration from the relative consensus among the original six member states that, as founder members of the original EC, had in common a similar level of economic development; some measure of postwar disillusionment with the nation state; a similar constellation of political forces and elites; a general realisation of the need to work together as neighbours, to maintain peace and to achieve a secure market for their products; and a common Judaeo-Christian heritage. This relative homogeneity no longer holds true.

The issue of which countries are considered to be eligible for membership is answered in part by reference to the nature of the economic and political systems. The criteria for membership were first set out in the European Commission document, *The Challenge of Enlargement*, and later at European Council summits. Article O of the TEU states that European identity is the basic criterion for membership of the EU. Article F of the TEU sets out that the Union (and, by implication, applicants) must respect both the national identities of the member states, whose systems are founded on the principles of democracy, and fundamental rights under the European Convention for the Protection of Human Rights and Fundamental Freedoms.[25] As Nicolaides and Raja Boean have pointed out, it is worth remembering that there is a distinction to be drawn between the formal membership criteria as stipulated in the Treaty, and the preconditions agreed at European Council meetings since the Treaty came into force. These are:

> ...stability of institutions guaranteeing democracy, the rule of law and human rights; respect for and protection of minorities; the existing of a functional market economy; the capacity to cope with competitive pressure and market forces within the Union; the stability to adhere to the aims of political, economic and monetary union.[26]

These criteria were formalised at the Copenhagen European Council in June 1993.[27] There will be protracted and difficult negotiations ahead for the Czech Republic, Estonia, Hungary, Poland and Slovenia, and later for others in East and Central Europe. It is clear that, more so than in previous enlargement negotiations, the applications from countries of the former Soviet bloc will be subjected to detailed scrutiny, in terms of those applicants' legal, political and economic institutions and procedures and in terms of economic as well as political criteria,[28] although the Commission stated in July 1997 that the five principal applicants would be in a position to 'satisfy all the conditions of membership'[29] in the medium term.[30]

Must, and can, all applicants accept the *acquis communautaire*—that is, the body of law, policies and decision-making methods of the EU developed since 1952? The Commission position is that new members must 'apply the *acquis* upon accession'[31] and states that the timetable for accession will depend on the progress made by the applicants in adopting and implementing the *acquis*. The dilution of the *acquis* is thus not negotiable, as the *acquis* implies the acceptance of both the rights and obligations of the Treaties and hence applicants are obliged to accept these as a precursor to membership. Must they accept all of it? Are there any 'opt-outs'? Should opt-outs be considered, and it is unlikely at this stage, is there then the possibility of a multi-speed and multi-tiered EU (for example on CFSP, neutrality, defence, membership of EMU etc.)? The debate on flexibility within the 1996–7 IGC examined the need to retain the *acquis communautaire* while retaining some flexibility for some member states.

Advantages of enlargement for the European Union

There has for some time been considerable discussion of the advantages and disadvantages of the widening of the EU's membership, and it is clear that there is no single position adopted by the member states on this issue. Rather, there are differing national perspectives which are closely linked with national interest, and each state's location in terms of geography, agricultural and other interests. What was beyond doubt was that with the completion of the 1996–7 IGC with its agenda of 'deepening', the negotiations on accession accelerated, with a focus on 'widening', i.e. the enlargement of EU membership.

From the EU's perspective, the advantages of the enlargement can be summarised as follows. First, there is the prospect of enhancing security in the region. Second, there is also the prospect of increased European prosperity. Third, there is the realisation that a larger EU would be more powerful and influential, and could speak and act on behalf of a larger number of member states in the international arena and as a larger trading bloc. The Agenda 2000 document of the European Commission states simply 'enlargement will enhance its (the EU's) influence.'[32] Fourth, and following on from this, the EU would be seen as a larger 'Europe', and not simply Western Europe, in a pan-European framework which would be dominated by the EU. In this regard, the EU documents tend to fall into the trap of identifying the EU with 'Europe', which the reader was warned against early in this chapter.

Disadvantages of enlargement for the EU

But there are also a number of potential disadvantages to enlargement from the EU's perspective. First, many 'deepeners' or federalists fear that an enlarged EU denotes a 'diluted' EU, possibly with several differing speeds of integration, and many member states travelling at a slower speed and hence delaying the deepening of economic and political integration.[33]

Second, there is a perception that the EU would become too large to be effective, and that its institutions would not be responsive to the large number of member states. Third, there is a fear of a dilution of benefits of membership, if more (especially poorer) countries were to share the EU Budget. Closely linked to this is the heterogeneity of EU regions and the fact that member states will require 'sectoral and regional adjustments',[34] while at the same time the Common Agricultural Policy is a continuing issue of concern.

Fourth, there is some apprehension that, if several speeds of integration were to eventuate among different groups of states, a phenomenon often also referred to as a Europe of concentric circles or differentiation, there could be a problem of EU institutions not speaking for all members. This could spell the end of the vision of collective responsibility among the member states. Others fear the creation of a new 'dividing line' in Europe, further to the east, with a differentiation still clearly maintained between East and West. Finally, the sense of some integrationists is that the entire process of deepening of integration would lose its momentum.

It has also become increasingly clear that the EU itself was in need of reform in preparation for further enlargement, reforming its CAP and other structural policies, and also ensuring that its Budgetary Own Resources are sufficient for the enlarged membership. The IGC of 1996–7 attempted to deal with some of these issues in terms of institutional reform. The Dublin II draft treaty of December 1996 pointed out that '...further enlargement of the Union affords both a unique opportunity and an important challenge. These are challenges which the Union must meet at a time when political institutions everywhere are under question by a well informed public.'[35] The document also states that '...it is necessary to prepare now for the larger and more diverse Union of the future so as to avoid paralysis and to preserve the capacity of the institutions to act.'[36] The European Commission's 1997 document entitled 'Agenda 2000: For a Stronger and Wider Europe' attempted in particular to analyse the issue of enlargement from financial, economic and security perspectives.[37] It is a major and significant attempt by the Commission to adapt to the changing internal and external environment and hence, for Commission President Jacques Santer, the EU 'must set about adapting, developing and reforming itself. Enlargement represents a historic turning point for Europe (sic), an opportunity which it must seize for the sake of its security, its economy, its culture and its status in the world.'[38] 'Agenda 2000' undertook to further examine EU institutional reforms, including a generalised system of qualified majority voting, by the time of the next enlargement.

Implications of accession for the applicant states

To date, applications to join the EU have been made by Turkey (April 1987), Cyprus (July 1990), Malta (July 1990),[39] Hungary (March 1994), Poland

(April 1994), Romania (June 1995), Slovakia (June 1995), Latvia (October 1995), Estonia (November 1995), Lithuania (December 1995), Bulgaria (December 1995), the Czech Republic (January 1996), and Slovenia (June 1996).

The European Commission's 'Agenda 2000' document recommends that accession negotiations commence with the Czech Republic, Estonia, Hungary, Poland and Slovenia on the one hand, and with Cyprus on the other.[40] Many East European countries, adhering to democratic principles and possessing free market economies, albeit with different rates of development, are already implementing the policies of the EU's Single Market and are examining ways to meet the EMU convergence criteria. Yet they are not in any way participants in EU decision making and have no assurance that they will become EU members.

Sander has referred to the practice of the spokes (individual countries) and hub (EU) of the wheel, whereby the Central and Eastern European states often have extensive bilateral ties and agreements as individual states with the EU, but not necessarily with each other, since the collapse of the COMECON system in 1991.[41] This induces a certain reliance of each of these states on the EU, whether under the Poland and Hungary: Aid for the Restructuring of Economies (PHARE) program and Association Agreements or via other agreements on aid, trade, advice and consultancy and TEMPUS educational exchanges.[42] It is anticipated that the applicant states will receive support from the cohesion and structural funds of the EU and these are detailed in the Commission's 'Agenda 2000' document. In addition, many applicant states apply with hopes of increased security, stability, prosperity and influence as members of a large EU. On the other hand, difficulties can be anticipated in dealing with the loss of recently acquired sovereignty, joining a club where the rules are already set and in implementing the single market.

The applicant states will be involved in a protracted set of accession negotiations, which will serve as a means to establish the new boundaries of the enlarged EU. They will also fundamentally alter the character of the Union, in terms of levels of diversity and cultural distinctness. The accession negotiations will provide the applicants with a deeper understanding of the institutional governance of the EU and its member states, and also the first major negotiating experience with the EU. It is during these negotiations between officials from the applicant states and the EU Commission and Council officials that any special conditions, temporary derogations and transitional periods are decided, as well as any budgetary provisions.[43]

It is not, however, to be assumed that all European states wish to join the EU. The Norwegian government has twice negotiated accession—in 1972 and 1994—and each time the public rejected membership in referenda. The Maltese

Labour party opposes Malta's membership, and it continues to look unlikely that Switzerland will join the EU, in the aftermath of a referendum which resulted in the rejection of membership of the European Economic Area.[44]

Finally, it is important to be aware that while membership of the EU, and the advantages and disadvantages related to it, is an important ongoing concern for many non-EU European countries, that this is neither the sole, nor necessarily the principal, concern of these countries. As just indicated, some may not join the EU. Some may do so at their own pace and not that of the EU. It is tempting to fall into the trap of assuming that the EU is 'Europe', as so much documentation of the EU has for so long equated the EU with Europe. However, it is critical to keep in mind that transition studies regarding the ECE are as valid as integration studies, that analyses of democratisation processes in the ECE states are as valid as those of the democratic deficit in the EU and Western Europe. Developing democracies and market economies are a dynamic source of research. The world of area specialists has been shattered, while transition, integration, citizenship and the 'new Europe' are the key concerns at this exciting time of 'the sudden shock of disappearing boundaries' which Gordon Smith has described.[45]

The structure of this volume

This volume explores the themes of boundary and identity from several perspectives, which cover most of what is known as 'Europe' from cultural, political, sociological, legal and historical perspectives. It is the result of a conference entitled 'Europe—Rethinking the Boundaries', held in September 1995 and organised by the Contemporary European Studies Association of Australia. The volume highlights the multiplicity of approaches and the complexity of the understanding of what is Europe, while at the same time serving to present a coherent theme of boundary which is both thought-provoking and comprehensive. It raises many questions and enters the debates on Europe's boundaries. It points to the need to stand back from the simple dichotomy of 'deeper' or 'wider' Europe, and examines the implications of the power bloc of the EU and the evolving political and economic systems in Central and Eastern Europe.

The contributors to this volume are all of European nationality or background and have a longstanding research interest in Europe. Yet they all live and teach in Australia, and hence have an unusual perspective on the European project and its critiques and challenges. They consider it from beyond the immediate daily minutiae of Europe, as their geographical and intellectual distance has provided them with a unique opportunity to reflect on the developments.

Leslie Holmes considers the theme of a 'clash of civilisations' with particular reference to understanding Europe in Chapter Two, a theme further developed by Jeremy Salt in Chapter Seven, with reference to the so-called 'Islamic threat'. Chapter Three by Philomena Murray examines the changing boundaries of the nation state's action in the context of EU membership. This is further explored with reference to the role of the Common Foreign and Security Policy in Christine Agius' chapter (Nine) on the 'war on neutrality', which examines the superpower Europe's interaction with the foreign policy stances of Austria, Finland and Sweden. The crucial issue of the changing boundaries and status of both states and foreign policy as state action is taken up as a theme by Chris Barrett (Chapter Eight) on German foreign policy and security.

The last few decades have seen the increased enlargement of the membership of the EC and the EU, a process reflected in the progressive stages of the European integration process. These are explored by F. Damaso Marengo in his chapter (Five) on the Mediterranean boundaries of the EU. Marengo places the Mediterranean enlargement and the possibility of further Mediterranean countries' accession to the EU in comparative perspective with the proposed enlargement eastwards. In Chapter Four, Rémy Davison examines this process in terms of future issues in forthcoming enlargements.

Glenda Sluga's chapter (Six) critically examines the implications of the practices of boundary-marking and ethno-territoriality in a historical and cultural perspective, examining in particular the Balkan boundaries and how history and identity have been 'written' into territory and formal boundary. She points to the tendency to understand culture in terms of ethnicity and democratic ambitions in terms of ethno-national sovereignty and the problems that these trends can cause.

These chapters illustrate that Europe is still in a period of change and challenge and that boundaries are being reconsidered from a variety of perspectives. They remind us that it is no longer appropriate to speak of the centrality of the nation state, the stability of borders and the importance of territory in absolute terms. The Europe on the verge of the twenty-first century is one based on transnational cooperation and rivalry, on supranational and subnational challenges to nationality and nationhood. It is a Europe of flux and changing boundaries, and which demands a reconsideration of the nature of political and social practice, as well as culture and civilisations.

Notes

1. C. Offe, 'Capitalism by Democratic Design? Democratic Theory Facing the Triple Transition in East Central Europe', *Social Research*, 38 (2), 1991.
2. Quoted in M. Rodriguez Salgado, 'Europe and 1992: In Search of Europe', *History Today*, 42, 1992, 15.

3. *Ibid.*, 11.
4. *Ibid.*, 15.
5. W. Wallace, *The Transformation of Western Europe* (London: Routledge, 1990).
6. *Ibid.*
7. C. Navari, 'Functionalism versus Federalism: Alternative Visions of European Unity', in P. Murray and P. Rich (eds), *Visions of European Unity* (Colorado: Westview, 1996).
8. For a full discussion of these issues see L. Holmes & P. Murray (eds), *Citizenship and Identity in Europe* (Aldershot: Dartmouth, forthcoming in 1998).
9. A. Amin and J. Tomaney (eds), *Behind the Myth of European Union: prospects for cohesion.* (London/New York: Routledge, 1995).
10. U. Bullman, 'The Politics of the Third Level', *Regional and Federal Studies*, 6 (2), 1996.
11. G. Marks, 'An Actor-centred Approach to Multi-Level Governance', *Regional and Federal Studies*, 6 (2), 1996.
12. J. Loughlin, 'Representing Regions in Europe', *Regional and Federal Studies*, 6 (2), 1996.
13. See D. Held, *Democracy and the Global Order* (Cambridge: Polity Press, 1995); D. Archibugi and D. Held (eds), *Cosmopolitan Democracy: An Agenda for a New World Order* (Cambridge: Polity Press, 1995).
14. D. Held, 'Democracy and the New International Order', in Archibugi & Held, *op. cit.*, 106–8.
15. M. Kaldor, 'European Institutions, Nation States and Nationalism', in *ibid.*, 94.
16. B. Buzan, 'Introduction: The Changing Security Agenda in Europe', in O. Waever *et al.* (eds), *Identity, Migration and the New Security Agenda in Europe* (London: Pinter, 1993).
17. P. Gowan and P. Anderson, 'Preface' in *The Question of Europe* (London: Verso, 1997).
18. See, for example, E. Meehan, 'The Debate on Citizenship and European Union', in Murray and Rich, *op. cit.*
19. *Ibid.*, 217.
20. See A. Smith, 'National Identity and the Idea of European Unity', in P. Gowan and P. Anderson (eds), *The Question of Europe* (London: Verso, 1997), esp. 339.
21. The incorporation of the GDR into the FRG in October 1990 was of course an addition to the EC and is regarded by some commentators as another enlargement.
22. *The Week in Europe*, European Commission, Dublin, 9-13 January 1995, 1.
23. R. J. Goebel, 'The European Union Grows: the Constitutional Impact of the Accession of Austria, Finland and Sweden', *Fordham International Law Journal*, 18 (4), 1995, 1092.
24. See C. Jeffery and G. Orcalli, 'The Regional Dimension of the European Union', *Regional and Federal Studies*, 6 (2), 1996.
25. Article F of the TEU states:
    '1. The Union shall respect the national identities of its Member States, whose systems of government are founded on the principles of democracy.
    2. The Union shall respect fundamental rights, as guaranteed by the European Convention for the Protection of Human Rights and Fundamental Freedoms signed in Rome on 4 November 1950 and as they result from the constitutional traditions common to the Member Sates, as general principles of Community law.
    3. The Union shall provide itself with the means necessary to attain its objectives and carry through its policies.'
26. P. Nicolaides and S. Raja Boean, 'The Process of Enlargement of the European Union', *EIPASCOPE*, 3, 1996, 6.
27. European Commission, Press Release IP/97/660, Doc 97/9, Brussels and Strasbourg.
28. Nicolaides and Raja Boean, *loc. cit.*, 6.
29. European Commission, Press Release IP/97/660, Doc 97/9, 12.

30. It is important to be aware that there has been considerable emphasis on the concept of stability with regard to the former Eastern bloc states. It has long been held by several EU actors, including the Commission, that membership of the EU for the ECE states would lead to stability in the region and form a buffer against unrest and economic uncertainty as well as guard against the possibility of a return to a form of communism.

31. European Commission, Press Release IP/97/660, Doc 97/9, 13.

32. European Commission, 'Agenda 2000: for a Stronger and Wider Europe', Doc 97/6, Strasbourg, 15 July 1997.

33. See, for example, the debate in the European Parliament of the Christodoulou report, A4-353/96, December 1996.

34. European Commission, Press Release IP/97/660, Doc 97/9, 12.

35. Conference of the Representatives of the Governments of the Member States, *The European Union Today and Tomorrow: Adapting the European Union for the Benefit of its peoples and Preparing it for the Future. A General Guideline for a Draft Revision of the Treaties*, Dublin II, Conf. 2500/96.

36. *Ibid.*, 115.

37. European Commission, 'Agenda 2000', *loc. cit.*

38. European Commission, Press Release IP/97/660, Doc 97/9.

39. Malta's application was subsequently withdrawn.

40. Cyprus's application has always been treated as distinct from those received from the Central and East European states of the former Eastern bloc.

41. Note however that the Central European Free Trade Agreement was established in 1992 and originally comprised the Visegrad Four (Czechia, Hungary, Poland and Slovakia). Slovenia joined in 1996, and the Ukraine has since expressed interest in joining.

42. H. Sander, 'Towards a Wider Europe: Eastern Europe's Rocky Road into the European Union', paper presented at the 1996 Contemporary European Studies Association of Australia (CESAA) symposium: 'Rewriting Rights in Europe', Melbourne, September 1996.

43. See Nicolaides & Raja Boean, *loc. cit.*, 8, for a discussion of the purposes of the accession negotiations.

44. See D. Thurer, 'Switzerland: the Model in Need of Adaptation?' in J.J. Hesse and V. Wright (eds), *Federalizing Europe? The Costs, Benefits and Preconditions of Federal Political Systems* (Oxford and New York: Oxford University Press, 1996). Switzerland rejected EEA membership by a majority of 50.3 per cent and with 16 of 22 cantons.

45. G. Smith, 'Seeking to understand European politics,' in H. Daalder (ed.) *Comparative European Politics: the story of a Profession* (London: Pinter, 1997), 152-153.

2 Europe's Changing Boundaries and the 'Clash of Civilisations' Thesis

LESLIE HOLMES

Introduction

Possibly the most widely debated article in Western political science in the first half of the 1990s was Samuel Huntington's 'The Clash of Civilizations?'.[1] It had as much impact in the mid-1990s as Fukuyama's 'end of history' thesis had in the late 1980s,[2] while Huntington's follow-up book published in 1996[3] only fuelled the controversy. In a sense, Huntington's article and book address many of the same major issues in world politics as Fukuyama's. Far from accepting that we have reached the end of history, however, the Harvard professor concludes that we are entering a new era of conflict, based not on ideology or economics, as in the past, but on cultural differences.

This chapter starts with an overview of Huntington's argument, primarily as elaborated in the original article, though with references to the book where appropriate. This is followed by a general critique of it. In the third and longest section, Huntington's argument is applied specifically to contemporary Europe; there is also speculation on future developments, and on how these are likely to reflect Huntington's concerns. Two main points are argued in the conclusions. First, while acknowledging that some of Huntington's thesis might be correct, it is emphasised that there are persuasive alternative explanations for most of the developments and events to which he refers, and that extreme caution must be exercised in applying simple, general paradigms (as Huntington himself describes his approach) to complex phenomena. Leading on from this, the second point is that there exists a real danger that the public policy proposals advocated by Huntington would increase the likelihood of his depressing scenarios becoming self-fulfilling prophesies.

Huntington's argument

Huntington's primary objective is to make sense of international relations in the post-Cold War era by identifying what he considers the single most important

19

source of tension. He argues that the root of most conflicts up to the eighteenth century was tension between princes. In the nineteenth century and up to the end of the First World War, the main source was tension between the peoples of nation states. And from the end of the First World War until about 1990 the significant conflicts were based on clashes of ideology—between fascism, communism and liberal democracy in the inter-war period, and between the latter two after the Second World War. In this third scenario, the main protagonists were not nation states in the classical European sense, although individual states did line up behind one or other banner.

In the post-Cold War period, nation states will remain the most powerful actors in world affairs, but the principal conflicts of global politics will occur between nations and groups of different civilisations:

> The clash of civilizations [a term Huntington acknowledges borrowing from Bernard Lewis] will dominate global politics. The fault lines between civilizations will be the battle lines of the future.[4]

Huntington further maintains that international politics were in a basically Western phase until the end of the Cold War, by which he means that the major conflicts were primarily between Western countries. This has begun to change in the 1990s, and the rest of the world has become part of the source of conflict. Countries beyond the West are no longer mere objects of Western colonialism, but have their own role to play in moving and shaping history. In place of the former Three Worlds, countries are grouped according to civilisations (i.e. shared cultural attributes):

> A civilization is . . . the highest cultural grouping of people and the broadest level of cultural identity people have short of that which distinguishes humans from other species.[5]

For Huntington, civilisations have both common *objective* elements— such as language, history, religion, customs and institutions—and *subjective* self-identification. The size of civilisations varies substantially. Most embrace several countries, whereas two are essentially based on one country. Huntington recognises seven or perhaps eight major civilisations in the contemporary world—Western, Confucian/Sinic,[6] Japanese, Islamic, Hindu, Slavic–Orthodox, Latin American, and possibly African.[7]

Having identified the major civilisations, Huntington lists six reasons why the major conflicts of the future will occur along 'cultural fault lines'. First, the differences are said to be real and fundamental; the most significant relates to religion, which is held to be more basic than political ideology.

Second, as the world becomes smaller, so the interaction between groups increases; this in turn means that individual groups become more aware both of their commonalities with groups of similar culture (which Huntington, following H.D.S. Greenway, calls 'kin-countries'), and of their distinction from groups with different civilisational background. Third, economic modernisation and social change is held to distance people from long-standing local identities. One ramification of this is that the nation state is weakened as a source of identity. It is in these circumstances that attachment to religion, especially fundamentalism, increases. Fourth, there has been a rise of civilisation consciousness, enhanced by the dual role of the West. On the one hand, the West is at the peak of its power; on the other, non-Western civilisations are returning to their roots. Whereas in the past, non-Western elites typically went to the West for their education while the masses remained close to their roots, there has in recent times been something of a role reversal. Thus, there has been a discernible indigenisation of elites at the same time as mass culture has come under much greater Western (especially US) influence. Huntington's fifth reason is that cultural characteristics are much less malleable than are political or economic ones. People are held not to choose their cultural characteristics in the way they can between ideologies or class. Once again, Huntington focuses on religion, when he argues that religious values are particularly deeply ingrained. Finally, economic (macro-)regionalism is increasing, which tends to reinforce civilisation consciousness at the same time as it decreases identification with the nation state.

In an essentially pessimistic manner, Huntington further maintains that conflictual notions of 'them' and 'us' are likely to increase in the future, as people define themselves ever more in ethnic and religious terms. The clashes of civilisations will occur at two levels—the 'micro' (between adjacent groups along fault lines) and the 'macro' (states or groups of states from different civilisations will compete for military and economic power, in the process promoting their political and religious values). The fault lines will be the flash points for crisis and bloodshed. Of all the fault lines, Huntington believes that the most significant in Europe may well be that identified by William Wallace, which focuses on the Eastern boundary of Western Christianity in 1500 AD.[8] By taking the year 1500, neither Wallace nor Huntington has to draw any distinction between Catholicism and Protestantism within Western Christianity.

Huntington goes on to argue that clashes along the fault line between Western and Islamic civilisations have been occurring intermittently over the past 1300 years. One significant example was the attempt by the Crusaders to bring Christianity to the Holy Land in the eleventh to thirteenth centuries, while the most recent major case was the Gulf War. While there may be conflicts between kin-countries in the future, these will be less intense and less likely to spread than conflicts between civilisations. Conversely, if there is to be a Third World War, this will be between civilisations.

To some extent building on earlier work, Huntington next argues that *the* most fundamental divide is between 'the West and the rest', a phrase he borrows from Kishore Mahbubani. He suggests that both democracy and human rights are essentially Western concepts that are unwelcome in most non-Western civilisations. Although some non-Western countries have sought to redefine their identities (Huntington cites in particular Russia, Turkey and Mexico), this usually results in wide-ranging confusion. Nevertheless, some countries can succeed in 'joining' the West, as long as they meet three criteria—the move must be supported by the country's elite; the general public must at least accept the move; and the dominant elites in the recipient civilisation (here, the West) must be willing to embrace the convert.

In the penultimate part of his article, Huntington produces a hierarchy of civilisations in terms of their chances of moving closer to the West. According to him, the obstacles are least for the Latin American and East European countries, while they are greatest for the Islamic, Confucian, Hindu and Buddhist societies. Indeed, he proceeds to argue that the most likely threat to the West emanates from a Confucian (Sinic) and Islamic military alliance. Although he acknowledges that this alliance he claims to have identified might be short-lived, he does emphasise that there is currently an arms race between it and the West.

The final section of Huntington's argument both summarises the preceding points and examines their implications for the West and Western policy-makers. He argues in favour of incorporating the two civilisations closest to the West (Latin America, Eastern Europe) and of cooperating closely with Russia and Japan. On the other hand, he again emphasises the threat from the Confucian and Islamic states, and urges vigilance and high military spending by the West to protect itself against other civilisations that seek to become modern without being Western. In contrast to the Fukuyama thesis, Huntington's denies the likelihood of the emergence of a universal civilisation. His is ultimately a bleak picture.

A critique of the Clash of Civilisations Thesis

Huntington's argument is a powerful and seductive piece—if often repetitive in its book-length version. It traverses the world and the centuries in a masterful way. It is a *tour de force,* and deserves to be taken seriously. As far as it goes, much of it is also persuasive. Since so much of it is speculative, it is difficult to disprove at this point in time. Nevertheless, many of the underlying assumptions and major assertions must be questioned; there are convincing alternative interpretations of the same events which may lead to very different conclusions and hence a very different world-picture. For the purposes of this analysis, nine aspects of the thesis will be considered.

First, many of the *generalisations* and *classifications* deserve to be challenged. For instance, the distinction Huntington draws between modernity and Westernism is not as clear as he believes; many would see these two phenomena as intimately related. Huntington distinguishes between economic and military modernisation on the one hand, and social and political Westernism on the other, citing Japan as an example of a country that has become modern without becoming Western. But this interpretation can be challenged. Certainly, Japanese society and politics are in important ways very different from American. But then so are French or Italian, and Huntington needs to show why he considers some of these cultural differences to be significant and others superficial. The classification of civilisations must also be questioned. For example, a case can be made for distinguishing Russia from the rest of the Slavic-Orthodox world, or at least from South-Eastern Europe. The fact that Huntington himself draws such a distinction—and, very confusingly in terms of his own civilisational divisions, refers to 'Eastern Europe'—when discussing future scenarios only highlights a problem in his original classification. Finally, doubts must be raised about the probability of a clash between Confucian (Sinic) and Western civilisations. With the notable exception of Tibet and one or two other western parts of the People's Republic of China (PRC), China has no tradition of aggressive expansionism or imperialism (unlike Russia, for instance), and Huntington often appears to be merely resurrecting the old racist 'yellow peril' theme.[9] The differences between the West and the PRC have been and remain primarily ideological; it is far from clear that the West has any *fundamental* differences with Taiwan, Hong Kong (at least until July 1997) or Singapore. Indeed, the USA publicly lent its support to Taiwan in early 1996 as the Republic of China came under threat from the PRC; this, too, must cast doubt upon the validity of Huntington's thesis.[10]

Second, there is on occasions a *selectivity* in Huntington's historiography. Thus the notion that wars up to the eighteenth century were mostly between princes rather than civilisations sits uncomfortably with the references to the Crusades. In the post-Second World War period, there have been many bloody conflicts that simply have not been as widely reported in the West as those that related to the ideological Cold War; this applies to several in Africa, most notably. This selectivity endorses Huntington's thesis, and perhaps helps to explain some of his own perceptions. But for his thesis to be more persuasive, Huntington needs to redress some of the perceptual distortion of the past, not endorse it.

Third, some parts of the argument appear to be peculiarly *time and place specific.* It is understandable that the argument reflects many of the concerns and the confusion of the post-Cold War era, as the New World Order has apparently soon proven to be the New World Disorder. But the temporal specificity should be more explicitly recognised. Huntington's article was published only four years after Tiananmen, two years after the Gulf War, and a little over a year from the outbreak of the Bosnian conflict that he sees as symptomatic of the conflict between 'the West' and Islam. Already by the mid-1990s, some of the edge of the Confucian and Islamic threats had been blunted. China's economic modernisation only highlights the tensions between its economic base on the one hand and its political, legal and ideological superstructure on the other; in the foreseeable future, it could well be more concerned with the resolution of these internal contradictions than challenging and threatening the West.[11] The collapse of the Soviet Bloc[12] and Empire, plus the encouraging developments in the Israeli-Palestinian relationship by 1995, meant that even countries like Syria—not to mention Iran—had sought better relations with the West. It would be extremely naïve, and itself very time-specific, to assume that such improvements will necessarily continue in some linear way; the deterioration in Israeli–Palestinian relations in 1996–7 exemplifies this. On the other hand, they are sufficient to highlight problems of specificity in Huntington's putative 'big picture'.

Fourth, the clash of civilisations thesis is excessively *reductionist.* There is too little attempt to provide alternative explanations of current and possible future clashes. While it is feasible—tempting even—to explain the 1990s war in Bosnia-Hercegovina in terms of the clash of civilisations thesis, to do so would be grossly to simplify a highly complex phenomenon that involves nationalistic, territorial, ideological, political and numerous other factors. Equally, it is just as likely that future major clashes will relate to limited resources as to clashes of civilisation. As Gleick[13] and others have convincingly argued, a major source of conflict in the next century is likely to be water; this could well lead to major tensions in the driest parts of the globe, including *within* the 'Islamic' Middle East and Africa. Moreover, as economies continue to develop in Asia, eastern Europe and Latin America, there could be an enormous increase in the global demand for oil; while science *might* devise acceptable alternative fuels for our motor-cars, there can at this stage be no certainty about this.

Closely related to this, and constituting our fifth point, Huntington's argument is often *unifaceted,* and may well be concentrating on epiphenomena rather than the most basic factors. Expressed differently, there is rarely any consideration of countervailing forces, even though (because?) these sometimes appear to be *stronger* than those identified by Huntington. For instance, although the

West claims to place great emphasis on human rights, basic common economic interests frequently outweigh this. The USA rattled its sabres at the PRC in 1994 over the latter's poor human rights records; however, despite its threats and the fact that Beijing refused to make concessions on this issue, Washington eventually renewed the PRC's Most Favoured Nation status. Similarly, for all its protests about human rights abuses in Indonesia, Australia signed a security agreement with Jakarta in December 1995, partly because of long-term vested economic interests.

Developing this point about underlying economic interests, it should be noted that Huntington inadequately explores the possibility that globalisation and the spread of economic rationalism will have a homogenising and counter-conflictual effect. He does allude to this, in his references to the impact of the West on mass culture around the world. But his argument that elites from the various civilisations are resisting homogenisation and closer cooperation across civilisations sits uncomfortably with recent developments in *cross-civilisational* regionalism and with significant examples of attempts at *reconciliation*. A prime example of the former is the progress made towards closer economic interaction within the Asia Pacific Economic Cooperation forum (APEC), while the (admittedly troubled) Israeli–Palestinian Liberation Organisation (PLO) Accords and the changes in South Africa act as counter-examples to the bleak picture being painted by Huntington. It is appropriate at this juncture to remember our earlier point about time-specificity; the latter two developments have occurred since Huntington wrote, and to exaggerate their significance would be to commit the same error of contemporaneous parochialism as he does. Conversely, they demonstrate clearly why the Huntington thesis must be approached with considerable caution.

Also leading on from the argument about reductionism, and constituting our sixth point, Huntington tends to be overly *deterministic*. His focus is primarily on structure, and there is little room for agency. While it is easy to attribute too much to individual agents and to detach them from underlying forces, it would be absurd not to acknowledge the importance individual leaders can have in domestic politics and, sometimes as a largely unintended consequence, in international relations. It *did* matter that Gorbachev was in charge in the USSR 1985–91, that Thatcher led Britain 1979–90, that Deng was the paramount Chinese leader from the late 1970s to 1997 and that Saddam Hussein was in charge in Iraq at the time of the Gulf conflict. While none of these politicians could have come to power in a vacuum and independent of social forces, and although they had to work within *some* constraints, their role and policies were not pre-ordained, and real choices were involved. One very important implication of acknowledging the role of agency is that agents can both provoke *and reduce* conflict. Identity is a considerably more subjective and mutable phenomenon than Huntington acknowledges.

Seventh, the argument is in places *inconsistent*, even confused. For instance, Huntington acknowledges that the boundaries of civilisations can change; if so—and it is so, to the extent that discernible civilisations exist in any meaningful way—then we need to know under what circumstances this occurs, and what the prospects are for such changes in the foreseeable future. Moreover, Huntington argues that the principal conflict in Europe is between Western Christianity on the one hand, and Eastern Orthodoxy and Islam on the other.[14] Yet the conflicts over the years between Serbs (mostly Orthodox) and Kosovars (mostly Muslims) or between Greeks (typically Orthodox) and Turks (predominantly Muslim) reveal clearly why caution must be exercised in linking Orthodoxy and Islam, or assuming that the tensions between them are necessarily less profound than those between either and Western Christianity. While some Croats argue that their fight against Serbia was on one level to defend Europe against Eastern Orthodoxy and Islam (i.e. in line with Huntington's grouping), many Serbs claimed in the early 1990s that they were defending Europe against Islam. It has to be acknowledged that at some points in his argument Huntington himself *recognises* that Orthodox Christians and Muslims can be in serious conflict;[15] but this acknowledgement merely endorses the point being made here about inconsistency.

Not only is it questionable to link Orthodoxy and Islam, but the notion that either, or for that matter the West or any of his other groupings, constitutes a single civilisational imperative cannot go unchallenged.[16] Let us consider here just Islam. Not only are there significant differences between the Arab and non-Arab Islamic states, but the substantial differences between, on the one hand, Libya, Iraq and Syria and, on the other, Saudi Arabia, Egypt and even Jordan are good indicators of the need to be extremely cautious in talking of 'the' Islamic civilisation.[17] As mentioned above, it is by no means inconceivable that there will be major conflicts between Islamic states in the next century, possibly relating to water and/or oil.

Two final examples of the ambiguities in Huntington's argument, and of his own reservations about his thesis, are his statements that, 'Differences do not necessarily mean conflict, and conflict does not necessarily mean violence'[18] and that the Confucian–Islamic military connection of which he makes so much 'may or may not last'.[19] In non-American English, this is an example of 'having a bob each way', and makes the clash of civilisations thesis far less persuasive as a predictor (and hence a guide to policy-makers).

Eighth, Huntington inadequately considers the *reasons for the hostility to the West* that unquestionably does exist at times in various parts of the world; to argue against over-generalisation about the non-Western world is not to deny that there is much antipathy to the West and Western concepts. In terms of elites turning against the West, there needs to be consideration of their own legitimation problems, for instance, and of ways in which these might be addressed. More generally, there needs to be proper consideration of the nature of post-colonialism, and of the terms and nature of international trade. Huntington claims not to be Western-centric, and that he is not regarding others merely as 'objects of study'. At times, he also appears to be criticising the arrogance and powerbrandishing of some Western states. Yet his whole approach is of the defensive Westerner. Indeed, the assumption that 'others' who do not share certain Western values are *ipso facto* hostile to the West is one of the most dangerous aspects of the argument in terms of its potential policy implications. There is no overt consideration of the possibility that 'hostility' may in some, perhaps many, cases be no more than a quite understandable desire to be left alone. The possibility that many non-Western cultures sometimes feel threatened by Western values and influences—even as they are also fascinated by them and by the communications technology that plays such an important role in transmitting them—must be fully explored; like almost any living being whose existence is endangered, those who believe their cultures are being threatened are quite likely to respond in negative and even aggressive ways.

Finally, and as the ninth point, Huntington's article can in important ways be seen as *irresponsible.* It has exerted a major influence on the debate about whether or not the West still has dangerous enemies; as John Esposito has argued, 'The defeat of communism has created a "threat vacuum" that has given rise to a search for new enemies'.[20] There is no question that Huntington intended his piece to be normative-prescriptive; it is meant to prove the existence of a threat in the post-Cold War era so that Western—particularly US—policy-makers will continue to pour vast sums of taxpayers' money into defence and defence-related research and development. Following on from the eighth criticism in particular, there is very little attempt to suggest ways in which the West could promote more harmonius relations.[21] Despite Huntington's claims to the contrary, this is a Western-centric argument. What Huntington has apparently failed to realise is that his kind of argument might actually play *against* Western interests, in that it either maintains or erects barriers that render war more likely.

It might be objected that for Huntington to have incorporated some or all of the above points would have required a substantial increase in the length of his article. Even if this is true, the fact that the full-length book does not address or overcome many of these issues suggests that Huntington is either unaware of the problems or else has chosen to ignore them. Since his argument is aimed *inter alia* at policy-makers, Huntington should have shown that alternatives to his essentially unilinear argument had at least been considered, on one level to render it more convincing.

Despite its several shortcomings, Huntington's argument is rich as a heuristic device, and in the next section, its application to contemporary and future possible developments in Europe is assumed to be as useful a way as any of attempting to understand these.

The Clash of Civilisations Thesis and Europe

Of Huntington's seven or eight civilisations, three (Western, Slavic–Orthodox, Islamic) dominate in contemporary Europe; if Russia is taken as *sui generis,* there is a fourth. Many of Huntington's specific observations about Europe appear to ring true; there is no intention in this analysis of throwing out the baby with the bathwater. A few examples will demonstrate this.

In *some* ways, the nation state is being transcended or substantially modified, as Huntington suggests. Clearly, both centripetal (integrative) and centrifugal (disintegrative) forces currently operate in Europe. Thus, Belgium federalised in 1993 and could yet break up; Czechoslovakia divided into two countries at the beginning of the same year; Yugoslavia and the USSR disintegrated at the beginning of the 1990s; and there are significant separatist or autonomist movements in Spain, the UK and Italy. On the other side of the coin, *very* faltering steps are being taken towards reconciliation of the two Irelands; Belarus and Russia moved somewhat closer together in 1996; while Germany unified in 1990.

But the examples cited in the last paragraph are all cases of *particular* nation states that have changed or are changing their boundaries. As such, they do not *per se* support the argument about the nation state being transcended. More significant are the developments within the EU. With the adoption of the Maastricht and Amsterdam Treaties, the member-states have agreed to a deeper level of integration and further limits on their own sovereignty. The EU has also been widened since Huntington wrote his article, with the accession of Austria, Finland and Sweden to the EU from January 1995.[22] Inasmuch as these countries also have to accept the terms of Maastricht, the point about limiting sovereignty has even wider applicability. Moreover, their joining is in line with Huntington's 'kin-country' argument, since all of the EU member-states are 'Western' (though Greece is Orthodox).[23] The kinds of development occurring within the EU have been part of the reason for claims by writers such as Hobsbawm, Touraine and Dogan that Western Europe at least has become or is becoming 'post-national'.[24]

Huntington's argument about kin-countries is also persuasive regarding Russo–Ukrainian relations. Tensions between the two most populous former Soviet republics were such that war appeared to some to be a real possibility in the early 1990s; yet this did not eventuate, and relations improved in the mid-1990s. Similarly, the decision by Belarus to seek a much closer relationship with Russia that resulted in the April 1996 treaty between the two countries could be explained in Huntingtonian terms.

Many of the moves towards closer economic cooperation taken by formerly communist states of Eastern Europe accord with the Huntington thesis.[25] Thus, it is mostly Slavic non-Orthodox Christian states (Czechia, Poland, Slovakia and Slovenia, plus the non-Slavic but also non-Orthodox Christian state of Hungary) that have formed what is in many ways the most successful economic grouping of former CMEA (Council for Mutual Economic Assistance) members, the Central European Free Trade Area (CEFTA), while the Balkan states have been excluded from this.[26]

Equally, the wars that erupted in the late 1980s and early 1990s—between Armenia (Christian) and Azerbaijan (Muslim); Croatia (Catholic) and Serbia (Orthodox); Serbs, Croats and Bosnian Muslims in Bosnia; Russians (Slavic Orthodox) and Chechens (Muslim)—all accord with Huntington's argument.

And many of Huntington's statements about racism in Europe ring true. For example, there is no question that many French, and not only supporters of Le Pen, are even more incensed if a terrorist bomb appears to have been planted by North African Islamic groups than if an equally destructive bomb were to be planted by alienated white non-Muslim groups. This said, the racism is not new, merely more intense in the 1990s. This point is explored further in the conclusions.

But while Huntington's argument *can* be used to explain the various relationships and developments just cited, there are alternative explanations, many of them at least as convincing as Huntington's. Ukraine and Russia are both nuclear powers, for instance; the leaders in Kyiv and Moscow appreciate the dangers of allowing their differences to escalate. Belarus has even worse economic problems than Russia; given the West's wariness about investing in the former, partly because of the growing tendency there towards dictatorship, it is not surprising that President Lukashenka has wooed Russia.[27] The disputes between Armenia and Azerbaijan, between Croatia and Serbia, and among the three main groups in Bosnia, can be interpreted at least as well in terms of territorial differences as 'clash of civilisation' factors (and in all cases appeared to have been more or less resolved *pro tem* by 1996). In sum, factors other than civilisation could provide just as convincing explanations of these phenomena as the 'clash' thesis, though they would be more individualised, and therefore perhaps less attractive to some, than the grand comparative approach adopted by Huntington.

At the same time, some recent developments in Europe run counter to the kin-country argument. Most notably, there are at least three sets of relationships which the kin-country thesis would suggest should bring 'divided' groups closer together, but in which this does not appear to be happening. Thus,

Hungarians within Hungary have so far demonstrated little enthusiasm for linking up with Hungarians in Slovakia, Transylvania or Vojvodina; Moldova has proven reluctant to move too close to Romania; and the Russian government has been lukewarm in its support for Russian separatists in the Crimea. All this could change, of course; but these cases do warn against over-hasty and simplistic reductionism.

What of Huntington's suggestion that East European countries should find it easier to join the West than should other states? The focus here will be on the major military and economic blocs in Europe, NATO and the EU respectively.

The most tangible signs of the end of the so-called Soviet Bloc[28] became visible in mid-1991, with the collapse of both the WTO (Warsaw Treaty Organisation) and the CMEA. Already in the dying days of the former, many of the East European states made clear their desire to join NATO. They did so not merely, nor even primarily, because of feelings of civilisation solidarity with the West, but rather as a way of minimising the chances that a revitalised USSR or its successor state(s) would reimpose its control over them.

NATO initially appeared to be highly enthusiastic about this new development. In November 1991, what could be seen as a half-way house was built, with the establishment of the NACC (North Atlantic Cooperation Council). This included all of the former Soviet republics except Georgia, as well as the East European states; for a very brief period, 'the West' and the Slavic Orthodox worlds or civilisations appeared keen to move much closer together.

But the West's initial enthusiasm soon waned. By late 1993, Russia was declaring its opposition to any incorporation of Central and East European states into NATO. Much of this change of policy can be explained in terms of domestic Russian politics, in particular Yeltsin's more hawkish stance in the aftermath of the violent closure of the Russian parliament in September– October. This said, the clash thesis *can* be invoked to interpret the dramatic shift, since these internal differences could be seen on one level to reflect Russia's 'torn' nature, of which Huntington makes so much.[29] Neither Russia's changed foreign policy, nor the disturbing results of the December 1993 Russian elections, scared the Central and East European states off the NATO track, however. On the contrary, the first application for NATO membership by a former component of the 'Soviet Internal Empire', Lithuania, was lodged in January 1994.

The West was by now becoming wary of being drawn too far into the conflicts between Moscow and its former satellites. It was in this context that President Clinton's proposal for a 'Partnership for Peace' arrangement was formally adopted by NATO in January 1994. But although all of the east European states except some of the former Yugoslav republics, and all of the former Soviet Union (FSU) states except Tajikistan, had joined the Partnership for Peace within a year, the scheme was clearly a compromise, and fell far short of the aspirations and expectations of many Central and East European states.

Many observers believed that Western concerns about both practical difficulties and Russian reactions would delay any further military integration of the CEE states. Yet in July 1997, following on from the publication in September 1995 of its 'Study on Enlargement',[30] NATO did invite three CEE states (Czechia, Hungary and Poland) to commence negotiations for full membership; 1999 was seen as the target date for admission of these countries. The process could yet encounter obstacles. Moreover, those CEE countries not invited to this first round of negotiations were bitterly disappointed, and Russia continued to have serious reservations about developments even after President Yeltsin had signed a 'Founding Act' in May 1997 that appeared to represent Moscow's acknowledgement of NATO's right to expand eastwards. Nevertheless, slow progress towards greater involvement of many CEE states in NATO *is* being made, at the same time as NATO continues to make concerted efforts to make the Russians feel they are at least being consulted about the whole process.

So far in this part of the discussion, 'the West' has been referred to as if it had one basic position. It is now necessary to examine 'the' Western position more closely. Huntington's notion that 'the West' subdivides into two main variants—the North American and the West European—is of some value in beginning to understand differences within NATO, since Washington tended to be more concerned with Moscow's feelings than did most of the West European states. But it can be too simplistic even to refer to the West European position. The UK has often sided more with the US than with its continental European neighbours, while France has tended to be the most distant from Washington of the major West European actors. The dominant country in Western Europe, Germany, has played a complex role. While being close to Washington, it has also enjoyed a warm relationship with many Central and East European countries. During the first half of 1995, the important differences between the US and dominant West European views were reflected in the confusion over Bosnia, including divergent opinions on how best to respond to Russia's (ultimately largely symbolic) support for the Serbs. It was therefore not surprising that the US eventually decided to seek a solution itself; even though the French insisted that the peace accord to a European war be signed in Europe, few did not appreciate that what by late 1995 looked like a real possibility for peace in Bosnia had been worked out in Dayton, Ohio.

The situation regarding economics and trade bears marked similarities to that of military integration. At about the same time as it became obvious to most (though not necessarily to Gorbachev) that the CMEA's days were severely numbered, a putative successor organisation, the Organisation for International Economic Cooperation, was mooted. But this was stillborn, largely because most of Comecon's former members were far more interested in joining the Western trading blocs than in revamping their existing arrangements.

Most post-communist states have in the 1990s chosen one or both of two options. The first is to create and/or join local macro-regional economic groupings. Some of these comprise exclusively post-communist states, while others involve both post-communist and West European countries. Among the more significant groupings are the Commonwealth of Independent States (CIS);[31] the Central European Initiative;[32] The Council of Baltic States;[33] and CEFTA.[34]

The second path is to seek closer ties with the major economic groupings of Western Europe, notably EFTA (the European Free Trade Association) and the EU. The former signed Free Trade Agreements with Bulgaria and Hungary in March 1993, following similar agreements with Czechoslovakia in March 1992 and with Poland and Romania in December 1992. There have also been much looser Declarations on Cooperation between EFTA and some of the other post-communist states (e.g. Slovenia, May 1992; Albania, December 1992).

The ultimate aim of all these states is not membership of EFTA, however, but the EU. In the early-1990s, most post-communist states saw a connection with EFTA as one way of moving closer to the EC, especially with the formation of the EEA (European Economic Area, comprising EFTA—minus Liechtenstein and Switzerland—and the EC/EU) in March 1993 and its operationalisation in January 1994. But with three of the major members of EFTA joining the EU in January 1995, there has been even less pretence by the post-communist states that EFTA is of much interest to them. Several countries have taken concrete steps to move closer to the EU. For example, Association (or Europe) Agreements were signed with the EC by Czechoslovakia, Hungary and Poland in December 1991, by Romania in February 1993 and by Bulgaria in March 1993. All of these took time to become operational. Thus, the Hungarian and Polish agreements became effective in February 1994, while the Bulgarian, Czech, Romanian and Slovak came into effect one year later. The three post-communist Baltic states signed such agreements in April 1995, while Slovenia initialled one in June. But several of these countries then went further and made formal applications for full membership of the EU; by June 1996, the list of applicants comprised ten post-communist states (Bulgaria, Czechia, Estonia, Hungary, Latvia, Lithuania, Poland, Slovakia, Slovenia and Romania). Hungary and Poland again led the way, submitting their applications as early as April 1994.

As with NATO, however, so the EC's apparent initial enthusiasm to welcome countries that had overthrown their communist systems soon declined. In the early 1990s, the recession that had already hit the Anglophone countries spread to Western Europe; in this situation, most EC countries became more wary about opening up their markets to the Central and East Europeans. There were a number of incidents, such as the temporary ban on the import of meat, livestock and dairy produce from Central and Eastern Europe in April 1993, that were perceived by the East Europeans as indicative of the West Europeans' reluctance to admit them to Western markets. Indeed, many in the east of Europe now saw the EC as hypocritical, in that it preached free market economics at the same time as, in practice, it raised barriers to free trade as a means of protecting its own economies. A prime example was the dispute over Polish cherries. The Poles sought to sell cherries cheaply in Western Europe, but were required to charge at least the same price as that of the cheapest cherries produced within the EC, thus rendering the Polish produce less competitive.

Despite these tensions, many Central and East European states knew they would have to maintain the pressure on their Western neighbours for closer economic ties if they were to develop and to avoid having to reorient their economies back towards the FSU. This helps to explain the Hungarian and Polish applications of April 1994, and the many subsequent applications to join the EU. The latter has found it difficult to resist such pressure, and in 1994 agreed to produce a set of criteria to be met by applicants before their applications would be seriously considered. This promise resulted in a 300-page White Paper that was adopted by the EU in May 1995 and which does provide a list of criteria. But the EU was still reluctant to indicate any target dates by when countries meeting the specified criteria might realistically expect to be admitted. In December 1995, it indicated that negotiations would probably commence in the second half of 1997. In July 1997, the EU Commission did indeed recommend the opening of negotiations with five CEE states (Czechia, Estonia, Hungary, Poland and Slovenia). Yet the months following this announcement revealed that there were still profound differences among the EU member-states on the timing and scope of enlargement, and it remains to be seen which countries will be admitted and when. The incorporation of even the strongest post-communist applicants is still some way off.

If the situation of the post-communist countries vis-à-vis the EU is compared with that of the Southern European states that moved from dictatorship to democracy in the mid-1970s, it might initially appear that the latter were treated much better. Thus the Greek transition from the colonels' regime began in 1974, and Greece was admitted to the EC in 1981. The Portuguese and the Spanish commenced their transitions in 1974 and 1975 respectively, and were admitted to the EC in 1986. Does their better treatment accord with Huntington's thesis?

While the apparently better treatment of the Southern European states might initially appear to be in line with the 'kin-countries' argument, closer analysis reveals that there are several other reasons—many of them at least as convincing as Huntington's thesis—why their situation was different from that of the Central and East European states. First, the scale and nature of their transitions was different. Greece had only been a dictatorship for some seven years, and had had much experience with democracy. While both Spain and Portugal had been dictatorships for decades, they like Greece had basically market economies, indigenous bourgeoisies, and largely settled borders,[35] and thus did not require nearly as comprehensive transformations as the post-communist states. Since the post-communist transitions are far more complex, there is *ceteris paribus* a greater likelihood that some of these countries might yet steer away from democracy (as Slovakia appears to many to have been doing since 1995); given that membership of the EU is open only to states that have liberal democratic systems, it becomes clearer why the EU has reservations. Second, there were only three of these Southern European transitional states; the ranks of the post-communist states applying for EU membership are likely to swell from the present ten. Finally, the situation of the EU has changed. It is now much bigger than it was when the Southern European states joined, and is attempting much deeper integration; its own complexification is a significant factor. Expressed another way, *some* of the problems facing the post-communist states as they attempt to enter Western 'clubs' relate more to problems within the 'club' than to the applicants themselves. And as a minor point, it should also be remembered here that Greece is an Eastern Orthodox country anyway, while most of the CEE applicants are predominantly Christian societies—all of which raises further questions about the kin-country argument.[36]

Before concluding this discussion of post-communist states' membership of the EU, the earlier point about the need to disaggregate 'the West' needs to be recalled. Thus Germany has tended to be the most welcoming of the EU states, while some of the Southern European states, perceiving themselves likely to be subject to greater competition in agriculture and even manufacturing if the Central and East Europeans join the EU, have been the least. Some countries that have benefited extensively from the EU's regional funds are also concerned that they will lose their benefits to the newcomers. Once again, vested economic interest provides at least as convincing an explanation of current attitudes as the kin-country argument.

Yet there is one major semi-European country whose relationship with the West and recent domestic developments might at first glance appear to provide strong evidence in support of Huntington's thesis. That country is Turkey. While officially a secular state, Turkey is very much a Muslim society, and was from June 1996 to June 1997 governed by a coalition in which the pro-Islamist Welfare Party was the senior partner. It can also be argued that the EU has consistently excluded Turkey from its ranks because of its different civilisational affiliations. Closer scrutiny reveals, however, a more complex picture than the simple reductionism of the clash of civilisations thesis paints.[37]

It is true that Turkey was in the mid-1990s being ruled by the most pro-Islamic, and in many ways most anti-Western, government since Turkey became a secular republic in 1922–3. The prime minister at that time, Necmettin Erbakan, declared his intention substantially to improve relations with the Central Asian republics and the Balkan states, and cited common history and spiritual links as a major reason for this. This is in line with Huntington's predictions about Turkey. But it took some six months to appoint Erbakan's government after the December 1995 parliamentary elections; while the Welfare Party had been the most popular party in those elections, it secured only 21.4 per cent of the vote, compared with just over 19 per cent each for the second and third most popular parties.[38] Only when relations between these latter two broke down, largely because of personal conflicts between Tansu Ciller of the True Path party and the then prime minister Mesut Yilmaz[39] of the Motherland Party, did a pro-Islamic dominated coalition take power. Not only did the vast majority of Turkish citizens not vote for the Welfare Party, but many of those who did apparently did so in protest at the ruling parties to that point. Hence, the significance of a move towards a Muslim-oriented party should be seen in context and not exaggerated. Moreover, the predictions of many observers that if Erbakan's government *were* to attempt to move Turkey too far away from the West, the pro-Western military would at least indirectly intervene in civilian politics, soon proved correct. In March 1997, the military issued a list of 'recommendations' to Erbakan's government, which in practice was akin to a set of directives. This, plus increasing civilian criticism of Erbakan's government, led to the latter's collapse and the return of Mesut Yilmaz as prime minister in June 1997.

It cannot be denied that there have been many tensions over the years between Turkey and the EC/EU, most of them relating to the latter's reluctance to admit the former to its ranks.[40] The reasons for this are several. An important one is that Greece, which has long had a troubled relationship with Turkey, has hindered moves towards a closer relationship between Ankara and Brussels. Another is that the EU is in theory supposed to comprise only European states; Turkey, like Russia, straddles Europe and Asia. But neither of these obstacles is insurmountable; were the EU enthusiastic about admitting the Turks, it could find ways to do so. Does this all mean that Huntington's thesis is correct? There is no question that it does provide an explanation; and Erbakan's statements cited above lend it weight. But other explanations are at least as convincing.

One is that Turkey has a considerably larger population than the Southern European countries admitted during the 1980s; even Spain's population is only some two thirds that of Turkey. Turkey is also a very poor country by European standards; in 1994, its per capita GNP was less than one third of Greece's, and just over a quarter of Portugal's. Hence, many within the EU fear that existing parts of the grouping will suffer, for instance in terms of losing micro-regional support, if such a large, poor country were to be admitted and hence eligible for EU funds.

Second, Turkey has a substantial problem with the Kurds. Parts of Western Europe, particularly Germany, have already suffered directly as a result of the Turkish–Kurdish conflict, and there are fears that other countries will be more directly affected if Turkey were to be admitted to the EU. The effects could be in terms of terrorism and/or Kurdish migration, both of which make many West Europeans apprehensive.

Third, and closely related to the second point, Turkey's commitment to democracy has been justifiably questioned on several occasions. Following a military coup, it was under a form of military rule anyway from September 1980 to December 1983; this was the third time since 1960 that the military had been directly involved in the country's politics. Although Turkey has had a form of parliamentary democracy since then, not only is its re-establishment relatively recent and the commitment to it still in question, but Ankara has frequently been accused of substantial abuses of human rights, particularly with reference to the Kurds.

Despite the differences between the EU and Turkey, it would be erroneous to assume that the former has taken no measures to bridge the gap. For instance, following a concession to Greece committing the EU to a deadline for consideration of Cypriot membership, EU foreign ministers signed an agreement with Turkey in March 1995 establishing a Customs Union between the two that was to become effective in January 1996. This was ratified by the European Parliament in December 1995, just days before the Turkish election, and became effective on schedule. However, the European Parliament's approval was subject to the condition that Turkey was to continue to be committed to democracy and to improve its record on human rights. Unfortunately, relations then deteriorated again in 1996, amid EU charges that the Turkish government was becoming even more abusive of human rights, particularly in connection with the Kurds. In September 1996, the EU voted to freeze some 53 million ECU of aid that was to have been granted to Turkey in 1997 until such time as Ankara started making concerted efforts to respect the rights of minorities. The military's clear involvement in civilian politics in 1997 only added to concerns about Turkey's overall political orientation.

Even *if* the tensions between Turkey and the EU were to be interpreted in terms of Huntington's thesis, however, there is no reason to suppose that these differences should or would lead to serious conflict. Turkey is a member of NATO, and it is highly unlikely that it would attack its fellow-states or *vice versa*. Of course, Turkey could leave NATO. Even if this were to happen, there is only the remotest likelihood at present that the government in Ankara would be foolhardy enough to declare war on its former allies. The possibility of the latter attacking Turkey is even more remote. The EU member-states have been criticised for not becoming sufficiently involved in the Bosnian conflict in the early-to-mid 1990s. One argument often advanced is that the West Europeans were unwilling to fight to defend Bosnian Muslims (which would be in line with Huntington's approach). But it is just as likely that the EU member-states were loath to become involved in *any* fighting beyond their borders; after all, they did not directly intervene in the fighting between Slovenia and 'Yugoslavia' (basically Serbia) or between Croatia and 'Yugoslavia' either. In short, while the EU may criticise the Turkish government and *vice versa,* this is quite different from there being a serious conflict or civilisation 'clash' between them.

Conclusions

While Huntington's thesis is seductive, and often persuasive, it is also potentially dangerous. One reason is that its very simplicity, though attractive, misleadingly glosses over many of the peculiarities and specificities of particular developments, cultures and relationships. In a follow-up article in response to his critics, Huntington acknowledges that his paradigm, as he calls it, neither accounts for all aspects of contemporary international politics nor can predict all future developments. Yet he goes on to say that the ability to criticise this or that aspect of his thesis is insufficient to invalidate it, and that the onus is on the critics to produce a better paradigm:

> A paradigm is disproved only by the creation of an alternative paradigm that accounts for more crucial facts in equally simple or simpler terms...[41]

This is to miss the point entirely of so much in the epistemological debates of recent years. It is to assume that we need a paradigm, almost any paradigm, even if this appears to be unwise or unjustified. It is as if Huntington is totally unaware that the sort of grand theorising in which he has engaged has come under profound scrutiny in recent years and been found to be often misleading or obfuscatory.

    While the damnation of grand theory by many post-structuralists and post-modernists sometimes goes too far, it is surely obvious that a paradigm or theory that is not only flawed *but that is also offered as a basis for major public policy making* is potentially dangerous. Thus, the most serious implication of Huntington's epistemological arrogance is that, if used as a basis for Western defence policy, it could help to turn the gloomy scenarios drawn by Huntington into self-fulfilling prophesies. Although the very fact that Huntington calls on 'the West' to make decisions in line with his recommendations reveals that he does recognise some role for agency, the structures within which these operate are held to be already well-formed and in many ways rigidifying. There is too little awareness of the fluidity of so-called civilisations, and of humanity's potential constantly to reconstruct and deconstruct them. Neither is there nearly sufficient acknowledgment of the fact that many Western societies are becoming more 'civilisationally pluralistic'; this point requires a little elaboration.

The path towards multiculturalism is proving to be a bumpy one in many parts of the world, Europe included. Groups that have long inhabited a given region/country sometimes find it difficult to adapt to an influx of peoples from other parts of the world with different cultures, particularly if this influx occurs quickly. Much of the racism in Western Europe during the 1990s can be partly explained in terms of the wave of immigration and population movement that related to both the collapse of communist power and the general softening of borders within the EC/EU. But there is a dynamic to this process. While it would be naïve and irresponsible to downplay the extent of racism in countries such as France, Austria and Germany (to name but a few), it should also be recognised that precisely this racism among some sections of populations has led others to counter this and, in the process, become more aware of those against whom racist attacks are directed. Many West Europeans are embarrassed by the concept of 'Fortress Europe', and seek to welcome and better understand refugees and other immigrants. The *millions* of Germans who protested in the streets in 1992 and 1993 against racist attacks constitute just one piece of evidence of this, the subsequent tightening of the German asylum laws notwithstanding. The process of multiculturalisation will continue to be problematic in Europe, as elsewhere; but as time passes and groups continue to intermarry and work together, so the possibilities increase that the significance of 'civilisational difference' will decline, especially if states adopt concrete measures to encourage multiculturalism.

Hence, if Huntington had devoted more of his article and book to constructive proposals for increasing understanding, tolerance and respect between groups both within and between existing political and cultural units, he might have contributed to a more civilised world, rather than one in which the West is encouraged to fear and arm itself against a potential enemy in the form of 'the rest'.[42] Such proposals would *also* have implications for policy on public expenditure. But these would be for greater spending on education and aid of various kinds rather than on weapons.[43] One does not have to be a post-modernist to advocate greater tolerance, merely someone wanting to make the world a safer rather than a more dangerous place to live in. And this is certainly in 'the West's' interest.

Europe's boundaries, both of states and of supranational organisations, are still very fluid. Indeed, they have been more fluid in the 1990s than for decades. There will continue to be tensions and even conflicts relating to these boundaries for the foreseeable future. There will also be tensions and conflicts between individual European countries, European macro-regions and 'the West' on the one hand, and individual countries and macro-regions on the other, well into the next century and probably beyond. But there will be many reasons for these tensions, and what will appear to be the dominant one in one case will be a marginal factor in another. Moreover, there will also be many instances of cooperation and improved relations—again for a number of reasons, including vested self-interest. The world is a much messier and more changeable place than Huntington wishes to acknowledge. Unfortunately, his desire for epistemological tidiness and simplicity could mean even more bloodshed than he appears to realise.

Notes

1. S. Huntington, 'The Clash of Civilizations?', *Foreign Affairs*, Vol. 72 (3), 1993, 22–49. A number of leading analysts—including Johns Hopkins Professor of Middle Eastern Studies Fouad Ajami, Singaporean Deputy Secretary of Foreign Affairs Kishore Mahbubani, Director of the Princeton China Initiative Liu Binyan and Georgetown Professor of Government Jeane Kirkpatrick—responded critically to Huntington's thesis in *Foreign Affairs*, Vol. 72 (4), 1993, 2–26.
2. F. Fukuyama, 'The End of History?', *National Interest*, 16, 1989, 3–18. See too F. Fukuyama, *The End of History and the Last Man* (New York: Free Press, 1992).
3. S. Huntington, *The Clash of Civilizations and the Remaking of World Order* (New York: Simon and Schuster, 1996).
4. Huntington, *loc. cit.*, 22.
5. *Ibid.*, 24.
6. Huntington used the term Confucian in his article, but changed this to Sinic in his book; the reason for this change is provided in Huntington, *op. cit.*, 45.
7. It is extraordinary that Huntington's own classification is so inconsistent, given that the notion of civilisations is the basis of his whole argument and that he had been working so long on his book. For instance, he argues on pp. 47–8 of the book that Buddhism does not constitute a major civilisation, yet includes it in his map of major civilisations on pp.26–7 (map 1.3), and lists it again on p.102. In response to criticisms that he had not included Judaism as a major civilisation in his original article, Huntington does at least focus on it in his book, and sees it as 'historically affiliated' with but distinct from both Christianity and Islam (p.48); yet he still does not state clearly how he would classify it. Many Jews would certainly baulk at the representation of Israel as an Islamic state on p.27. Given the situation in the Middle East, and its potential to be the starting point of

major conflict in the future, this blurring is a serious flaw in Huntington's analysis. Huntington cannot decide whether or not there is yet an African civilisation; the use of the word 'possibly' in front of African is Huntington's, not the present author's. But perhaps the most bizarre aspect of his elaboration of civilisations is the fact that Huntington completely omits (forgets?) Orthodoxy in his brief descriptions of the world's major civilisations on pp.45–8 of his book, even though he clearly includes it in a list towards the top of p.45 and in map 1.3; in terms of his own sequencing, there should have been some consideration of this civilisation between 'Western' and 'Latin American'.

8. W. Wallace, *The Transformation of Western Europe* (London: Pinter, 1990), esp. 16–21.
9. I am indebted to Jean Blondel for reminding me of this concept when he read through the draft of this chapter.
10. One of those who has criticised Huntington's thesis has argued that the attempt to integrate Hong Kong into the PRC will be 'particularly disruptive'—see R. Bartley, 'The Case for Optimism: The West Should Believe in Itself', *Foreign Affairs,* 72 (4), 1993, 17.
11. For conflicting views on whether or not the Chinese communist power system is likely to collapse see J. Goldstein, 'The Coming Chinese Collapse', *Foreign Policy,* 99, 1995, 35–52 and Y-S. Huang, 'Why China Will Not Collapse', *Foreign Policy,* 99, 1995, 54–68.
12. See footnote 28 below.
13. P. Gleick, *Water in Crisis* (Oxford: Oxford University Press, 1993), esp. 107.
14. Huntington, *loc. cit.,* 30–1.
15. *Ibid.,* 33 and 35; Huntington, *op. cit.,* 269–72.
16. It is acknowledged that Huntington sometimes recognises at least three or four subdivisions of Islam—Arab, Turkic, Malay, and, in his book, Persian (see *loc. cit.,* 24; *op. cit.,* 45). Nevertheless, he still ultimately treats Islam as a homogeneous entity.
17. See the chapter by Jeremy Salt in this collection.
18. Huntington, *loc. cit,* 25.
19. *Ibid.,* 47. See too Huntington, *op. cit.,* 238–45, esp. 239–40.
20. J. Esposito, 'Political Islam: Beyond the Green Menace', *Current History,* 93 (579), 1994, 19.
21. At the very end of his article, Huntington (*loc. cit.,* 49) does call on the West 'to develop a more profound understanding of the basic religious and philosophical assumptions underlying other civilizations and the ways in which those civilizations see their interests'. However, given the overall thrust of his argument, this call is essentially a platitude; this is borne out by the fact that the same concluding section contains a number of specific proposals about Western defence policy. See too Huntington, *op. cit.,* 312, which reveals clearly Huntington's 'insider' and 'outsider' mentality, as does his rejection of multiculturalism (*ibid.,* 318).
22. On all this, see the chapters by Philomena Murray, Rémy Davison, and Christine Agius in this volume.
23. It is not clear from Huntington's analysis exactly how a non-Slavic Orthodox country is to be classified in civilisational terms, though he does claim (*op. cit.,* 162–3) that Greece 'is not part of Western civilization'.
24. E. Hobsbawm, *Nations and Nationalism since 1780* (Cambridge: Cambridge University Press, 1992); A. Touraine, 'European countries in a post-national era' in C. Rootes and H. Davis (eds), *Social Change and Political Transformation* (London: UCL Press, 1994), 13–26; M. Dogan, 'The Decline of Nationalisms within Western Europe', *Comparative Politics,* 26 (3), 1994, 281–305.
25. Subject to the point made earlier that many of the Central and East European states do not fit neatly into any of his civilisation groupings.
26. Whether or not Slovenia constitutes a Balkan country is a fiercely contested issue; many Slovenes themselves prefer others not to consider their country part of the Balkans.

27. It should be noted, however, that many Belarusians have protested against their leader's overtures to Moscow. Moreover, Belarus's ever more dictatorial system was subjected to increasing criticism from the Yeltsin regime in late-1996 and 1997.
28. Many Central and East Europeans whose states were never part of the USSR have recently been emphasising that they resent the application of the term Soviet (Outer) Empire to their countries. Given this, and the fact that the nature of the relationship between Moscow and most of the East European capitals during the communist era was in important ways different from the relationship between West European states and their colonies (even allowing for differences between *these)*, the arguably less loaded term Soviet Bloc is used here.
29. For Huntington, 'torn' countries are those that cannot decide to which civilisation they belong—see Huntington, *loc. cit.,* 42–5 and *op. cit.,* 139–54.
30. Key passages from this are reprinted in *Transition,* 1 (23), 1995, 19–26.
31. All of the FSU states except Estonia, Latvia and Lithuania; although relatively little has happened so far, a formal proposal to create an Economic Union of the CIS states was made in May 1993.
32. Created in January 1992, and originally comprising Austria, Croatia, Czechia, Hungary, Italy, Poland, Slovakia and Slovenia; Bosnia-Hercegovina and Macedonia subsequently joined, and it was agreed in May 1996 to admit in addition Albania, Belarus, Bulgaria, Romania and Ukraine.
33. Established in March 1992, this comprises ten states, including Germany, Denmark, Poland, Russia and the three FSU Baltic States.
34. December 1992—comprising the Visegrad Four plus, since January 1996, Slovenia.
35. There are disputes, of course, such as that between the Basques and the Spanish authorities, or between Greece and Turkey; but the scale and nature of these is different from many of those that have pertained in some of the post-communist countries in the 1990s. It is worth noting in this context that, of the 27 post-communist states of CEE and the FSU, 22 are newly sovereign.
36. Questions can be raised about the validity of Huntington's assertions concerning the growing attraction of religion around the world. In Europe, at least, there is some significant evidence to the contrary. Many long believed that the Poles were a deeply Catholic nation; but in the 1990s, the Roman Catholic Church's anti-abortion stance is seen by several analysts as a key factor explaining what many had predicted would never happen—enough Poles freely voting for parties connected to the former communists (who were generally pro-abortion) to bring such parties to power (September 1993).
37. See too Jeremy Salt's chapter in this volume.
38. Moreover, the Welfare Party's vote represented only a 4.5% improvement on its performance in the 1991 elections, so that any notion that there had been a huge swing to the Islamists would be misguided. For a recent brief overview of the divisions *within* Turkish society, which endorse Huntington's notion of it as a 'torn' society, see M. Hakan Yavuz, 'Turkey's "Imagined Enemies": Kurds and Islamists', *The World Today,* 52 (4), 1996, 99–101.
39. The main reason for these tensions in the spring of 1996, apparently, was that Yilmaz would not support Ciller in her denial of allegations of corruption. In a cynical display of vested interest politics, the Welfare Party supported Ciller in June 1996, even though it was precisely this party that had made the allegations against Ciller in the first place (in April). But the party achieved its objectives, securing the position of senior partner in the governing coalition.
40. Turkey had an Association Agreement with the EC from 1964; but this was suspended in 1981 because of the military coup in Turkey. Relations improved again once military rule was replaced by a parliamentary system, and Turkish workers were free to seek work within the EC from 1986. Turkey applied for full membership of the EC in 1987; but the EC ruled in December 1989 that conditions were not yet appropriate for Turkish membership.

41. S Huntington, 'If Not Civilisations, What? Paradigms of the Post-Cold War World', *Foreign Affairs,* 72 (5), 1993, 187.
42. It is instructive to note that Huntington states on p.130 of his book that 'It is human to hate'.
43. For a balanced view of both 'the Western' and 'the Islamic' worlds, which criticises both yet argues persuasively why initiatives in understanding must emanate from the West, see A. S. Ahmed, 'Towards the Global Millennium: The Challenge of Islam', *The World Today,* 52 (8–9), 1996, 212–16.

3 The European Transformation of the Nation State

PHILOMENA MURRAY

Introduction

When the European Community (EC) was first created, the national state actors did not intend that it would replace or even weaken the nation state. However, many idealists of the period, whether federalist or neo-functionalist, *did* aspire to some form of radical transformation of the nation state, and even its supplanting by a supranational body with competences which would be transferred from the nation state to a new supranational, federal focus of power and public policy. The purpose of this chapter is to examine the transformation of the West European nation state into a 'member state' of the European Union (EU), within the process of cooperation known as European integration. There has been considerable examination of the role of the nation state in the EC and EU, and one of the most influential and incisive analysts has been Alan Milward.[1] This chapter takes as its starting point Milward's contention that the creation of the EC was a part of that 'postwar rescue of the European nation state, because the new political consensus on which this rescue was built required the process of integration, the surrender of limited areas of national sovereignty to the supranation'.[2] It then examines the manner in which the nation state of Western Europe has been transformed into a type of member state, adapting and modifying Alberta Sbragia's use of the term 'member state'.

Milward points to the historical specificity of the important post-war era, especially 1945 to the late 1960s. He suggests that the EC rescued, bolstered and ultimately saved the nation state, particularly in the form of social and economic benefits. These benefits have accrued to the nation state as a result of EC membership. However, as Hartley has pointed out, Milward neglects to deal with the security and even the political elements of the desire for post-war European cooperation.[3] So for Milward the nation state's rescue has been material, economic and social, rather than based on political or security concerns. In addition, while many of his observations hold for the period up to the late 1960s, they are less valid since that time.

Contentions regarding the role of the nation state feature in a divisive debate regarding the entire integration process in the EU.[4] Many analyses of the EU and its relationship with the nation state are based on an essential division. Either there has been a withering away of the state's power, or there has been a strengthening of that power, as a result of EU membership. These analyses are normative to a degree. They often say what should happen and what might have happened, rather than analysing what has actually happened. For example, those analysts who favour further cooperation, with increased pooling of sovereignty of the constituent states of the EU, sometimes called integrationists, interpret the role of the nation state as subservient to the EU primacy of law and competences. Those who suggest that there has been a strengthening of the nation state as a result of EU membership tend to be intergovernmentalists, neo-realists, or, in some cases, revisionist historians like Milward. As already noted, Milward suggests that the EC rescued the nation state. Unlike many integrationists and especially federalists, he argues that the EC never had a chance of replacing the nation state.

On examination, interpretations of what has happened to the nation state tend to be about what *should* happen to the nation state. There are expectations that the nation state should participate in the pooling of national sovereignty in a federalising EU, according to many federalists for example. While there is no problem with federalists holding this position, or with intergovernmentalists holding that the nation state should not contemplate any further pooling of sovereignty, a problem arises when analysts are highly normative in their perspective—to a degree that they fail to clarify and differentiate between the issue of whether the nation state *has been* strengthened or weakened on the one hand and, on the other, whether it *should be* strengthened or weakened. The possibility of a third position, that the state has been neither strengthened nor weakened, but simply changed, tends not to feature much in these arguments.

The state remains the central concern of many analysts, and its role has been examined comparatively in terms of criteria such as sovereignty and effectiveness. The symbiosis of the nation states with the EC guarantees that the nation state will survive, for Milward. However, he does not explore the huge significance of the oft-quoted interdependence of the nation states and the long-range implication of the Maastricht Treaty and the Single Market's project of economic integration.

This chapter illustrates that the nation states of the EU are constituent members of a dynamic fluid political and economic structure and thus the issue of the nation state is an evolving one, as the EU itself is evolving. The nation states are not simply nation states—they are also member states, that is, constituent members of an international system of governance which involves shared competences at the supranational level of decision-making in the European Union. The conflict regarding the integrationist agenda of some institutions of the EU (such as the European Parliament and European Commission) and the more sovereignty-minded states (such as the United Kingdom and Denmark) will continue to be a tension within the EU structure. Sbragia suggests that it is no longer appropriate to talk of nation states in the EU but, rather, of member states.[5] This chapter thus examines changing boundaries of the nation state in terms of the transformation of the nation state in the EU into a member state, in the context of the integration process. It suggests that the member states engage in cooperation in a manner that the nation states in the international arena at large do not—a sharing of competences and of national sovereignty in common policies above the arena of the nation state. It analyses the transformation of the nation state into member state in terms of politics, law and economics.

Finally, it is argued that a definitive analysis of the role of the nation state is ultimately a question of interpretation and of national interests. It is worth noting that there is a certain circularity to, and a normative nature and element of vested interests in, the arguments regarding the role of the nation state in Europe that renders a definitive position—strengthened or weakened—both impossible and spurious. It is impossible to state that the nation state has been strengthened or weakened as it is not feasible to ascertain what a nation state would have been like if it had *not* been in the EU and largely spurious because the fifteen nation states will continue to remain in the EU as it suits their interests. Nugent has correctly pointed out that, despite some reservations by some states, each member state has 'made the judgement that membership enhances its ability to achieve certain objectives'.[6] It is impossible to come to a decision or position on the role of the nation state in the EU and its future, as many analysts try to do, as no such decision is possible, just as there is no single paradigm for the analysis of the nation state.

Milward's argument

The value of Milward's original study has been to contribute to this fascinating debate on the role of nation states in Western Europe and on the integration process. The integration process refers to the pattern of cooperation among state governments and institutions in order to ensure completion of objectives such as a single market, a common monetary system, common policies and a common and superior body of law. It is worth quoting Milward's interesting thesis:

Our lives in western Europe for almost two hundred years have been moulded by the nation state...Changes have occurred since 1945 which give citizens of European countries real cause to ask whether national government, which has so long shaped the basic organisational framework within which they live, will or should be allowed to continue to do so .... there has grown an actual, rather than merely an abstract, alternative to government from the national centre.[7]

Further, the fact that established nation states should voluntarily contemplate political unification is a 'political change of the first magnitude' according to Milward. The oft-presented antithesis of supranationalism versus the nation state is, in Milward's view, false. He argues that 'there is no such antithesis and that the evolution of the European Community since 1945 has been an integral part of the reassertion of the nation state as an organisational concept'. Milward unfortunately fails to adequately define this concept, which causes problems with the definition and context of his hypothesis.[8] This is Milward's principal hypothesis and he seeks to prove that the nation state has managed to reassert its primacy in terms of allegiance and support of citizens. Indeed Milward regards the EC as the buttress of the nation state and an indispensable part of the post-war construction of the nation state. He subscribes to the position that 'the process of integration was deliberately conceived and developed to preserve the nation state by supporting a range of new social and economic policies whose very purpose was the resurrection of the nation state after its collapse between 1929 and 1945'.[9]

Without the EC, says Milward, the nation state could not have offered its citizens the same measure of security and prosperity which it had provided hitherto and which justified its survival.[10] This is in fact difficult to test as we do not know how nation states would have developed without the EC. In some ways it is as much a moot point as the Cecchini report on the cost of non-Europe which preceded the implementation of the Single Internal Market.

Milward sees the nation state as having rescued itself, with a sweeping extension of its functions, and reasserted itself as the fundamental unit of political organisation.[11] The EC, then 'only evolved as an aspect of that national reassertion and without it the reassertion might have proved impossible'. So for Milward, the nation state created the EC precisely because it was essential to its revival and at the same time the EC is a part of that national reassertion. If that is the case it would be necessary to query the reassertion of the nation state in those countries which do not in fact belong to the EC. The development of the EC and the process of European integration, is, for Milward, a part of the postwar rescue of the European nation state. Milward is correct in positing this rescue as part of a new political consensus which required a process of integration involving the surrender of limited areas of national sovereignty to the 'supranation', although the latter is not defined by Milward. He regards the process of European integration as serving the nation state. This is in some aspects undoubtedly true as the nation states created the EC (and decisions are made in a largely intergovernmental capacity) because it suited their national interests, interests which have been the subject of numerous analyses. Nevertheless the argument can read rather glibly. National interests, especially of the elites, were of course involved in creating the promise of European Union and the ever closer union of the peoples of Europe. What Milward did not take issue with, and could have, was the insistence of the nation states on the importance of the rhetoric of European Union and closer union, despite their repeated blatant disregard for it. So the nation state continued to pursue national interests within the EC. The EU was to continue to espouse the myth of the ever closer union of the peoples of Europe while at the same time the pursuit of national interests by the member states was to have unintended consequences.

The role of the nation state in the EU

The EU is characterised by economic interdependence and is a major actor in the globalisation of the economy and trade relations in particular. The EU has even gone beyond general international trends of transnational monetary relationships by attempting, under the TEU, to develop transnational and supranational relations whereby the national economy is increasingly more porous, and decisions regarding fiscal and monetary policy are made at several levels. The creation of EMU (Economic and Monetary Union) is envisaged under the Maastricht Treaty by 1999.[12] Davidson suggests that if the EMU program is carried out, the Community will move towards a 'federal system of economic government'.[13] This has immense implications for public policymaking if the focus shifts from the state to a federalised EU.

The interdependence of the economies of the nation states of Europe and the world at large is a transformation that is a continuing one, one that cannot ever return to the relative impermeability of the nation state of early this century. It is a commonly accepted fact that the nation state in the European economy is no longer a fully independent actor. National boundaries have little economic relevance in the EU. Economic transactions take place across borders and there is a freedom of movement of labour and an international mobility of all the factors of production in what, in effect, constitutes the largest frontier-free market in the world.

The post-Second World War era saw a desire for a cessation of nationalist hostilities among many nation states' leaders in Western Europe.[14] There was a desire for a merging or pooling of sovereignty in the EC. This would involve joint competences to make policy which applied to all constituent states. 'It was no coincidence that the effort towards European cooperation started with the European Coal and Steel Community (ECSC) since these two commodities were at the heart of traditional war making capacity. It was assumed that if these resources could be brought under joint control, it would be extremely difficult for these countries to fight each other in the future.'[15] The EC was founded in order to aid the recovery of national economies and to facilitate French influence over Germany. It was also founded with the objective of achieving peace and an ever closer union among the peoples of Europe. It was characterised by institutions which were both supranational and intergovernmental. It was not a distinct project to undermine the nation state, nor was it designed explicitly to strengthen the nation state. The first phase of postwar interstate cooperation took many forms, the strongest being the communities of the EC, as there was a Treaty-based decision to merge powers or legal competences to a body above the nation state. This body was to be controlled to a large extent by the nation states.

By the 1960s, an era of interdependence in economic terms saw the nation state reasserting itself. The states soon recovered economically from the disasters of war. They became accustomed to regular transnational, interstate negotiations and developed a means of working that came to be known as the Community method. This was based on mutual economic benefit. 'Whereas traditional international relations, governed by consensus, are based on the presumption that states mistrust each other, the development of a system (in the EU) governed by majoritarian decision-making has to be based on mutual trust.'[16] Intra-Community trade increased enormously during this early period of post-war reconstruction, so well analysed by Milward. The states also discussed various projects for closer political cooperation. Most of these projects failed due to the intransigence of at least one member state in its desire to protect national interests. Nevertheless the cooperation among states on economic issues such as the creation of the Common Agricultural Policy, and free trade in the area and other common and harmonised policies had political implications for the state, as it necessitated cooperation on policymaking and intergovernmental consultation. It has always been impossible to maintain a neat division of the EC into economic and political sectors. The economic was also political and so this is a false distinction. It is one which Milward ignores as he fails to address the political issues of integration in the 'rescue' of the nation state.

With membership of the EC, the states became accustomed to cooperation. Decisions relating to agriculture, fisheries and coordination of monetary policy were taken in Brussels by the Ministers of national governments on the basis of proposals from the European Commission. The 1970s saw an increase in the scope and number of EC policies and this led to the first rewriting of the

Treaty structure of the EC in the Single European Act. In addition, the EC had built upon a body of law that, as a result of a series of court cases, was established as having primacy over national law. This legal dimension of the EC was central to the change of the nation state to member state. The treaties signed by each of the member governments in the 1950s were transformed into a body of international law which was binding on its member states and their citizens.[17] EU law takes precedence over national law, is directly applicable in the states, and is binding on those to whom it is addressed.[18] Wallace correctly points out that the 'sharpest and most formal incursion into national sovereignty has been the acceptance of European Community law as superior to domestic law in all areas of Community competence under the Treaties'. He sees the high level of compliance in the EC and beyond as 'one of the most remarkable and distinctive aspects of West European regional integration over the past twenty five years'.[19]

This process of legal, economic and even political integration has not had the same effect on all the member states. Indeed it can be misleading to discuss the transformation of *the* nation state in the EU, as the nation states differ according to size, population, economy, growth rates, democratic experience and model of government, for example. In addition, it is important to recall that the nation state system is more robust in some cases than in others and that the nation states differ in patterns of elite cooperation, in powersharing and in institutional frameworks for the achievement of their goals.[20]

William Wallace has pointed to many of the problems with the concept of the state in the EC context. He suggests that 'some of the underlying tensions within the European Community have stemmed from the different concepts of the state held by both major and minor EC members' and that the EC represents a rather unstable compromise between these different concepts of the state and state action.[21]

If not the nation state, what?

It must be kept in mind that no alternative to the state was ever seriously considered during the post-war era of reconstruction which Milward and others examine. It is a matter of historical record that the federalist option presented by Spinelli and the European Federalist Movement wished for the abolition of national sovereignty. However, this was not considered a workable option in the 1940s and 1950s for the policymakers.[22] The weakening of the nation state was not an objective of the founders of the European Community. Bullman has pointed out that 'since the 1950s, the European Community developed in a way in which the nation states kept the rule book firmly in their hands'.[23] The remarkable interrelationship of nation state and Community was to ensure national dominance by way of the Council of Ministers, the major policymakers. The objectives of a political union were placed to one side, while ensuring an element of supranationalism was evident in the institutions of the European Court of Justice, the Commission and Parliament. Thus, quite rapidly, the EC's authority was to rest largely with the states. The Community never provided any organisational structure that would ultimately replace the state. Normative proponents of federalism did so aspire, however, and so the debate on the national perspective versus the supranational one was to become a feature of regular discussion on the EU's role and future development.

Although the nation state has undergone changes since membership of the EU, it certainly has not changed beyond recognition due to European Community or EU membership. By and large, it has had its economic wellbeing enhanced considerably. Wallace suggests that nation states no longer control national economies in Western Europe.[24] The states are committed to certain economic changes—such as the creation and implementation of a Single Market—because it is to their advantage. They are less committed to political change in the governance of the EU itself. There is especially a reluctance to grant what would amount to polity status to the EU—except in some academic debates.[25] There is however a current reconceptualisation of sovereignty, accountability, citizenship and the traditional roles of the nation state.[26] Increased moves to economic integration mean that the nation state is part of an interlocking network of relationships which are increasingly political, especially since the Maastricht Treaty's influence on justice, police and internal affairs, finance, foreign and defence policies and economic union.

The economic integration of markets had not initially led to a political integration of high politics. Yet, the logic of a European Union project, that is, a governmental EU if all the objectives and promises of the Maastricht TEU are implemented, is that it could well replace the nation state's key functions. However, it needs to be asked if that is in fact necessary. The nation state has changed in method but the principle has not really changed. The nation state is still the major actor in EU and in international affairs. The promise of a federal EU remains a feature of the EU but the tenacity of national interests is still evident in the predominantly intergovernmental cooperation among the member states.

The member states dominate decisionmaking in a number of ways. The EU maintains intergovernmental traits, as seen in the pillar structure of the Maastricht Treaty on European Union. The success of the EU depends on the support of the states for its actions, especially new action under Article 235 of the EEC Treaty and in new policies and the changes brought about by Intergovernmental Conferences (IGCs). The EU changes its method of working by intergovernmental means, that is, by joint decisions of the member states in the Council or European Council. The decision to render it supranational must ultimately be a decision by the member states in an intergovernmental capacity.

There is no government or polity at the EU level because until now there has never been any consensus on the need for such a political union. The need has never been expressed by the nation states as they still retain the support of the citizens for the state.[27] It is a feature of the debate on the nation state in comparative perspective that the legitimacy of the nation state is under question. The state's legitimacy is being undermined as citizens have begun to question the powers that have already been ceded to the EC/EU. Since Maastricht, many citizens object to the handing over of these powers and even question the legitimacy of the states' actions in doing so. Maastricht opened up the citizens' eyes to the way the EU is, in a sense, taking power from the nation state. The citizens now question the legitimacy of the nation state to act on their behalf in handing over states' rights of sovereignty and autonomy, which tend to be discussed as if they are indivisible.

The public debates in the member states since 1992 have shown that the permissive consensus on the European integration process is no longer prevalent. There is considerable opposition to the elitist approach of decisions being made by national governments, decisions which may require a further alteration of the nation state's status into that of a member state. The debate after the Maastricht TEU was signed by national governments suggests that the EU entered a period of questioning of the 'member state' status of the nation state. The Danish 'No' vote in the first referendum of June 1992 and the second 'Yes' vote in May 1993, by a tiny margin of approval, led to a reassessment of the European integration process. The debate before the referendum in France in September 1992 focused on the nature of sovereignty. Even the Irish referendum debates, which resulted in a more comfortable majority in favour of the Maastricht amendments to the EC's Treaty base, also revolved around the issues of sovereignty and the imposition of EC law and citizenship. These debates have been part of wider examination of the EC's redefining of national identities in the Maastricht Treaty.

The relationship between the nation state and the EU

The relationship between the nation states and the Community/Union has changed substantially over the last 45 years. Sbragia sees a 'gradual embrace' of the two—nation state and Community—as having taken place at the level of elites, policy and politics to the extent that she sees a 'blurring of the distinction made between the "Community" and the '"nation state" that agreed to form that Community in the first place'.[28] Sbragia suggests that it is at these three levels that there is evident a 'gradual knitting together of the

Community and the states that compose it', namely, elite, policy and politics.

At the elite level, there has been a gradual integration of nationally based elites—governmental, business and judicial—into the Community with domestic level policymakers dealing with the Brussels decisionmakers in a routine manner. In terms of policy she points to the "redistributive and social regulatory element", namely the move from an economic community into non-economic, social areas. The third factor that Sbragia sees as a dimension of the gradual embrace of nation state and Community is that of politics, namely the politicisation of the Community brought about by the debate on the TEU.

Sbragia presents a convincing argument that the relationships of the nation state and EC will become both more politicised and more contested. She sees this as part of the transformation of nation states into member states. This transformation has already taken place in many aspects of policy. This begs the question of whether there is anything distinctively different about the nation state in the EC as compared with the nation state in the international arena or in international relations in general. This is a question worthy of more comparative research and this chapter points to certain aspects only, as we shall see in the next section.[29] Like all nation states, the member states see sovereignty as a central principle and the state will remain a contested concept in international relations.

As early as the 1970s, it was clear that the West European nation state was part of a Community of governance that operated both above and alongside the nation state. Coombes saw the most relevant features of the Community's legal system as:

* Community law is independent of the member states in the sense that it can be of direct incidence and may not require further enactment by member states' public authorities to be fully binding on both public and private bodies and individuals.

* It takes precedence over the law of the member states in the sense that the Court of Justice established by the treaties is the final authority in interpreting it; the role of the Court in developing the Community's legal framework is a political aspect of major significance.

* Community law is also generative, consisting not only of binding provisions of the treaties but also of secondary legislation which the Community's independent institutions are empowered to enact, and of 'unwritten' law produced by decisions of the Court of Justice.

These three features both limit the competence of political authorities in the member states participating in the Community and also 'create a measure of political authority in the Community's own institutions'.[30]

Examining the transformation: the characteristics of the member states of the EU

The transformation of the nation state in the European integration process is one which has been gradual, gradualist and functionalist while it had an aim which was transnational and even supranational in promise. This section examines in closer detail some features of the transformation of the nation state within the EU. The transformation is characterised by the following features:

A. The member states have merged control over many aspects of their independent high and low politics, for example social, foreign, monetary, military, and economic policy. There has been a partial transition from independent economic policies to common policies such as social policy, CAP, energy and the environment. Nugent points out that, in the areas of agriculture and external commercial policy, the EU system results in 'the role of the states being reduced to those of intermediaries'.[31]

William Wallace made the following comment about the EC in the early 1980s and it is still apposite:

> The Community commands resources, distributes benefits, allocates markets and market shares, and adjudicates between conflicting interests—all on a modest scale, within limited sectors, but all taking it into the central issues of politics.[32]

This is still the case in essence, although it is far from modest. The EC has created the Single European Act, the Single Market, the TEU and the Amsterdam Treaty and the EU has increased its membership of states, the number and scope of its policies, and the shared competences in areas covered by the institutions and the Treaties, resulting in a recasting of the role of the nation state to a highly involved member state, participating in decision making in the EU in the Council, European Council, Committee of Permanent Representatives (Coreper) and specialist committees.

B. The member states are part of an integrated single market to the extent that all decisions relating to the free movement of goods, persons, capital and enterprise are made at EU level and not at national levels. There is a transparency and porous nature to the national boundaries in all economic transactions. The states are members of the largest frontier-free market in the world. There is free movement of all the factors of production (labour, capital, enterprise, goods) of the 15 EU states.

C. The member states participate in policies of resource redistribution. There is a substantial transfer of funds across borders, administered by the European Commission in cohesion policies. These consist of allocating financial aid for disadvantaged regions, periphery regions, regions in the process of de-industrialisation. It also has preferred groups for attention, such as the long term unemployed, youth unemployed, and to an extent women.[33]

D. The member states are part of an organisation that has its own resources, that is, its own annual budget of approximately 80 billion ECU. While this is small compared to national GNP, and hence cannot change the nation state fundamentally, it is nevertheless a substantial resource of the EU for implementing policies.

E. The member states are obliged to comply with the binding nature, direct applicability and primacy of EU law. National law is no longer the last resort, although this is a matter for contention by the member states. EU law has primacy over national law and it takes direct effect once the law is approved by the national government representatives—Ministers or Ambassadors—in the meetings of the Council of Ministers and its preparatory committees such as Coreper, which consists of the Permanent Representatives of the EU member states, who attempt to streamline decisionmaking and come to agreement on issues before they are approved by the national Ministers.

It is this characteristic of European law that is so striking about the EU and so much in contrast with distinctly intergovernmental law. What is also remarkable is that by and large compliance is accepted as the norm, although there are lists of states which infringe EC law in the EU Bulletin each month, that is, those countries against whom cases have commenced for infringement of EU law.[34] EU law is so accepted in national courts that it is increasingly common for national courts to refer legislation as a matter of course to the European Court of Justice for a preliminary ruling as to its acceptability and compliance with EU law.

The EU has legal authority—if not legitimacy—and in the 1980s Jacques Delors predicted that up to 80% of all economic and social legislation affecting nation states would emanate from the EC by the end of the twentieth century.

F. Under the Maastricht Treaty, there is a provision for coordination of all foreign policies into a Common Foreign and Security Policy (CFSP), altering traditional notions of sovereignty.[35] While this does not constitute a common policy as yet, it denotes united positions on defined issues.

G. Maastricht also provides for intergovernmental cooperation on internal affairs, justice and police matters in the pillar of the TEU entitled Justice and

Home Affairs (JHA) with the elaboration of common policies on policing, visas, the fight against drugs and terrorism, and issues relating to refugees and migrants. In addition, it has established a Europol system of police information and cooperation. However, it is clear that there are grave problems of accountability of this largely secretive mechanism, and the fact that it can be seen as a continuation of the Schengen agreement on the closing of external borders to migrants and refugees makes it necessary to subject the EU to scrutiny on the nature of these intergovernmental negotiations which are not accountable at national or at European level.[36] There is little involvement or scrutiny by the European Parliament or Commission with regard to these policies and there is little accountability or evidence of checks and balances in the EU's intergovernmental mechanisms.

H. There is provision for a single European currency and a single European Central bank by 1999, as set out it the Treaty on European Union and in the Madrid European Council Conclusions of December 1995. The states must however comply with the convergence criteria in order to gain membership of the EMU.[37]

I. Maastricht provides for European citizenship which is based on national citizenship and for the first time gives formal rights of voting and standing in local or European Parliament elections in another member state for all EU nationals. This citizenship issue has been the subject of a great deal of debate and criticism.[38] The citizenship provisions do not apply to non-EU migrants.

J. There is regular EU coordination at all international meetings such as the United Nations, General Agreement on Tariffs and Trade (GATT)/World Trade Organisation (WTO) and Organisation for Economic Cooperation and Development (OECD) throughout the world.[39] In addition, the member states are represented by European Commission delegations throughout the world in over 120 diplomatic missions and also by the Commission in international negotiations on behalf of the nation states in GATT or WTO. All issues relating to Competition Policy are managed by the supranational Commission. This is of course not to state that the member states adopt a hands-off approach to these international negotiations. It is clear that the EU consists of nation states who have their own national interest as their primary motivation. In the case of the CAP reform in the context of the Uruguay Round in the 1990s, the French and Irish governments attempted to influence discussions of the CAP and to gain the best possible deal for their farmers.

The process of integration has thus had some unintended consequences for the nation state. The process of integration which is often referred to by

Milward is assumed to be the means by which the nation state was bolstered and strengthened. There is little doubt that the development of the Community in social and especially economic terms saw an increased harmonisation among the original six member states of their policy approaches and even in some cases the creation of common policies like the CAP. However, the development of what is called the Community method sees the development of a separate 'identity' according to some analysts, or at least a separate policy network and even what can be called Community governance, which includes the *acquis communautaire*. One way in which the nation state is transformed is the legal element of the *acquis*. The Community developed its legal system to become a largely supranational and independent body of law so that the EC and EU became in many ways defined by its independent legal character.

An unintended consequence of the integration process, however, has been a reassertion of the nation state, particularly—though not exclusively—by de Gaulle in the 1960s, and continued by British and Danish governments. This was regarded as a negative development in the integration process by those nation states—such as Belgium, Italy, the Netherlands and Luxembourg— that have sought to promote a rejection of intergovernmentalism in favour of a federal supranationalism. Milward was in fact correct in regarding nation states as reaching an achievement of independence and assertion of national primacy in the period 1945–68, with the nation state having its highest point in the late 1960s.[40] This was to be diminished as the integration process advanced from the 1980s onwards.

In addition, the process of integration led to a way of behaving that was not distinctly related to the nation state, but rather related to patterns of community and networks which were forecast by Karl Deutsch in the 1960s. There was a new network of elites who may not have seen the EC as the focus of their primary loyalty (as the neofunctionalists had predicted), but who did see it as the focus of their lobbying and influencing of transnational policy. Lobbyists for businesses and regions, for example, actively interact with the EU in order to influence national and EU agendas and to improve their national situation.[41] The farmers' lobby is the most apposite example.

The nation state was transformed in its relationships (if not in its organisation) by the EC. The dominant role of the nation state has been challenged. The EU does carry out certain functions that used to be the exclusive domain of the nation state. Further, the TEU creates an incipient CFSP. There is the possibility of joint defence which in many ways redefines traditional notions of sovereignty.[42]

The future of integration

The gradual politicisation of the EU has meant that its policies are now increasingly under public scrutiny, although still far from being a transparent process, and its policy scope has increased immeasurably since the 1980s, as codified by the Single European Act and the Maastricht TEU. The boundaries of EU and nation state action have thus been a subject of debate. The boundaries of governance have also changed within the EU.

It is difficult to predict the future of integration in the EU for at least two reasons. The first is that the analysis of the EU is dealing with contemporary national, as well as EU, politics. So it was difficult to predict the impact of domestic considerations, for example, on the decisions to be reached in the 1996 Intergovernmental Conference. The second reason is 'the lack of any real notion of an end-product of the process'.[43] The end goal of the EU project has never been clearly defined. It is well known which plans failed in the past. However, the ideal of European Unity, or European Union, is itself the subject of much divisive debate, and this has been a feature of the European Unity ideal since at least the 1930s.[44]

The centrality of the member state

The nation state remains central to the European Union. It is the state which defines the future structure of the Union, through the mechanisms of IGCs and in the Council of Ministers and European Council although in an integration framework. It will be important for the states to address the issue of Union legitimacy. If the EU were simply interstate or intergovernmental, then legitimacy, normally associated with the nation state, would not be an issue. However, as intergovernmental negotiations result in the increased scope of activity for the EU, then there are problems for European Union legitimacy and even national identity boundaries. The legitimacy problems of the EU to date have been made clear in the unwillingness of the citizens of nation states like Denmark or France to accept the integration project as expressed in the SEA or the TEU. In addition, legitimacy is also associated with democracy and the issue of reconciling democratic principles to the EU is an important one and an increasingly pertinent one as the EU encroaches on policy scopes in areas such as EMU, defence and foreign policy.

Of course one must be cautious in using terms such as democracy and legitimacy, as there is a risk of succumbing to the tendency of treating the EU as a type of actual state or polity that must conform to certain conditions or criteria such as democratisation. Legitimacy implies several factors. It appears to imply the acceptance by the citizens of the government and of decisions and of the office holders. There is very little acceptance at the EU level of the decisionmakers in the EU and even this is very difficult to gauge as decisionmakers of the EC can be punished in national polls for a variety of reasons. One of the reasons for the debate on legitimacy and acceptance of the EU regime is that the permissive consensus, referred to by many writers on European integration, including Milward, has been eroded to the extent that it is no longer acceptable to talk of such a consensus vis-à-vis the 15 member EU as it was with the less complex EC of six or nine member states in the past.

There is a clear information deficit in the EU and there is equally a clear comprehension deficit concerning it. The complexity of the EU renders loyalty to it difficult and even identification with it almost impossible, while at the same time multiple identities are evident. The creation of a type of polity is therefore not possible in terms of participatory norms if there is a general incomprehension. This, as Kerremans has pointed out, has rendered the EU vulnerable to public opinion and to criticism of its actions. Kerremans has suggested that the EU's legitimacy, such as it exists, is in part an aggregative legitimacy of the member states as national representatives, and there is a certain logic here as the EC was founded by the states and the member states remain the dominant if not sole actors.[45]

Any decisions taken by the national representatives at IGCs must be transparent and supported by the citizenry. Decisions relating to the functioning of the Maastricht TEU or the EU in general are often regarded, quite correctly, as encroaching on national sovereignty. If that is the case that has to be recognised and its benefits made absolutely clear. The secrecy of elite office-bearers making decisions had, until 1992, reinforced a sense of virtual invulnerability among those decisionmakers in the Council and that has led to fears of a loss of national sovereignty. Milward's arguments have value, in pointing out that the process of European integration has benefited the nation state and that a certain amount of loss of national sovereignty was necessary in order to gain these benefits of EU construction.

The member states remain the pivotal actors at intergovernmental fora, not the supranational institutions. National interests dominate. Nevertheless, national interests still to a large extent concur on the importance of increased European economic integration. The 1996–7 IGC does not address the possibility of the EU being a superstate, even if Milward does call the EU that. It will not create a European nation. Increasingly IGCs will result in consultation of the populace before the ratification of their results. The permissive consensus is so fragile that this consultation is essential.

There will be no fundamental renegotiation of the transformation already achieved of the nation state to member state. There has been a negotiation of the proposal to make two particular policies intrinsic to sovereignty a more integrated part of the EU Treaty. These two policy areas are CFSP and JHA. Here cooperation takes place in an intergovernmental manner and is not subjected to the scrutiny of the EU institutions. Should the proposals that these policies be integrated into the EU proper be taken on board, we may see a transformation on a large scale towards a supranational polity. Should this not take place, the member states will retain this measure of national sovereignty. Either way, these member states cannot revert to their former status as independent 'nation states'.

Notes

1. See, for example, A. Milward, *The European Rescue of the Nation State* (London: Routledge, 1992); A. Sbragia, 'From "Nation State" to "Member State": The Evolution of the European Community', in P. Lutzeler (ed.), *Europe After Maastricht* (Providence/Oxford: Berghahn Books, 1994); D. Smith and O. Osterund, 'Nation State, Nationalism and Political Identity', *Working Paper No. 3*, Advanced Research on the Europeanisation of the Nation state (ARENA), (University of Oslo, 1995); J. Olsen, 'European Challenges to the Nation State', *Working Paper No. 14*, ARENA, (University of Oslo, 1995); P. Schmitter, 'If the Nation state were to Wither Away in Europe, What Might Replace It?', *Working Paper No. 11*, ARENA, (University of Oslo, 1995); J. Olsen, 'Europeanization and Nation State Dynamics', *Working Paper No. 9*, ARENA, (University of Oslo, 1995); H. Hinsley, 'The European Community: a body politic or an association of states?', *The World Today*, 45 (1), (1989); J. Pinder, 'The European Community and the Gaullist fallacy', *The World Today*, 45 (4), (1989).
2. Milward, *op. cit.*, 4.
3. A. Hartley, 'How the European Community really came about', *The World Today*, 50 (1), (1994), 19.
4. The European Community has been known as the European Union since 1 November 1993 when the Maastricht European Union Treaty was ratified.
5. A. Sbragia, *loc. cit.*
6. N. Nugent, *The Government and Politics of the European Union* (London: Macmillan, 1994), 434. He suggests that the main priorities are 'the promotion of economic growth and prosperity, the control of economic and financial forces which are not confined to national boundaries, and the strengthening of political influence'.
7. A. Milward, *op. cit.*, 1.
8. Ibid., 2–3.
9. A. Milward, 'Allegiance—The Past and the Future', *Journal of European Integration History*, 1 (1), 1995, 11–12.
10. Ibid., 3.
11. Ibid., 3.
12. Title VI of the *Treaty on European Union*, Council of the European Communities, Commission of the European Communities (Luxembourg: OOPEC, 1992), especially Article 109j. See also Conclusions of the Madrid European Council, December 1995, concerning deadlines for the achievement of EMU.
13. I. Davidson, 'Europe between nostalgia and utopia', in J. Story, (ed.), *The New Europe:*

60 *Europe: Rethinking the Boundaries*

Politics, Government and Economy since 1945 (Oxford: Blackwell, 1993), 491.

14. P. Murray and P. Rich (eds), *Visions of European Unity* (Colorado: Westview, 1996).
15. N.P. Gleditsch, 'Democracy and the Future of European Peace', *European Journal of International Relations*, 1 (4), 1995, 547.
16. A. Duff, *Reforming the European Union* (London: The Federal Trust and Street and Maxwell, 1997) 18.
17. M. Shapiro, 'The European Court of Justice', in A. Sbragia (ed.), *Euro-politics: Institutions and Policymaking in the 'New' European Community* (Washington: The Brookings Institution, 1992), 123.
18. There have however been challenges in recent years to this primacy, as well as a need to clarify the hierarchy of norms in law; all this was debated, but only to a limited extent, at the 1996 Intergovernmental Conference.
19. W. Wallace, 'Rescue or Retreat? The Nation State in Western Europe 1965–1993' in P.Gowan and P. Anderson (eds), *The Question of Europe* (London: Verso, 1997), 44.
20. This is explored in more detail in P. Murray, *The European Union: A Supranational Polity?* (forthcoming).
21. W. Wallace, 'Theory and Practice in European Integration', in S. Bulmer and A. Scott (eds), *Economic and Political Integration in Europe* (Oxford: Blackwell, 1994), 274.
22. See P. Murray, 'Spinelli and European Union' and C. Navari, 'Functionalism Versus Federalism: Alternative Visions of European Unity', chapters in Murray and Rich, *op. cit.*
23. U. Bullman, 'The Politics of the Third Level', *Regional and Federal Studies*, 6 (2), 1996, 3.
24. Wallace in Gowan and Anderson, *op.cit.*, 37.
25. See F. Traxler and P. Schmitter, 'The Emerging Euro-Polity and Organized Interests', *European Journal of International Relations*, 1 (2), 1995; Schmitter, *loc. cit.*
26. L. Holmes and P. Murray (eds), *Citizenship and Identity in Contemporary Europe* (Aldershot: Dartmouth, forthcoming in 1998); A. Linklater, 'Citizenship and Sovereignty in the Post-Westphalian State', *European Journal of International Relations*, 2 (1), 1996.
27. See, however, support in public opinion polls for European integration in C. J. Anderson and K. Kaltenthaler, 'The Dynamics of Public Opinion toward European Integration, 1973–93', *European Journal of International Relations*, 2 (2), 1996, 175–99.
28. A. Sbragia, *loc. cit.*, 70.
29. J.A.Camilleri and J. Falk, *The End of Sovereignty?: The Politics of a Shrinking and Fragmenting World* (Aldershot: Elgar, 1992).
30. D. Coombes, *The Future of the European Parliament* (London: Policy Studies Institute, 1979), 42–3.
31. N. Nugent, *op. cit.*, 434.
32. Wallace, 'Europe as a Confederation: the Community and the Nation state', *Journal of Common Market Studies*, 21, 1982–3, 61.
33. See however the critiques of cohesion in M. Tomaney and A. Amin (eds) *Beyond the Myth of European Union* (London: Routledge, 1995).
34. See, for example, Chapter 7, 'Community law', particularly the section on infringement proceedings in European Commission, *Bulletin of the European Union*, 1–2, 1995, 115–16.
35. See C. Agius' chapter in this volume.
36. See M. Anderson, M. den Boer and G. Millar, 'European Citizenship and Cooperation in Justice and Home Affairs', in A. Duff, J. Pinder and R. Pryce (eds), *Maastricht and Beyond* (London: Routledge, 1994); L. Feteke and F. Webber, *Inside Racist Europe* (London: Institute of Race Relations, 1994); and T. Bunyan (ed.), *Statewatching the New Europe* (Nottingham: Russell Press and Statewatch, 1993).
37. For a critique of the convergence issue, see Tomaney and Amin, *op. cit.*

38. Meehan, 'Citizenship and the European Union', in Murray and Rich, *op. cit.* and E. Meehan, *Citizenship and the European Community* (London: Sage, 1993). See also Linklater, *loc. cit.*
39. G. Edwards and S. Nuttal, 'Common Foreign and Security Policy', in Duff, Pinder and Pryce, *op. cit.*
40. A. Milward, 'Etats nations et communauté: le paradoxe de l'Europe?' *Revue de synthèse*, July/September 1990, 255 quoted in Wallace, 'Rescue or Retreat . . ' in Gowan and Anderson, *op.cit.*, 28.
41. See C. Jeffery (ed.), 'The Regional Dimension of the European Union: Towards a Third Level in Europe?', special issue, *Regional and Federal Studies*, 6 (2), 1996; and S. Mazey and J. Richardson (eds), *Lobbying in the European Community* (Oxford: Oxford University Press), 1993.
42. See C. Agius' chapter in this volume.
43. T. Christiansen, 'European Integration between Political Science and International Relations Theory: the End of Sovereignty *EUI Working Paper*, RSC 94/4 (Florence: European University Institute, 1994), 2.
44. Murray and Rich, *op. cit.*
45. B. Kerremans, 'Integration, Legitimacy and Institutions in the European Union', paper presented at the ECPR Workshop on 'Democratic Representation and the Legitimacy of Government in the European Community', Madrid, 1994.

4 An Ever Closer Union? Rethinking European Peripheries

RÉMY DAVISON

Introduction

The European Union's (EU) fourth enlargement of January 1995 represented the completion of a decade-long transformation of the relations between the European Community (EC)/EU and the European Free Trade Association (EFTA) states, a process which commenced with the landmark Luxembourg Declaration of 1984. The Corfu Summit of June 1994 represented the high-tide mark of West European integration; it was anticipated that the wider Western Europe, encompassing the EU12 and the four EFTA applicants (Austria, Finland, Norway and Sweden), were moving towards an even closer union. A resemblance to the first enlargement of 1973 emerged however: in November 1994, the Norwegian electorate rejected EU membership in a referendum. In 1972, Norway had taken an identical course, if not under identical circumstances. The 1995 result was an EU enlarged to 15 member states, not 16 as expected.

The institutional dilemmas of a wider Western Europe are manifold. How much wider can the EU become before changes are disequilibrating? How much more fragmented may Economic and Monetary Union (EMU) become before the attempt at monetary and financial integration is abandoned as an idealistic aberration of the 1980s and 1990s? To what extent does enlarging the boundaries of the EU affect the process of integration?

It is apparent that multiple logics drive EU integration. However, some of these logics prompt fragmentation rather than convergence. In the structure and process of inter-state bargaining, the key objectives of the integration process become increasingly blurred as actors seek to secure relative gains in order to offset potential losses. The European bargain, historically underpinned by a customs union, the Common Agricultural Policy (CAP), a Paris–Bonn axis, the Luxembourg Compromise and German industrial power, is under threat of dissolution as multifarious challenges to the *acquis communautaire*[1] emerge. These include a difficult EMU convergence process; enlargement; member states' economic divergence; and an increasing degree of institutional

63

fragmentation at the policy-making level. Furthermore, new peripheries have emerged on the EU's borders, several of which are part of the Union itself.

This chapter commences with a brief discussion of the economic fault lines which exist between the European core and its peripheries. The following section examines briefly the theories relating to integration and enlargement. It also details the Luxembourg Declaration, and the convergence of EC–EFTA policy-making in the wake of the Single European Act (SEA) and the Single Internal Market (SIM) programme. The chapter then moves to a cost/benefit analysis of the implications of EU enlargement from 12 to 15 member states, with reference to the impact of the European Economic Area (EEA), together with an examination of the problems associated with EMU in an expanded EU. Finally, the conclusion suggests that, in the absence of *sui generis* logics of integration, the process of enlargement and the development of new peripheries, in combination with *dirigiste* integration 'from above' are more likely to prompt fragmentation of the European political economy than convergence.

Competing European peripheries

As Ernst Haas has stated,[2] it is not possible to analyse European integration without some reference to international relations theory. It is, however, possible to critique the development of the EU from the perspective of the various dependent relationships or asymmetries which exist between the states and markets of the European core and periphery. The EU15 itself is characterised by a core–periphery relationship, where the Mediterranean enlargements plus Ireland comprise states whose recent history reflects dependent underdevelopment. To some extent, this may also describe parts of southern Italy and, in the medium term, the East German enlargement of the Federal Republic of Germany (FRG).[3]

Asymmetries are also evident when analysing the EU–EFTA relationship. EFTA states felt compelled to seek an European Economic Area (EEA)[4] agreement owing to the magnetic market power of single market Europe. EFTA states benefited both economically and socially from their association with the EU. Market access was improved, trade barriers to capital goods imports were eliminated, and EFTA business acquired greater access to the more competitive and lucrative EU financial markets. Two-way Foreign Direct Investment (FDI) and portfolio investment also gained from the EU–EFTA nexus. According to Wijkman, various EFTA states fall into either 'core' or 'periphery' categories (see Table 1).[5] However, it is debatable whether the UK, due to the size of its economy, should be included with the northern periphery, having left EFTA in 1973. Certainly, its non-adherence to EMU places it on the fringes of the EU monetary system (see Table 2), but it is highly questionable whether the UK economy is of only marginal importance. It is striking that the core Europe and Northern periphery categories in Table 1 approximate the EC6 and EFTA7 membership of the 1960s.

Table 1
Core and periphery regions in Europe

Core Europe	*Northern Periphery*	*Southern Periphery*	*Eastern Periphery*
Germany	Sweden	Greece	CEE states[d]
France	Norway[c]	Portugal	
Benelux	Finland	Spain	
Austria	Denmark	Turkey	
Switzerland[a]	Iceland[c]	Former	
Italy[b]	Britain	Yugoslav	
	Ireland	states	

[a] Not a member of the EEA or EU.

[b] With certain reservations, given Italy's southern periphery and exceptionally high debt-to-GDP ratio. See also Table 2.

[c] Member of EEA but not EU.

[d] The former CMEA states (minus Mongolia, Cuba and Vietnam), including the Baltic republics of the former USSR (Estonia, Latvia, Lithuania).

Source: Adapted from P. Wijkman, 'Patterns of Production and Trade', in W. Wallace (ed.), *The Dynamics of European Integration*, (London: Pinter, 1991), 95.

Economic relations in the EU are characterised by core-periphery relationships. This was reflected in the trade/investment links in the 1950s and 1960s between the original six member states of the EC (hereafter EC6 etc.) and the EFTA states.[6] In each case, dominant states emerged. In the EC6, France, West Germany and Italy benefited most from the cartelisation of coal and steel, while the UK established a dominant position within EFTA. During the 1960s, the EC6 [7] transformed agriculture with the implementation of the CAP. With the completion of the Customs Union in 1968, the framework for an EC6 trade bloc was established. During the same period, the UK was finding that EFTA was a limited market for trade and investment expansion, and on two occasions (the first immediately after EFTA's formation) sought

EC membership. Within EFTA, the United Kingdom remained on the European periphery, as it was unable to compete effectively within key EC market sectors.

The dependence some EFTA states had upon the UK was evidenced by the applications for EC membership made by Denmark and Norway, both EFTA members, and by Ireland, which were made at the same time as the UK (1961 and 1967). For states outside the EC, growth levels below the EC average appear to drive attempts to gain EC membership. Similarly, in the absence of economic crisis, the pressures which force states to seek integrationist solutions to national problems subside. In 1960–1, Norway's growth was more than five per cent lower than the EC6 average, while in 1992, Norwegian growth was only slightly behind that of the EU12 (see Figure 4). By 1994, the transaction costs associated with membership were rejected by the Norwegian electorate in a referendum. In marked contrast, the economic difficulties encountered by Finland and Sweden (less so Austria) during the late 1980s and early 1990s gave further impetus to the necessity for further integration with the EU12 (see Figure 4).

Enlarging and widening the boundaries of European integration: the background

Analyses of EU integration and enlargement fall into several categories. This chapter will refrain from recapitulating theories familiar to students of EU integration (for example, the realist, neofunctionalist, liberal and Marxist perspectives).[8] Conversely, certain theories of international integration view the process differently, arguing that the focus should be upon the development of non-discriminatory trade blocs.[9] Other theorists regard integrative widening as part of a trend that began with the development of the 1992 Internal Market project.[10] Game theorists regard the EU as an international regime in which multi-level processes (sub-national, national and international pressures) force states into collective intergovernmentalist bargaining processes. In turn, these pressures often develop integrationist momentum, as smaller states are increasingly marginalised by the expansion of discriminatory trade and financial regimes.[11] In this respect, notions of an 'inner six' (EC) and an 'outer seven' (EFTA) have conditioned West European relations in many respects since the inception of the European Coal and Steel Community (ECSC) in 1951. By contrast, neorealist theories of international relations stress the importance of state interests, structural constraints on states' actions, and the transaction costs associated with international cooperation.[12] However, the approach here conjectures that Europe comprises several competing peripheries, some of which form part of 'core Europe'. This means that while the European core notionally comprises the EU member countries, the reality is that wide variations exist in terms of economic performance and, indeed, levels of economic development. Variations on this theme include the notion of 'Europe of many circles', *Europe à deux vitesses* and *Europe à la carte*. In a sense, the European Economic Space (EES), EEA and the EU's Pre-Accession Phase White Paper[13] regarding Central and Eastern Europe represent the multiple frameworks under the which the EU has attempted to foster a process of European politico-economic convergence, under the rubric 'European integration'. This implies that the development of an inner European 'core' of dominant EU states is integrally linked with the German economy through such processes and institutions as EMU and the European Monetary Institute (EMI) (see Table 2). In this manner, the German economy and the Deutschmark (DM) provide the nexus of this arrangement, with Austria, Sweden, and the Benelux countries as satellite states, and France and Italy as participants in a centrifugal process.

The late 1980s not only witnessed an emergence of complementarity in the policy-making agenda between the EC12 and the EFTA6, but also the development of a potentially much greater enlargement framework. This was exemplified by the membership applications of Turkey[14] (1987), Cyprus (1990) and Malta (1990). The 'Austrian defection' from EFTA took place in 1989, when the Austrian authorities did not consult their EFTA partners over Austria's EC membership application. In truth, the Austrian move should not have come as any surprise; business had acted quickly to establish itself within the SIM, and it would be highly competitive by 1992. This paved the way for not only further EC applications from Finland, Norway, Sweden and Switzerland, but also the establishment of the EEA in 1992. In effect, this created a single economic area, comprising two trading blocs where there would be freedom of movement in goods, services, labour and capital.

The collapse of the Soviet East European empire in 1989, and the Council for Mutual Economic Assistance (CMEA) in 1991, provided not only eastward expansion possibilities for the Federal Republic of Germany (FRG), but a queue of prospective new applicants for membership of the EC. Following the rapid marketisation of the Visegrad economies (Poland, Czechoslovakia, Hungary) in the early 1990s, these states (or their successors) have looked westward for integration, although their economies (particularly Poland) remain to some extent locked into trade relationships with Belarus, Ukraine, the Baltics, and Russia. The incorporation of Central and East European states, and even some former Soviet states, into the EC had been mooted since the late 1980s. But further expansion of the EU is unlikely to take place before 2002, and the dilemma of EU eastern enlargement is rooted in the complex strategic relationships which still exist between the Russian Federation and the west.

The tensions which exist in the status and membership of NATO, together with NATO's belated intervention in the Serbo-Bosnian conflict, raised tensions between Russia and the NATO allies. In the short to medium term, it is the military/strategic equation which must be resolved before the EU can absorb a Central and East European (CEE) enlargement. Once this is complete, the first order questions become economic in nature, rather than politico-strategic.

Table 2
Variable geometry: fast-track EMU members and states
unlikely to achieve convergence criteria by 1999

Inner Eight	*Outer Seven*
Germany	Britain
France	Denmark
Benelux	Greece
Italy[a]	Spain
Austria	Portugal
Norway[b]	Finland
	Sweden

[a] Unlikely to achieve EMU convergence criteria in short-to-medium term due to exceptionally high level of public debt.
[b] Less likely to achieve convergence with EMU due to referendum on EU membership in 1994.

The Luxembourg Declaration

The Luxembourg Declaration demonstrated that the new logics of convergence overflowed into the EC-EFTA relationship. From 1985, the Delors Commission gave considerable practical economic and market substance to the Cockfield White Paper. Prior to the Single European Act (SEA), the EFTA states had been afforded considerable assistance as a result of the UK's EC membership. The United Kingdom remained the EFTA members' leading economic partner. But the SEA illustrated the fact that the EC was determined to follow a more institutionalist path to European union, albeit a *dirigiste* one. Throughout its first term, the Delors Commission mapped out a relatively coherent and rapid path towards EC integration and, in view of their asymmetrical dependence upon the EC's course of action, the EFTA states were bound to follow. The Luxembourg Declaration had an important consequence: it provided the basis for the EEA (1984, formalised between EC and EFTA 1989), which itself was the foundation for the EEA agreement of May 1992.[15]

The UK's participation in the SEA negotiations meant that the EFTA states could no longer expect a preferential trading relationship with their former partner. In the meantime, EFTA ranks were thinning; Britain and Denmark had left as early as 1973 and in 1986 Portugal joined the EC. From the mid 1980s onwards, the EFTA6 were obliged to take collective action in order to guarantee an effective market presence within the projected Single Internal Market (SIM). As the 1992 SIM process gathered speed after 1987, the EFTA6 found it necessary to adopt most of the SIM measures articulated in the Cockfield White Paper, the 'four freedoms' (goods, services, capital, labour) and the harmonisation and common policies complementary with the completion of the SIM by 31 December 1992. Essentially, the EFTA6 recognised the 'cost of non-Europe'; that is, the costs to EFTA merchandise and service sectors which would accrue if the EFTA governments chose to remain outside the core EC12 orbit. In effect, the EFTA6 had little choice but to adopt the EC's harmonised product standards, competition policy and rules on financial transactions. As a result, the EFTA states from 1986 liaised with the EC Council of Ministers with a view to forming a EEA. This assumed a more concrete form in the EC-EFTA High Level Contact Group which negotiated the joint use of the EC's unified customs document. This was formalised by the EC-EFTA 'Single Administrative Document' in 1989.

Symmetry or asymmetry? Analysing the costs and benefits of the EEA and the fourth enlargement

Measuring the costs and benefits of EU enlargement in terms of gross trade dependence, it emerges that Britain is potentially the greatest beneficiary of the EU-EFTA enlargement. As a destination for exports, UK trade with the EFTA4 applicants comprises the highest proportion of total trade (as a percentage of exports) in the EEA plus Switzerland.[16] As a whole, the EU makes a 6% gain in population, while GDP achieves a 9% boost, due to higher than average GDP per capita in the former EFTA states.[17]

The fourth enlargement proved beneficial to Austria, Sweden and Finland insofar as institutional representation is concerned. In the EU Council of Ministers, vote weighting for the three new members of the EU15 was distributed disproportionately to population, resulting in Sweden and Austria receiving four each and Finland three in the 87 vote Council. Germany, following unification in 1990, did not receive any further voting power, despite its absorption of the five new East German *Länder*. In the European Parliament, Austria secured 21 MEPs, Finland 16, and Sweden 22. However, given the party-political allegiances of the Members of the European Parliament (MEPs), the net effect of the new members' parliamentary representation is likely to be minimal.[18] The enlargement of the EU also means that the revolving presidency of the European Council will be held less frequently by individual member states. However, the EP regards this as a means by which the Commission may take over certain functions of the Council and 'presidentialise' the institutional decision-making process.[19]

Many studies on the wider EU have focused principally upon the costs and benefits associated with the accession of the EFTA states, and the member states of the EEA. Baldwin[20] sees substantial benefits for the EFTA states as a result of closer economic integration with the EU. He argues that few direct market liberalisation benefits will flow to EFTA states which join the EU, but notes that their ability to affect EU economic policy measures was severely limited within the EEA. This in itself acted as a stimulant for the EFTA states to seek membership of the EU, as EFTA itself was too limited in quantitative terms as a single 'domestic' market for EFTA exports.

Figure 1
EU Agro-budgetary outcomes for 1995–98*

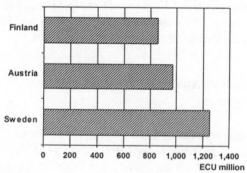

* Budgetary estimates.

Source: CEC, *XXVIIIth Annual General Report on the Activities of the European Communities 1994* (OOPEC, 1995).

The 1994 referenda on the European Union produced three 'Yes' votes and one 'No' vote among the EFTA applicants. The Norwegian rejection had been expected for some time, and came as no surprise to observers. As Figures 1 and 2 demonstrate, the EFTA3 achieved substantial agriculture rebates from the EU Budget for the 1995–8 triennium. However, this is unlikely to persist beyond 1998. Once the initial adjustment phase is completed, the EFTA3 will become net contributors to the EU Budget.

Figure 2
Projected general budgetary revenues deriving from enlargement 1995–1998*

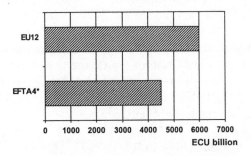

* Including Norway, prior to the referendum on accession to the EU. The figure shows revenues accruing to the EU12 Budget from the EFTA4 contributions. In addition,it shows the total net budgetary position for the EFTA4 after contributions and rebates.

Source: CEC, *XXVIIIth Annual General Report on the Activities of the European Communities 1994* (OOPEC, 1995).

This is the price the EFTA countries were forced to pay for admission to the EU. The integration of the EFTA3 together with the EEA signatories— which were already *de facto* client states of the EU — with the EU was a crucial step in the establishment of a single economic unit in Western Europe. As the EFTA states are advanced industrial economies with strong EU business and financial links, and since they have adopted most of the SIM proposals governing harmonisation, the EU–EFTA–EEA nexus has several structural implications for the global economy, namely:

*   Greater internal demand fuelled by direct access to EU markets for EFTA consumers (a boost in supply side due to gains in efficiency and consequent decreases in corporate transaction costs).

*   Increased negotiating powers in the World Trade Organisation (WTO).

*   Reduced reliance upon the US and Japan as destinations for exports due to further trade concentration, the elimination of competition, of investment restrictions and of distortions within a 17-member EEA.

*   The application of the Common External Tariff [CET] in the former EFTA states, which is likely to decrease further the EEA states' reliance upon US and Japanese imports, while reducing levels of FDI deriving from third countries.

The evidence suggests that the EU has focused predominantly on intra-EU trade. In 1990, two-way trade totalled ECU1.081 trillion (see Figure 3). In 1993, total EU–EFTA merchandise trade was almost $US260 billion. By 1994, intra-EU trade accounted for around 70% of the Union's total trade. The initiatives of the SIM suggest that intra-EU trade will be consolidated further. The 1992 adoption of the EEA Agreement between the EU12 and EFTA, together with the assumption of Union membership by the EFTA3, resulted in another $US200-plus billion that was added to the EU GDP total. This is offset by the fact that EFTA members of the EEA are heavily dependent upon the EU as their largest destination for exports, although the balance of trade between the EU12 and EFTA6 gave the EU an annual surplus in merchandise trade of around $US6.4 billion in 1993.[21] Given Austria, Norway and Sweden's already-extensive linkages with the German economy and currency, a relatively rapid assimilation of the EFTA3 with the EU is likely, although Finnish convergence with EMU is likely to proceed more slowly. These integrative processes are likely to deepen further the EU's dependence upon its own domestic market as the predominant source of demand.

Figure 3

EC12 and EFTA5 exports, 1990 (in millions of ECU)

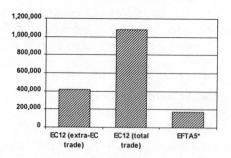

* EFTA5 denotes EFTA minus Iceland and Leichtenstein

Source: CEC, *Eurostat: Basic Statistics of the Community* (29th ed., OOPEC, 1992),Table 6.13, 288.

The EEA Agreement of 1992 exemplified the core-periphery relationship which had developed between the EU and EFTA countries over three decades. Previous EFTA members had joined the EC in order to capitalise on the growth and development opportunities which were greater in the EC than EFTA. Similarly, the EEA began the process of full integration into the widened boundaries of the EC.[22] The EEA process was disrupted, however, by the

Swiss referendum, which rejected the Agreement. This immediately created a number of budgetary problems for the EC, as Switzerland's contribution to regional development comprised 27% of the EFTA–EEA total.[23]

The areas not covered by the EEA included customs union, external relations, structural instruments, regional policy, industrial policy and taxation. The Maastricht Treaty on European Union (TEU) further complicated matters; the TEU covered EMU, foreign and security policy, and justice and home affairs. Accession negotiations following the Commission's Opinion additionally covered financial and budgetary provisions and the re-weighting of voting in the EU institutions.[24]

Explaining why some states attempt to join trade blocs while others refrain is more complex. However, economic performance is at least one important factor which may be tested. As Figure 4 demonstrates, all applicants for EC/EU membership except Portugal had growth rates below the EC/EU average in the year of application. In the year following accession, all new member states had growth rates which exceeded the EC/EU average, with the exception of Denmark (below) and Greece (equal to average). Although in the case of the 1995 enlargement, Austria's growth was only slightly behind that of the EU12, the gap in the case of Sweden was larger (2.1%) and in Finland's case was substantial (8.1%). In the cases of Sweden, Finland and Norway, this gap was particularly serious given the depth of recession in the EU economies at the time of application (1991/92).

Figure 4
Growth differentials between applicant countries and the EC/EU, year prior to application (% GDP)

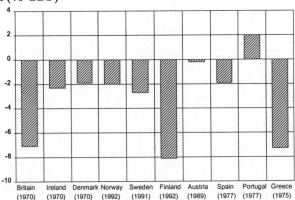

Source: IMF, *IMF Yearbook, 1984*, (IMF, 1984); IMF, *IMF Yearbook, 1991* (IMF, 1991); CEC, *European Economy: Annual Economic Report 1991-92* (OOPEC, 1992); OECD, *OECD Economic Outlook* (OECD, 1992).

This suggests that declining economic performance may be one major factor linked with the integration process. In Britain's case, the gap between the EC's and the UK's economic performance grew throughout the 1960s, which was an influential factor that forced the Heath government into a disadvantageous bargaining position on EC membership in the early 1970s.

This goes some way towards explaining why the CEE states on the periphery of the EU have demonstrated a particular interest in EU membership. The interest CEE states have in the EU is naturally financial. States which possess significantly lower per capita GDPs, after decades of gross income disparity between Western and Eastern Europe, have a strong incentive for gaining membership of the EU. Recent applications from CEE states include the Visegrad countries (1994), and Slovakia, Romania, Latvia, Bulgaria, Croatia, Estonia and Lithuania (1995) [See further Table 3]. As a result, the EU established a negotiations group with a view to determining the terms of entry into the Union. However, given that average per capita GDP in the CEE countries falls well below the EU15 average, full membership of the Union is highly unlikely in the short to medium term. This is why the Commission White Paper on CEE suggests that the Common Agricultural Policy (CAP) will not be included in any eastward enlargement of the EU. According to several estimates, enlargement encompassing the Visegrad states alone would require almost a doubling of the current EU Budget, without even taking into consideration other complex political and economic problems associated with further enlargement.[25]

However, EU states are, at the same time, interested in the development of a new European periphery in Eastern Europe, where labour-intensive manufactures may be transferred, while undercapitalised CEE industries are acquired by EU firms. The rapidity with which Volkswagen acquired a controlling stake in Czech industrial giant Skoda soon after 1989 demonstrated the tremendous interest EU firms have in cementing a position in new CEE markets, while controlling key industrial sectors in CEE. German involvement in CEE acquisitions has been particularly notable in the Czech Republic, Hungary and Poland. In another example of the 'peripheralisation' of a sector of the European economy, it will be difficult for CEE states to move beyond a dependent relationship with the EU due to the extent of EU firms' control over CEE industrial sectors. Ersatz capitalism is already developing in the CEE countries as former state enterprises exchange debt for equity.[26] The EU's CEE policy can be seen as avoiding responsibility for CEE reconstruction and, in fact, increases the likelihood of dependent development.[27] The Commission's current intention is to implement the 'four freedoms' in the applicant CEE states,[28] but without the massive capital transfers to the CEE states which would be associated with full membership of the EU.

Table 3
Applications and association agreements with the EU

Country(ies)	Current arrangements with EU	EU application status
Bulgaria	Europe Agreements (1992)	Applied for membership
Croatia		Applied for membership
Cyprus		Applied for membership
Czech Republic	Europe Agreements (1991)	Applied for membership
Estonia		Applied for membership
Greenland		Withdrew from EC[a]
Hungary	Europe Agreements (1991)	Applied for membership
Iceland	EFTA/EAA	
Latvia		Applied for membership
Liechtenstein	EFTA/EEA	
Lithuania		Applied for membership
Malta	Association Agreements	Applied for membership
Norway	EFTA/EEA	Withdrew EU application
Poland	Europe Agreements (1991)	Applied for membership
Romania	Europe Agreements (1992)	Applied for membership
{Russian Federation		
{Kazakstan	{Partnership and Cooperation	
{Belorussia	{Agreements (from 1993)[b]	
{Ukraine		
Slovak Republic	Europe Agreements (1991)	Applied for membership
Slovenia		
Switzerland	EFTA	Withdrew EEA/EU application
Turkey	Association Agreement	EU application 'left on table'[c]

[a] Greenland (as part of the Danish state) withdrew from the EC in 1984. It remains associated with the EC under Part IV of the Rome Treaty.

[b] The Partnership and Cooperation Agreements have grown incrementally. 1993 represents the commencement date of the negotiations.

[c] Turkey's application was effectively vetoed by the Greek government.

Note: Europe Agreements are, in effect, association agreements with the EU. They permit specific and limited market access to certain EU market sectors, in addition to limited financial assistance.

Despite the absence of a concrete EC-EFTA agreement in the 1980s, EFTA firms moved quickly to establish themselves in the EC internal market. EFTA could not exist without a major trading partner and adoption of EU financial and trade harmonisation regulations was essential if EFTA states were to compete in the SIM. Thus, the EC-EFTA convergence process was initially business, rather than government-driven, partially due to the dominance of intra-industry trade in Western Europe, where manufacturing industries displayed relatively high levels of interdependence. This was particularly true of large industrial firms which lacked vertical integration, and were thus reliant upon large networks of small and medium-sized enterprises (SMEs) supplying a range of intermediate and finished goods and services. The outcome of this rapid shift by EFTA firms meant an increase in the pace of market integration between the EC and EFTA economies, thereby inducing EFTA member governments to seek new forms of accommodation with the EC. In the first instance, the EFTA6 sought an extension of the SIM legislation so that harmonisation between EC/EFTA would be achieved without EFTA having to assume the full burden of the *acquis communautaire*.[29] The SIM now covers almost the entire West European landmass. It dominates the global merchandise export market with over ECU 1 trillion in exports, compared with ECU 309 billion for the US and ECU 226 billion for Japan in 1990. In manufactured exports, the EU12 almost doubled the US/Japan total combined.[30]

The export figures suggest that the EU is excessively dependent upon exports; and, second, that it is predominantly reliant upon third countries as export markets. Neither assumption is correct. In the first instance, as we have seen above, around two-thirds of the trade is conducted *within* the EU and EFTA. This, in simple terms, effectively protects two-thirds of the EU market, rendering it in essence a *domestic* market (see Table 4 and Figures 5–9).

The EFTA4 (Finland, Norway, Austria and Sweden) applications for membership demonstrated a widespread concern for FDI flows and investment divergence. Despite the EEA, national governments of the EFTA states became increasingly concerned that the Nordic states and Austria would be marginalised by competition for markets which were largely dominated by German, British and French firms.

The second Norwegian rejection of EU membership reflected several factors. First, opposition groups campaigned strongly on fishing rights and 'excessive' Norwegian contributions to the EU Budget. Second, Norway is dependent upon the EU as an export destination, although less so as a percentage of GDP than, for example, Germany. Third, as a member of the EEA, Norway receives most of the benefits and few of the compromises associated with EU membership. Fourth, as mentioned above, Norwegian growth did not lag far behind the EU average at the time of application. For these reasons, it is scarcely surprising the Norwegian electorate voted against EU membership.

With the exception of Finland, which possessed special trading arrangements with the former USSR, the EFTA states were notable for their trade dependence upon the EU as a whole. In 1986, Austria directed 60.1% of its exports to the EC, Norway 65.1%, and Switzerland 54.9% (see Table 4). The shattering of the late 1980s growth bubble in the early 1990s recession hastened the promulgation of an EEA agreement between the EU and EFTA, although Switzerland was ultimately not a participant in the process, following a referendum on the EEA.

Table 4
Exports to EC member countries, 1957-86[a]

	1957	1974	1981	1986
EC Countries				
Belgium	46.1	69.9	70	72.9
Denmark	31.2	43.1	46.7	46.8
France	25.1	53.2	48.2	57.8
West Germany	29.2	53.2	46.9	50.8
Greece	52.5	50.1	43.3	63.5
Ireland	N/A.	74.1	69.9	71.9
Italy	24.9	45.4	43.2	53.5
Luxembourg	-	-	-	-
Netherlands	41.6	70.8	71.2	75.7
Portugal	22.2	48.2	53.7	68.0
Spain	29.8	47.4	43.0	60.9
UK	14.6	33.4	41.2	47.9
EFTA				
Austria	N/A.	N/A.	N/A.	60.1
Finland	N/A.	N/A.	N/A.	33.3
Iceland	N/A.	N/A.	N/A.	N/A.
Norway	N/A.	N/A.	N/A.	65.1
Sweden	N/A.	N/A.	N/A.	50.0
Switzerland	N/A.	N/A.	N/A.	54.9
Third Countries				
Canada	8.3	12.6	10.7	6.8
Japan	N/A.	10.7	12.4	14.8
Turkey	N/A.	N/A.	N/A.	44.0
USA	15.3	21.9	22.4	24.5
USSR	N/A.	N/A.	N/A.	12.9

[a] Expressed as a % share of total exports of exporting country.

Source: CEC, *Eurostat*, various issues; *OEEC/OECD, National Accounts Statistics*, various issues, 1957–87.

Figure 5
EU countries' trade with EFTA states: 1993 imports and exports
(as reported by EU countries)

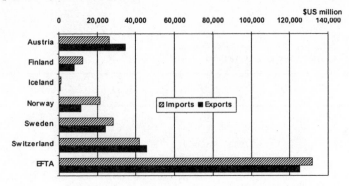

Source: EFTA, *EFTA Trade in 1993: Statistical Tables* (Economic Affairs Department, 1995), Tables 18, 22.

Figure 6
EFTA countries' trade balances with EFTA and EU states, 1993

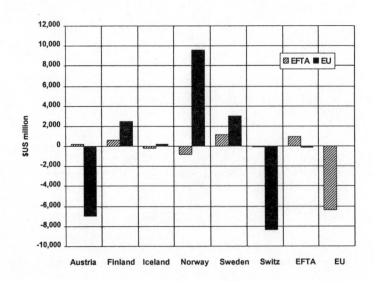

Source: EFTA, *EFTA Trade in 1993: Statistical Tables*, (Economic Affairs Department, 1995), Table 6, 10.

Figure 7
EFTA6 exports as a percentage of GDP: 1987

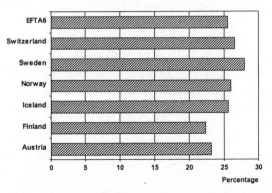

Source: OECD, *National Accounts Statistics*, (OECD, 1988).

Figure 8
EFTA6 Trade with EU12: 1986 Exports as a percentage share of total exports of exporting country

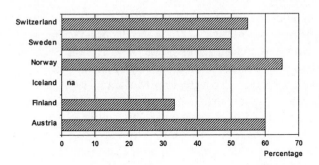

Source: CEC, *Eurostat*, various issues; OEEC/OECD, *National Accounts Statistics*, various issues, 1987.

In post-war Sweden, as in all of the EFTA states, an export-driven economy has been the key to the country's steady growth cycle. Until the late 1980s, the Swedish model appeared to provide a 'middle path' between market capitalism and socialism, achieving an equilibrium which appeared to ameliorate the worst aspects of both systems. In 1989, the Swedish public sector accounted for approximately 60% of GDP,[31] thus demonstrating the central role played by the state in the economy. This encouraged private-sector investment to move beyond Sweden, which had negative effects on the economy by the end of the 1980s. In 1990, direct investment by Swedish public and private sector enterprises in the EC amounted to 10 times that of EC direct investment in Sweden.[32] Divergence of investment away from Swedish enterprises, and into more profitable off-shore ventures, resulted in a systematic disinvestment in Swedish productive capacity and a substantial growth in unemployment. Sweden's economy was stagnant and the emergence of the world recession in the early 1990s impacted severely upon the ability of the Swedish public sector to cope with the creation of new employment in a depressed global export market.

Key sectors of the Swedish economy were markedly affected by the downturn in the EC economies. The automobile industry, which accounted for some 4.8% of the total workforce in 1995, was especially hard hit. Truck and turbocharger exports to the EC by Volvo, and aerospace technology, aircraft, aircraft engine and car exports from Saab-Scania were drastically curtailed as EC competitors rationalised product lines and cut overheads in order to deal with the problems of surplus capacity. More costly, specialised producers like Volvo and Saab experienced extreme difficulties competing with larger firms such as Opel, Renault, VW, Fiat, BMW, Daimler-Benz and Airbus. Large falls in exports to the crucial US market were also recorded from 1990. As Wells and Rawlinson noted, Saab and Volvo also experienced considerable production difficulties as a result of relatively high levels of worker absenteeism, job turnover and poor productivity.[33] In the midst of far stronger competition from EC countries, the under-capitalisation of Volvo and Saab was evident, and this led Volvo to seek an abortive merger with Renault,[34] while a controlling interest in Saab was acquired by General Motors in 1992.[35]

Swedish business was forced to undergo a rapid readjustment in the recessed economic environment of the early 1990s. This, more than any other single factor, shaped the Swedish government's attitude towards integration with the EU. The EEA was a necessary structural re-orientation of the EFTA economies, ensuring these states embraced the 'four freedoms' of the SIM 1992 project. In view of the EU's drive towards harmonisation, certain areas not covered by the EEA meant that in order to provide an enhanced and competitive business environment, the EFTA states were obliged to further their EEA gains by applying for accession to the EU.

The EU-EFTA agreement on the EEA Agreement meant that the EFTA countries adopted some 1,400 EC laws and regulations. These principally concerned the 'four freedoms'. Effectively, this extended the EC internal market to include all EFTA market sectors, with the exception of agriculture and fisheries, which are not part of the liberalised EU market. The Swiss referendum rejecting the EEA complicated EU-Switzerland economic relations. Despite its failure to adopt the EEA, Switzerland remains part of the broader

EES, and has made notable efforts to harmonise some of its regulations with those introduced by the EU Commission as part of the SIM programme. Much of the impetus for the regulatory changes came from Swiss firms that wish to retain a strong presence in the SIM. Swiss transnational corporations (TNCs) have substantial industrial and financial interests in the EU. This is particularly true of firms such as Asea AB of Sweden and BBC Brown Boveri Ltd. of Switzerland which merged in August 1987 to create Asea Brown Boveri (ABB). As a result, for EFTA firms, competitiveness in, and harmonisation with, the EC was critical to their success in the SIM. Firms were therefore important players in the EFTA countries' shift towards full EU membership. The future growth of firms like ABB was inextricably bound up with inclusion without discrimination in the SIM. As 'outsiders' in the SIM, Swedish and Swiss firms required further integration with EC business, especially as strong competitors, mainly from Germany and France, also existed in the electrical equipment industry where ABB's key interests lay. These product sectors included process automation systems, robotics, high-speed locomotives, and environmental and pollution control equipment.[36] Firms like ABB rely heavily upon the EU as an export destination, and the Swiss economy remains highly dependent upon EU market sectors such as machinery and electronic equipment, as these manufactures comprise over 27% of total Swiss exports.

In terms of EU-EFTA3 industrial linkages, the prospects for increased technology exchanges, mergers, and joint ventures appear promising, particularly with regard to Swedish heavy industries. This is best exemplified by the European automobile industry. Throughout the 1980s, Volvo-DAF (Netherlands) engaged in a successful joint venture operation. This was further exemplified by the Volvo-Peugeot-Renault joint venture on componentry based at Douvrin in France. Saab-Scania entered into a model-sharing agreement with Lancia, Alfa-Romeo and Renault (the Typo 4). In addition, the Swedish vehicle manufacturing and aerospace industry has been further integrated with German design and manufacturing facilities as a result of General Motors' (GM) control of Saab-Scania in the early 1990s. GM Europe's Opel subsidiary (Germany) now supplies and shares engines and components with Saab. Saab's aerospace arm has also engaged in significant R&D agreements and hi-technology trade with British Aerospace. The level of intra-industrial trade and R&D collusion, facilitated by the emergence of a single market, has resulted in efficiency and productivity gains in the last decade, demonstrating that the EES and EEA have provided an enhanced environment for business.

The EU remains a key export destination for the remaining EFTA states of Iceland, Liechtenstein, Norway and Switzerland, with over half of their total exports going to EU countries, of which Germany and France were the largest recipients (see Figure 9). Norway and Switzerland cannot be ruled out as prospective members of the EU or EEA.

Figure 9
EFTA exports to the EU as a percentage of total exports, 1995

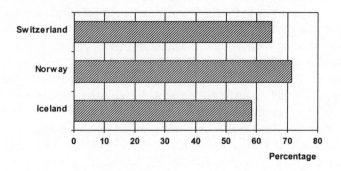

Source: EFTA, *Thirty-fifth Annual General Report of the European Free Trade Association, 1995* (EFTA, 1996).

EMU, financial convergence and enlargement

EMU was and continues to be a critical factor in the development of full economic integration within the EU. At the same time, the strict convergence criteria attached to Stage III of the EMU process also persuaded both electors and governments that monetary union was not in their national interest. This was made explicit prior to the fourth enlargement by the Danish and British governments in the protocols opting out of EMU which were attached to the Maastricht Treaty in December 1991, and in their final form in November 1993. Conforming with Stage III would have been problematic for most of the EFTA states. Most of the EFTA economies demonstrate marked volatility, particularly as they are profoundly affected by changes in both EC economic policies and, more directly, by German monetary policy shifts and DM realignments. As Qvigstad notes,[37] only Austria and Norway complied with EMU convergence conditions in 1991, while Finland, Switzerland and Sweden were constrained by high inflation and monetary policy laxity. Finland also announced a currency devaluation in late 1991, thereby placing it outside EMU parameters for at least two years following the announcement of irrevocably-fixed exchange rates.[38]

The monetary convergence process between the EC and EFTA had commenced well before any formal application for membership of the Community was submitted, as a result of the EFTA4's linkages with the currency 'snake' of 1972–9.[39] After 1979, the EFTA states generally aligned their currencies with the basket of currencies which comprised the European Monetary

System (EMS). However, due to tight German fiscal policy, various EFTA states have periodically moved away from the Exchange Rate Mechanism (ERM) and allowed their currencies to float freely. The exception to this rule is Switzerland. The Swiss central bank (which also represents Liechtenstein) had a record comparable with the Bundesbank in terms of monetary discipline until the early 1990s. A loosening of fiscal policy in the FRG following unification resulted in a greater amount of offshore DMs as the German government introduced a broad fiscal stimulus into the GDR in 1990. Capital outflows from Germany due to increased imports, combined with a reluctance by the Swiss central bank to tighten monetary policy, resulted in unusually high inflation in Switzerland (peaking at 6.3% in 1990, the highest since 1984). This compared unfavourably with all other EFTA states, with the exception of Sweden with a rate of 10.5%.[40] It meant that Switzerland fell around 2% outside the inflation parameters necessary for convergence under Stage III. It is especially notable that Austria, Norway, Sweden and Switzerland effectively constitute a European DM zone.[41] Although the Swiss franc is a floating currency, it is periodically realigned with the DM, which suggests a high degree of Swiss monetary dependence upon Bundesbank policy and DM fluctuations.[42] Similarly, Swedish dependence upon German economic policy was never more visible than in the EMS currency crash of September 1992. Interest rates during the crisis rose as high as 500%, and the Swedish finance minister commented that 'the sky's the limit on interest rates' in an attempt to defend the krona.[43]

The cost of EU membership in terms of excise and VAT revenues has been considerable for Austria and Finland. VAT revenues for Norway and Iceland would have also declined had they assumed EU membership. Prior to the EEA Agreement, EFTA revenues from VAT and excises did not differ a great deal from the EC12 mean as a percentage of GDP (6.8% [EC]; 7.5% [EFTA]).[44] However, considerable differences existed between VAT revenues in the EC12 and EFTA6 as a proportion of total government revenue. In the EC12 in 1989, no state derived more than 20% of its revenues from indirect taxes, whereas dependence upon VAT and excises was particularly significant for Finland (33% and 14% respectively), Iceland (34% and 7%), and Norway (22% and 15%).[45] The elimination of border controls between the EU15 in January 1995 meant that some revenues have decreased and this has had some significance for Finland. It also at least partly explains why Iceland opted out of EU membership, while the Norwegian government pressed for the adoption of the EC Commission's 'destination principle' (i.e. that VAT rates would be paid in the importing country at the national rate).[46] The liberalisation of taxation regimes and the harmonisation of VAT as a result of internal market implementation suggests that the fourth enlargement members of the EU will experience problematic fiscal shortfalls in the medium term which will, in turn, have an impact upon their ability to participate fully in EMU.

The EEA was essentially a medium-term instrument, designed to harmonise the most important areas (the four freedoms, transport etc.) with the EU's single internal market. It provided the basis for a more extensive renegotiation of the EU-EFTA relationship; the EEA also permitted the inclusion of states (such as Switzerland and Norway) which chose to remain outside the parameters of the EU, as a means by which some semblance of integration might be attained. The Swiss rejection of the EEA also reflected a suspicion of the *acquis communautaire*, and a reluctance displayed by the Swiss financial sector to absorb the excessive liquidity that is symptomatic of the EU financial system and, consequently, to 'import' inflation. However, Switzerland, Liechtenstein, Iceland and Norway continue to possess free trade arrangements with the EU, although in the longer term, the absence of an EEA (Switzerland) and the non-accession of Iceland and Norway suggests that the lack of convergence (and, in all probability, increasing divergence) in areas such as taxation, industrial policy, and EMU will increasingly promote not merely a multi-speed and disparate EU, but one which will become difficult to integrate in market terms.

Figure 10
EFTA4*/EC12 inward and outward FDI flows, 1988
(1990 prices and exchange rates)

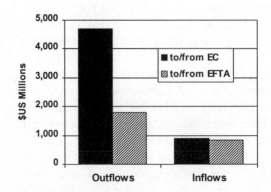

* EFTA4 denotes Austria, Finland, Norway and Sweden. Data unavailable for Iceland and Switzerland.

Source: BIS, *Investment Outlook* (BIS, 1990).

As Figure 10 shows, FDI flows from the EFTA4 were relatively small in 1988, as were EC12 FDIs in EFTA. However, Switzerland alone accounted for almost $US6 billion in FDIs, raising the total of EFTA6 investments to over $US10 billion. These investments also account for relatively high levels of employment in the host blocs. For EFTA, the EU remains the most important host region with over 690,000 EC-based employees of EFTA firms prior to the establishment of the EES framework in 1989. In 1988, 58.8% of EFTA FDIs went to the EC, while 53% of total direct investment flows originated from the EC12. For Sweden and Switzerland, the EU is a key region for FDI placement, although this trend has begun to recede in the wake of Swedish accession to the EU.[47] This partially demonstrates the extent to which Swedish TNCs provided the impetus for Swedish membership of the EU.

In Austria, total investment stock has consistently outpaced outward FDI flows, and the rate of investment in Austria has increased since the EEA Agreement and Austria's assumption of EU membership. Like Sweden, membership has also seen a reduction in the flow of outward FDI to the EU. In contrast, Switzerland's non-membership of the EEA and the EU has seen increases in EU FDIs in the Swiss economy. It appears reasonable to make correlations between levels of integration and FDI trends. As Pelkmans argues, there appears to be a direct link between high levels of market protection and increased FDI flows.[48] This may also give an indication as to why Japanese firms' FDIs (as opposed to market shares) in the EU and EFTA are relatively large.

? Central Eastern Europe

Conclusions: convergence and divergence in the wider western Europe

The fourth enlargement did not significantly reconstitute the European bargain, although it extended the EU's northern and central European peripheries. The states remaining immediately outside the framework of the EU (such as the CEE countries) comprise a more challenging agenda. However, the Pre-Accession White Paper explicitly ruled out membership for the CEE countries in the short to medium term.[49] The EU states are not interested in massive increases in the EU Budget to accommodate CEE agriculture. Nor is it in the interest of the EU's southern periphery (Spain, Portugal, Greece) to compete with the CEE for manufacturing investment. EU institutions would have to be enlarged substantially to cope with the CEE states (as well as Cyprus). As the EU grows larger, the Union becomes 'watered down', as the Commission phrased it.[50] CEE adjustment to the EU Internal Market is the pre-requisite for membership accession. However, the EU sees alignment with the SIM as the CEE countries' own responsibility.[51] For the EFTA applicants, this was not difficult, as they were all advanced industrial states. It is clearly difficult in the medium term for CEE countries to achieve EU levels of development.[52] As a result, CEE states will remain on the European periphery as an exploited resource base for EU transnational firms for the foreseeable future.

The widening of the boundaries of the EU is problematic. The accession of the EFTA3 and the EEA states merely extends the principle of European union to a number of developed market economies. Institutional gridlock remains in the form of national domination of decision-making, the 'democratic deficit', and an absence of system-reforming logics which permit Union 'widening' to have some congruence with notions of 'deepening' integration. But Eurobarometer surveys, close referenda results, and popular rejections of EU membership suggest a deeper malaise within the Union.

The initial Danish rejection of Maastricht; the close-run French referendum; rejection of the EEA in Switzerland; and the bare majorities regarding accession in Sweden and Finland reflect electors' reservations concerning the longer-term objectives of the entire European enterprise. Because EU *dirigisme* is characterised by elite domination, the SIM and EMU are regarded as business and finance-oriented at a time when the EU economies are experiencing high unemployment and low or zero growth.

In terms of the institutional dynamics of the EU, sceptics of European integration remain unconvinced by the measures adopted to ensure transparency in Council deliberations and decision-making.[53] This does not represent any trend towards the abandonment of the Council or Commission's *dirigiste* tendencies; more accurately, the most democratic body, the EP, has made information and public scrutiny far more readily accessible than have the non-elected bodies of the EU.[54]

The solution, however, is not simply to overcome the democratic deficit; nor is it merely a problem soluble within the confines of intra-EU diplomacy. More accurately, the present EU *malaise* is symptomatic of wider global problems, symbolised by the fragmentation of the Cold War order, and a US struggling against the threat of a post-hegemonic international system. The EU as a trading bloc remains the most insulated market in the world economy, although the costs of retaining external barriers and maintaining a discriminatory trading regime are rising appreciably. The EU needs to be viewed in a wider global context, as the process of integration is not self-generating or *sui generis*, but a *response to international structures and constraints*.[55]

The response has come from the core EU states in the form of the development of new peripheries outside the EU (principally the CEE countries). The EU core states (chiefly Germany and France) have succeeded in incorporating the various European peripheries into the wider Western Europe, whilst marginalising possible challengers such as Britain. The UK remains outside the EMU process and therefore its ability to influence EU institutions such as the European Monetary Institute (EMI) will be severely limited. The fourth enlargement completes one of the many circles in EU integration, namely, the consolidation of the DM zone which now includes Austria, Finland and Sweden. These states are bound even more closely with the German economy and financial system.

As a whole, the enlargement process demonstrates the difficulty of an integration process which seeks to widen its boundaries while also dealing with the issue of 'deepening' the institutional process of integration. Market integration alone does not develop sufficient momentum to push forward integration into more complex areas such as EMU and social policy. The emergence of a multitrack EU insofar as EMU is concerned exemplifies this. Integration cannot comprise widening alone; it must be matched equally with corresponding logics which deepen the Union. For integration to function effectively, it must necessarily consist of mutually-reinforcing frameworks. To this end, integration must be linear rather than cyclical; should patterns emerge which permit one logic (e.g. economic) to dominate the other, then disequilibrium (i.e. fragmentation and potential disintegration) is the result. While this cyclical framework persists, EU integration on all levels is likely to remain stagnant, uneven, and characterised by competing and conflictive peripheries. In a sense, we return to the Europe of the 1960s; Europe 'at sixes and sevens'. This is ultimately the long-term result of a rapid enlargement process. As Raymond Barre commented at the time of the first enlargement, 'The Rome Treaty was designed for a Community of six. It reflected their interests, aspirations and habits, and not those of the United Kingdom'.[56]

Notes

1. The *acquis communautaire* refers to the norms, procedures, rules and practices which comprise the European Communities. It is especially relevant in the enlargement context, as Accession Treaties bind new member states to the Communities' conventions and these enter into force once membership is assumed. The Report of the Three Wise Men, submitted to the European Council in November 1979, gave *de facto* recognition to the principle of an *acquis communautaire*, which was given legally-binding status in the Articles of Accession in each of the four EU enlargement agreements of 1972, 1979, 1985, and 1994.

2. For a seminal articulation of the neofunctionalist position, see especially E.B. Haas, 'The Challenge of Regionalism', *International Organization*, 12 (1958), 440–58; Haas, *The Uniting of Europe* (1958); Haas, 'International Integration: The European and the Universal Process', *International Organization*, 15, 1961, 366–92; Haas, *Beyond the Nation state* (Stanford: Stanford University Press, 1964), esp. 65; Haas, 'The Study of Regional Integration: Reflections on the Joy and Anguish of Pre-Theorising', *International Organization*, 24, 1970, 607–46; and Haas, 'Turbulent Fields and the Theory of Regional Integration', *International Organization*, 30, 1976, 173–212.

3.   For perspectives on dependency, see A.G. Frank, *Capitalism and Underdevelopment in Latin America* (New York: Monthly Review Press, 1967); and Frank, *On Capitalist Underdevelopment* (New York: Oxford University Press, 1975); I. Wallerstein, *The Capitalist World Economy* (Cambridge: Cambridge University Press, 1979), esp. ch. 4; and P. de Schoutheete, 'The European Community and its subsystems' in W. Wallace (ed.), *The Dynamics of European Integration* (London: Pinter, 1991).

4.   Switzerland originally signed the EEA, but its ratification was prevented by a 1994 referendum. Of the six EFTA members between 1973 and 1995, only Iceland, Liechtenstein, Norway and Switzerland remain. See CEC, *Agreement on the European Economic Area* (Brussels: OOPEC, 1992).

5.   See P.M. Wijkman, 'Patterns of Production and Trade', in Wallace, *op. cit.*, 104.

6.   *Ibid.*, 104.

7.   Comprising Belgium, France, West Germany, Italy, Luxembourg and the Netherlands.

8.   For a neorealist perspective on EU integration, see J.M. Grieco, 'The Maastricht Treaty, Economic and Monetary Union and the neo-realist research programme', *Review of International Studies*, 21 (1), 1995, 21–40. For a recent treatment of neofunctionalism, see J. Tranholm-Mikkelsen, 'Neofunctionalism: Obstinate or Obsolete? A Re-appraisal in the light of the New Dynamics of European Integration', *Millennium*, 20 (1), 1991, 1–21. For a neoliberal perspective, see A. Moravcsik, 'Preferences and Power in the European Community: A Liberal Intergovernmentalist Approach', *Journal of Common Market Studies*, 31 (4), 1993, 473–524. Few Marxist analyses of the EU exist, but for a penetrating critique see S. Holland, *Uncommon Market: Class and Capital in the European Community* (London: Macmillan, 1980).

9.   This is often termed 'open regionalism'. For perspectives on the development of rival trading blocs, see R.G. Cushing et al (eds), *The Challenge of NAFTA: North America, Australia, New Zealand and the World Trade Regime* (University of Texas, 1993); R.C. Hine, 'Regionalism and the Integration of the World Economy', *Journal of Common Market Studies*, 30 (2), 1992, 115–23; J. Whalley, 'CUSTA and NAFTA: Can WHFTA Be Far Behind?', *Journal of Common Market Studies*, 30 (2), 1992, 125–41; C. Fred Bergsten, 'APEC and the World Economy: a Force for Worldwide Liberalization', *Foreign Affairs*, 73 (3), 1994; L. Csapo, '1992: The European Challenge to the World', *Occasional Paper*, (Monash University, July 1989); P. Nell, 'EFTA in the 1990s: The Search for a New Identity', *Journal of Common Market Studies*, 28 (4), 1990, 327–58; and P. Wijkman, 'The existing bloc expanded?' in C. Fred Bergsten and M. Noland (eds), *Pacific Dynamism and the international economic system* (Institute for International Economics, 1993).

10. See W. Sandholtz and J. Zysman, '1992: Recasting the European Bargain', *World Politics*, 42 (1), 1989, 95–128; M. Zinkin, '1992 and All That', *International Relations*, 10 (1), 1990, 55–71; Wallace, *op. cit.*; I.B. Neumann, 'The European Free Trade Association: The Problems of an All-European Role', *Journal of Common Market Studies*, 28 (4), 1990, 359–77; and T. Wieser and E. Kitzmantel, 'Austria and the European Community', *Journal of Common Market Studies*, 28 (4), 1990, 431–50.

11. See R. Putnam, 'Diplomacy and domestic politics: the logic of two-level games', in P.B. Evans et al (eds), *Double-edged Diplomacy: International Bargaining and Domestic Politics* (Berkeley: University of California Press, 1993), 431–68; M.G. Cowles, 'Setting the Agenda for a New Europe: the ERT and EC 1992', *Journal of Common Market Studies*, 33 (4), 1995, 501–26; A. Moravcsik, 'Negotiating the Single European Act: national interests and conventional statecraft in the European Community', *International Organization*, 45 (1), 1991, 19–56; Moravcsik, 'Preferences and Power in the European Community: A Liberal Intergovernmentalist Approach', *Journal of Common Market Studies*, 31 (4), 1993, 473–524; and F. Laursen, 'The Community's Policy Towards EFTA: Regime Formation in the European Economic Space (EES)', *Journal of Common Market Studies*, 28 (4), 1990, 303–25.

12. See K. Waltz, *Theory of International Politics* (Addison-Wesley, 1979); and Grieco, *loc. cit.*

13. See CEC, *White Paper on the Internal Market and the Pre-Accession Phase for the Admission of Central and East European Countries* (Brussels: OOPEC, 1995).

14. The Turkish application has been 'left on the table' as it is highly unlikely that Greece would permit Turkish accession, mainly due to disputes concerning sovereignty over Cyprus, as well as islands in the Aegean.

15. In the EEA Agreement these included: agricultural and fishery products; customs union; coal and steel products; workers' rights of establishment, economic and monetary policy cooperation; common transport policy; state aid; social policy; consumer protection; environment; and company law. For further details, see CEC, *Agreement on the European Economic Area* (Brussels: OOPEC, 1992). For a quantitative analysis of various smaller EFTA and EC states' participation in EC/EU activities, see H. Compston, 'Union Participation in Economic Policy-Making in Austria, Switzerland, The Netherlands, Belgium and Ireland, 1970–1992', *West European Politics*, 17 (1), 1994, 123–45; and M.O. Hosli, 'Admission of the European Free Trade Association states to the European Community: effects on voting power in the European Community Council of Ministers', *International Organization*, 47 (4), 1993, 629–43.

16. OECD, *National Accounts, Country Statistics 1987* (OECD, 1988); and EFTA, *EFTA Trade in 1993: Statistical Tables* (Paris: Economic Affairs Department, 1995).

17. F. Granell, 'The European Union's Enlargement Negotiations with Austria, Finland, Norway and Sweden', *Journal of Common Market Studies*, 33 (1), 1995, 117.

18 . However, a strengthening of the EP environmental lobby and policies on fisheries, pollution and logging are likely to be affected in the longer term, given their sound record on environmental policy, where standards are generally higher than the minimum set down by the Commission.

19. See European Parliament, *Resolution on the functioning of the Treaty on European Union with a view to the 1996 Intergovernmental Conference— Implementation and development of the Union*, A4-0102/95 (Brussels: OOPEC, 1996), para. 21 (ii).

20. See R.E. Baldwin, 'The Economic Logic of EFTA Countries joining the EEA and the EC', *EFTA Occasional Paper No. 41* (Geneva: EFTA, 1992).

21. EFTA, *EFTA Trade in 1993: Statistical Tables* (Geneva: EFTA Economic Affairs Department, 1995), Table 6, 10.

22. EFTA, *Thirty-Third Annual Report of the European Free Trade Association* (Geneva: EFTA, 1994), 6.

23. F. Granell, *loc. cit.*, 122.

24. *Ibid.*, 122.

25. See 'The EU goes cold on enlargement', *The Economist*, 28 October 1995, 59–60. See also H. Field, 'Eastwards Enlargement and the European Union', *School of Economics Working Papers*, No. 6 (Brisbane: Griffith University, 1996).

26. The extent to which CMEA states were in debt to western financial institutions was evident well before the collapse of communist regimes in Eastern Europe. East–West European financial linkages could be traced back to the Brandt doctrine of *Ostpolitik* in the early 1970s. By 1990, Poland's net foreign debt exceeded $US40 billion. See *IMF Financial Statistics 1990* (Washington DC: IMF, 1991).

27. German investment and resources have been increasingly diverted towards some Central and East European (CEE) countries since the early 1990s, which itself has had a negative impact on the EU as a recipient of German outward FDIs. Although this has slowed the process of economic rejuvenation in East Germany, certain CEE countries—such as the Czech Republic, Poland and Hungary—have been recipients of increasing levels of German FDIs. As competitive advantage has shifted to Eastern Europe (particularly in terms of semi-skilled and skilled labour), states on the EU's southern periphery (Portugal and

Spain in particular) are likely to experience FDI scarcity as more EU production shifts to low-cost manufacturing bases in CEE countries.

28. See CEC, *White Paper on the Internal Market and Pre-Accession Phase for CEE Countries*, *op. cit.*

29. This point is also made in the White Paper concerning CEE enlargement—see *ibid.*, Executive Summary and Part 2.

30. See OECD, *National Accounts, Country Statistics 1986* (Paris: OECD, 1987); CEC, *Eurostat* (Brussels: OOPEC, 1987); and CEC, *Eurostat: Basic Statistics of the Community* (29th ed., Brussels: OOPEC, 1992).

31. CEC, 'The Challenge of Enlargement: Commission Opinion on Sweden's Application for Membership', *Bulletin of the European Communities*, Supplement 5/92, (Brussels: OOPEC, 1992).

32. *Ibid.*

33. P. Wells and M. Rawlinson, *The New European Automobile Industry* (London: Macmillan, 1994), pp.67–8.

34. The Renault-Volvo merger (effectively a Renault takeover) was not concluded following a last minute Volvo decision not to enter into the agreement.

35. As of October 1996, the Wallenburg family indicated it was prepared to divest itself of its remaining 50% interest in Saab-Scania to GM, following losses totalling almost $US2 billion since 1992. However, GM's stake, which includes the majority of the preferential voting stock, means that GM has controlled the day-to-day operations of the firm since 1992.

36. ABB, *Annual Report* (ABB, 1988).

37. J.F. Qvigstad, 'Economic and Monetary Union: A Survey of the EMU and Empirical Evidence on Convergence for the EC and the EFTA Countries', *EFTA Occasional Paper No. 36* (Geneva: EFTA, 1992), 22.

38. This means that a currency must remain within the 2.25% ERM band for 2 years and must not be devalued against any other member currency for the same period. Stage III commences from 1 January 1999, provided a 'critical mass' of states fulfils the convergence criteria. This means that nine of the fifteen member states must fulfil the EMU criteria (public budgets, public deficits, interest rates and currency stability) for Stage III to commence. See CEC, *Amendments to the EEC Treaty—Economic and Monetary Union—as agreed in the Council of Maastricht on 10 December 1991* (Brussels: OOPEC, 1992); and CEC, *Green Paper on the Practical Arrangements for the Introduction of the Single Currency* (Brussels: OOPEC, 1995).

39. The 'snake' was the EC's fixed exchange-rate system introduced following the United States' suspension of dollar/gold convertibility (August 1971) and the Smithsonian Agreement (December 1971). The snake drew both EC and non-EC countries (including Norway and Sweden) into a managed currency system, although the volatility of European capital markets led to the establishment of the EMS in 1979. However, the 1970s experience drew smaller European economies (Austria, Benelux, Denmark, Norway, Sweden, Switzerland) to 'shadow' the DM, or at least maintain relative parity with DM fluctuations and, therefore, West German monetary policy.

40. OECD, *Economic Outlook 50* (Paris: OECD, 1994).

41. Although the EU Commission welcomed Norway's shadowing of the ECU (rather than the DM) in 1990 in order to prepare Norway for EMS membership, the reality is that the ERM and ECU value reflects DM weightings in the basket of currencies. Norwegian monetary policy is also closely tied to German interest rate realignments. See P. De Grauwe, 'Is the European Monetary System a DM Zone?', *CEPS Working Document*, No 39, (1988).

42. See Union Bank of Switzerland, 'European Monetary Union by 1999', *UBS International*

Finance, 22, 1994/5, 1–8; and 'Swiss Economy Still on Track', *UBS International Finance*, 22, 1994/5, 9.

43. See *Time*, 28 September 1992.
44. Author's calculation from data in IMF, *International Financial Statistics* (Washington DC: IMF, March 1990).
45. *Ibid.*
46. CEC, *Agreement on the European Economic Area, op. cit.* See also C. Bright (ed.), *Business Law in the European Economic Area* (Oxford: Oxford University Press, 1994).
47. As Sapir asks, 'What is the extent of Swedish investment outflows that can be attributed to Sweden's failure to join the internal market?'. See A. Sapir, 'Sweden: Effects of EU Membership: A Comment', *The World Economy*, 17 (5), 1994, 679–81.
48. See J. Pelkmans, 'Is Protection due to Financial Instability? A Skeptical View', in P. Guerrieri and P. Padoan (eds), *The Political Economy of International Cooperation* (London: Croom Helm, 1988); and Pelkmans, 'Is Convergence Prompting Fragmentation? The EMS and national protection in Germany, France and Italy', in P. Guerrieri and P. Padoan (eds), *The Political Economy of European Integration* (New York: Barnes & Noble, 1989), 100–44.
49. The Pre-Accession White Paper was adopted at the Essen European Council in December 1994. See CEC, *White Paper on the Internal Market and the Pre-Accession Phase, op. cit.*
50. See CEC, *Commission Opinion on Reinforcing Political Union and Preparing for Enlargement* (Brussels: OOPEC, 1996).
51. CEC, *White Paper on the Internal Market and the Pre-Accession Phase, op. cit.*, Executive Summary.
52. Some data suggest that it will take approximately 30 years for the best-performing CEE countries to reach the 1996 levels of GDP per capita income and debt-to-GDP ratios of the worst-performing EU states. See 'The EU goes cold on enlargement', *The Economist*, 28 October 1995; and Field, *loc. cit.*
53. See European Parliament, *The New Treaties, European Parliament Proposals* (Brussels: OOPEC, 1993); CEC, *Resolution on the functioning of the Treaty on European Union with a view to the 1996 Intergovernmental Conference—Implementation and development of the Union*, A4-0102/95 (Brussels: OOPEC, 1996); and CEC, *Standard Eurobarometer*, 2 June 1993 (Brussels: OOPEC, 1993).
54. See European Parliament, *The New Treaties, European Parliament Proposals.*
55. For a summary of the neorealist position on international structures and balances of power, see Waltz, *op. cit.*, chaps. 6–7.
56. Quoted in M. Rutherford, *Can We Save The Common Market?* (Oxford: Oxford University Press, 1981), 34.

5 The Mediterranean Boundaries of the European Union

F. DAMASO MARENGO

Introduction

Of all contemporary theorists of international integration, only Karl Deutsch and his associates (1957) have paid systematic attention to the role of boundaries. Deutsch defines an integrated Community first and foremost as a 'security community'. He conceptualises boundaries as variables relating the inside and the outside in a dynamic fashion. The inside exists insofar as there is an outside: the existence of what is within is predicated upon the existence of what is, or is left, or is pushed without. It is, according to Deutsch, the development among a group of people of a perception of otherness from the rest of the world or, at least, the relevant world, which leads to their affirmation of a sense of identity among themselves and, eventually, the establishment of a community, a 'security community'.[1]

The notion that perceptions of 'otherness' precede—historically, psychologically, and socially—perceptions of 'identity' is controversial. In this chapter, I accept that this notion contains a fundamental truth without proving it. However, while Deutsch's, or Deutsch-type notions of 'security community' provide a philosophical underpinning to my present treatment of boundaries in the process of European integration, it does not provide an analytical framework.

In this chapter I intend to relate the variables 'boundary' and 'power' in the process of European integration, having regard to the distribution of power among the EU's member states, the power of the Union as a whole, and the power relationship between the Union and the rest of the world, with particular reference to the EU's neighbours. Firstly, I examine the way boundary lines were drawn and re-drawn at the various stages of the process of European integration, and try to identify the historical reasons for this. I then proceed to re-conceptualise these reasons in my own terms. In the second part of the chapter, I analyse the reasons behind the current proposals to re-draw the EU's Mediterranean and eastern boundaries. I then speculate on the consequences that the proposed boundary re-drawings would have on the

93

EU's internal equilibria, and suggest that the proposed re-drawing of the EU's eastern boundary would consolidate Germany's economic and political leadership of the Union and thus have considerable implications for the current distribution of power within the Union. The concluding remarks raise the question as to whether the criteria adopted for the proposed re-drawing of the Mediterranean boundary could not be followed for the re-drawing of the EU's eastern boundary too. Further, which compensatory mechanisms are member states that stand to lose out from the proposed re-drawing of the eastern boundary likely to ask for and be before they might agree to a revision of the EU's eastern boundary?

The European Union's boundary lines at the various stages of the process of European integration

The 1952 Boundaries

For a generation, from the establishment of the European Coal and Steel Community in 1952 until the Community's first enlargement in 1973, the Community's external boundary was the unbroken line separating the Six from the rest of the world. From within the context of an interpretation of the Community as a by-product of the Cold War, one could argue that the eastern boundary was the crucial stretch of the Community's external boundary. Ideology would have been the criterion followed in drawing the Community's boundary.

Others, including myself, without disputing the influence of the Cold War on the Community's origins, would, however, argue that the Community's crucial boundary was the Channel. That boundary distinguished from all others those European countries ready to share a certain approach to democratic and economic consolidation in the ideologically divided world. Only the Six founder states were willing to subscribe to that approach.

In processes of international integration, boundaries can be drawn having in sight the world within or the world without. The Community's first boundary was drawn having the world within in sight. The boundary was open to all those European countries willing to share a certain approach to contemporary domestic and international life. The defining features of that approach were: political democracy; the pledge to rule out force as a means of settling disputes among members; a belief that one member's economic prosperity could not be achieved at the expense of the economic prosperity of another member, but, on the contrary, was conditioned upon the prosperity of all. Thence emerged the decision to build among themselves a customs Community which would cover the entirety of the members' economic activity, including agriculture.[2]

The 1973 Boundaries

By 1973 the United Kingdom, Ireland, and Denmark had come to accept the Community's approach. The Community's western and northern boundaries were accordingly re-drawn. Among the European countries which could then conceivably share the Community's approach, only the Scandinavian countries still remained outside. The Community's boundaries had therefore almost achieved their maximum possible extension. In the decade that followed, the Community's approach remained the same; however the situation in the greater European environment, or in relevant portions of it, changed.

The 1981 and 1986 Boundaries

The Scandinavian countries were not prevented by any ideological or structural reasons from joining the Community and remained outside of their own choice.[3] However, the Mediterranean European countries had been shut outside the Community's southern boundary because, while sharing—to an even greater degree than the Scandinavian countries—history, tradition, and culture with the Community's member states, they had rejected their democratic political values. In the 1970s these countries (Greece, Spain, and Portugal) made decisive progress towards restoring democracy, and by the end of the following decade they had all joined the community.

As a result, the Community reached in one direction, for the first time, its natural boundary, since it now included all, or virtually all, the countries which arguably belonged to it geographically, historically, and culturally. Southward the Community had reached what, in historical terms, one could regard as its permanent boundary. Relations with countries lying outside could be properly regarded, from the Community's perspective, as external relations.

On the other hand, the Commnity's boundary to the North could still be regarded as temporary and ill-defined. The Community's boundary to the East was, instead, well defined within the current political context: as such, it was essentially a politico-ideological boundary, rather than a geographical-historical one.

The 1990 and 1995 Boundaries

Today, while the Union has fully embraced the South, it has not done so *vis-à-vis* the North. Two Nordic countries, Norway and Iceland, are still outside the EU's boundaries. Moreover, it is on the EU's side of the northern boundary that one meets the most serious doubts about the current standing and future ambitions of the Union: as evidenced, for instance, by the opt-outs requested by the governments and the lack of enthusiasm shown by the peoples in some member states in the aftermath of the Maastricht negotiations.

It is, however, at the EU's eastern boundary that the most dramatic events of the last decade, particularly the collapse of the Soviet Empire, took place. These events have already made possible major re-drawings of the EU's eastern and north-eastern boundaries. On 3 October 1990 the former German Democratic Republic, having joined the Federal Republic of Germany to form a united Germany, became an integral part of the Union. On 1 January 1995, Austria, Finland, and Sweden officially joined the Union.[4] But the major re-drawings of the EU's eastern boundary are perhaps yet to come.

A complete re-drawing of the EU's eastern boundary implies a major revision of the criteria according to which the EU's boundaries have so far been drawn and re-drawn. The EU's eastern boundary was originally conceived as a politico-ideological boundary; it became, by implication, an economic and socio-cultural boundary too. It was not a security boundary though, to the extent that Europe's security boundary to the East, within the context of the Cold War and the bipolar world, was of NATO and not of the EU.

The revision of the EU's eastern boundary would not imply a simple re-drawing of the boundary line, but a change in the nature of the boundary itself. If the countries, former satellites of the Soviet Union currently knocking at the EU's doors, were to become part of its eastern boundary, including them would *ipso facto* become a security boundary. If such a scenario were to become reality, it would give the Union, for the first time, a security boundary: that is, a boundary which would require the Union to give as much attention to what happens outside, as to what happens inside it. I shall shortly discuss an alternative approach to boundary re-drawing, namely the Mediterranean approach, and compare it with the approach proposed for the re-drawing of the EU's eastern boundary.

Boundaries and the process of European integration

Drawing on the findings of this brief historical survey, we ask the theoretical question of what role, if any, did boundaries, as given, play in the process (pace, direction, and speed) of European integration?

The initial stage

The boundary which drew the line between the Six's approach to contemporary domestic and international life and rival approaches advocated by the United

Kingdom and its northern allies made possible the Community's consolidation. This consolidation resulted from focusing the undivided attention of the Six on the major task ahead, dismissing once and for all the temptation of destructive and disruptive alliances. The boundary thus represented a protective wall rather than a springboard. To the extent that its purpose was not so much to keep outsiders out as to discourage insiders from peeping outside, the boundary represented a screen rather than a wall.

The boundary quickly and effectively fulfilled its function and soon became obsolete, or its original function distorted. As soon as the UK (and Denmark and Ireland) began earnestly knocking at the EU's door and vowing to accept the essentials of the Community's approach, the boundary became a barrier to keep them out. It was turning into a protective or defensive boundary, where there was no perceived need for protection or defence, at least on the part of the majority of the Community's members. To this extent, the boundary became internally divisive, contrary to what it was when originally drawn, and as such dysfunctional.[5]

The first three enlargements—1973, 1981, 1986

With the accession of the United Kingdom and Ireland, the Community lost a sharply defined boundary to the West. Meanwhile its southern and northern boundaries turned, slowly but surely, into springboards for expansion. The Community entered a new phase where its major concern was no longer integration *per se*, but, rather, trading power. This trend was, of course, particularly in evidence outside the Community's boundaries where the Community flexed its muscles in its relations with third countries, with which it negotiated treaties of cooperation and trade, and began building a power basis for itself in international arenas, where it claimed for its member states, and for itself, a growing share of the benefits of international trade.

The struggle for power shaped behaviour inside the Community too, where the Commission, in a sense, moved from a role of motor for integration on behalf of a plan under the control of an élite which included itself, to a role of powerful bureaucracy mainly catering to itself, on occasion in opposition to its member states' interests. Other Community institutions, including the European Parliament, became overwhelmingly concerned with their own place in the Community's institutional power structure. Between 1952 and 1986, the EC's northern and southern boundaries were moved to the optimal outer limits.

The post-Cold War enlargements—1995 and beyond

It is tempting to view the current situation on the eastern boundary also in terms of the EU's potential expansion, the eastern border being the last along which the Union can still consider expanding without sacrificing its identity, however that may be defined as European identity.

It is important to remark that the series of events which created the preconditions for the re-drawing of the EU's eastern boundary were entirely outside the EU's influence and took place without its participation. Indeed, it could be argued in retrospect that events outside the EU's control made possible the 1981 and 1986 revisions of the Mediterranean boundary. However, such external events (the ousting of the colonels in Greece, and the developments that followed the deaths of the Spanish and Portuguese dictators) were not entirely outside the Community's and its member states' influence and calculations. Although not provoked by the Community, they were anxiously awaited by it.

Further, the re-drawing of the EU's eastern boundary currently under discussion was never contemplated in a coherent manner in any blueprint for the EU's further development, although members remained open to any democratic European state under Article 237 of the EEC Treaty and Article O of the Maastricht Treaty. De Gaulle's vision of a Europe 'from the Atlantic to the Urals' was never to be operationalised in concrete political terms. On the other hand, while the revision of the EU's eastern boundary of the kind proposed in the 1990s was never operationally contemplated, its implementation is likely to disturb the EU's internal equilibria: not only those affecting the EU's leadership, but also the EU's rank and file.

Only the EU's first boundary revision was implemented in the expectation that it would have important consequences for the EU's leadership. The inclusion of the United Kingdom was then thought likely to provide an alternative to France's leadership of the Community. The current proposed revision of the EU's eastern boundary has been seen in some quarters as likely to strengthen Germany's position within the Union and make it the sole leader, rather than the joint leader with France as is currently the case, and to an extent reduce France's role in the EU's leadership.

There is, however, an important difference between the two instances. In the first instance, the expected outcome was the entry onto the stage of a new player, the United Kingdom, thought likely to compete with an existing player, France, for the EU's leadership and possibly to create the opportunity for a mediating leadership role for other players, particularly Germany. The current boundary revision could, instead, tilt the balance in favour of one of the two current leaders and against the other.

The proposed revision of the EU's eastern boundary is also likely to affect, in a negative way, the interests of the EU's smaller members, to the extent that it would inject, net of the increase in the EU's resources, fresh competition for the allocation of the EU's budget expenditures. This, of course, marks a further difference with the 1973 enlargement, which brought in the United Kingdom and Denmark, net contributors to the EU's resources, and which more than compensated for Ireland's expected drawing upon them.

Thus, the current proposed revision of the EU's eastern boundary is comparable to the 1981 and 1986 revisions of the EU's southern boundary. The two revisions led to the inclusion of new competitors for the EU's resources, without a balancing influx of fresh funds. However, the drain on the EU's resources was expected to be compensated, in the medium term, by the taking off of the new members' (especially Spain's) economies, boosted by participation in the Community, and the expanded market they would thus offer for the old members' industrial exports. Moreover, there was to be a reassessment of the contributions to the Community budget at this time.

The present Mediterranean boundary of the Union

To a large extent as a reaction to the proposed re-drawing of the EU's eastern boundary, a proposal emerged from within the Union itself which would join to the EU, without actually re-drawing its boundaries (except for the possible membership of Malta and Cyprus), the non-EU Mediterranean countries, through the creation of a Mediterranean Free Trade Area of which the Union as a whole would constitute the core.[6] What are the implications of this proposal for the notion of the EU's boundaries?

First, it should be noted that attention is being drawn to the EU's southern boundary not for the purpose of reaching out for new members, but of re-focusing the EU's attention on its existing southern members and their problems. The move finds its justification in a perception that the epicentre of the Union is moving northward and, it is expected, eastward. Second, the problems that the EU's southern members allegedly experience, or are likely to experience, originate from events taking place, or likely to take place, not within the EU, but outside its boundaries. I refer to Islamic fundamentalism, whose main epicentre seems currently to be moving to Algeria and the other Maghreb countries, with a secondary epicentre in Egypt.[7]

Within this context, the purpose of the Mediterranean Free Trade Area is to offer financial aid and trade opportunities (although limited in the agricultural sector) to the non-EU Mediterranean countries, in an attempt to promote their economic development and, with it, political stability. It is anticipated that this would in turn steel their societies against the temptation of Islamic fundamentalism. The proactive policy pursued in the economic field through the free trade area is complemented by a reactive and defensive policy pursued in the military field. There is a regional consensus among the EU's Mediterranean countries, led by France, that an Islamic fundamentalism victorious in Algeria would quickly spread to all Maghreb countries and engulf the whole region, with major repercussions in the territories of the EU Mediterranean States.

To counter the security threat related to Islamic fundamentalism, France, Italy, Spain, and Portugal have recently created a Euro-Mediterranean Force (EUROFOR) within the framework of NATO and the Western European Union (WEU). EUROFOR has mainly defensive purposes. However it would also, upon request, carry out peace-keeping and humanitarian missions. These missions could, in principle, take place anywhere in the world. But, presumably, they would be particularly likely in the Mediterranean itself, were there to be local conflicts encouraged by Islamic fundamentalism that could provoke the slaughter of local populations and the mass exodus of the survivors towards Europe.

The Mediterranean Free Trade Area, which will include the 15 EU member states and the non-EU Mediterranean countries plus Jordan, also contains, from the EU's perspective, an offensive trade promotion element. This could become important if the economies of the non-EU side of the Mediterranean were to take off. Once established, the Euro-Mediterranean Free Trade Area would be the largest of its kind in the world.

Within this context, a further element is likely to make an impact, radically different to that of Islamic fundamentalism, on the policies, societies, and economies of the Mediterranean countries, and which presumably played a role in prompting the proposal for the Mediterranean Free Trade Area, namely, a peaceful solution to the Arab–Israeli conflict through the creation of a Palestinian state. By tying the Mediterranean to it through the establishment of the Euro-Mediterranean Free Trade Area, the Union would stand greatly to benefit from such a development.

The question of the present boundaries of the EU and the future of European integration

The Euro-Mediterranean Free Trade Area, as a plan embracing both EU members and non-members, is by no means a new idea. A predecessor to it was the European Economic Area (EEA).[8] The essence of such plans is to create a sphere of influence and a network of client states which lie, and will most likely remain, outside the EU, but are expected to adopt most of the EU's policies, such as the Single Market, to provide a reservoir of support for the

Union and its members in international organisations, and to provide a protected market for the EU's exports. They offer to the non-Union members, in exchange for all this, a privileged access to the EU's economic power and significant market.

There is, though, a significant difference between the EEA and the Euro-Mediterranean Free Trade Area. The EEA was conceived, at least in part, as a response to the requests in the late 1980s and early 1990s of a group of European states for membership of the Union.[9] For the non-European members of the proposed Euro-Mediterranean Free Trade Area Union, Union membership is not an option. Because of this, the Euro-Mediterranean Free Trade Area is more openly an expansionist agreement than the EEA.

While the Euro-Mediterranean agreement obviously tends to favour those of the EU's member states which have greater interests in the Mediterranean, it does not seem to affect the distribution of power within the Union and the relative weight of its member states. It is therefore a safe agreement, unlikely to have negative side effects on the Union and its members, but likely to increase the influence of the Union as a whole, especially at the international level. Internally, the agreement has the purpose of making secure, or more secure, one of the Union's boundaries under threat from feared external disorders and unwanted immigration. This is an objective which is in the interest of all members of a Union where people and goods, including illicit goods and illegal residents, move freely.

Against this no-risk expansionist model proposed for the EU's Mediterranean boundary, there is another model that is proposed for the Union's eastern boundary. The proposal is to re-draw the EU's eastern boundary with a view to incorporating a group of countries which are anxious to be included and which can conceivably be included, having regard to these countries' cultural, historical, geographical, political, and economic background. Of course, significant differences exist among these various countries and between these countries and the EU's current members, and these need to be taken into account through a more or less lengthy transition period fixed for each of them before finally joining the Union.[10]

Likewise, no major objection to these countries' eventual membership of the Union originates from the international environment. This development, like that of NATO enlargement to include eastern and central European states, is known to be looked upon with some concern by Russia. However, it is hoped that Russia could be reassured by the incorporation of suitable conditions in the final individual agreements. On the other hand, the Eastern European countries knocking at the EU's door have made abundantly clear that they would not accept any solution short of full Union membership, and would reject a proposal along the lines of the Euro-Mediterranean model.

But is the proposed revision of its eastern boundary uncontroversial within the EU? We have seen that the Euro-Mediterranean plan was born as a reaction by the EU's Mediterranean members to a perceived shift of the EU's focus and resources towards its eastern boundary. A revision of the EU's eastern boundary is likely to disturb the EU's present equilibria and redistribute power within the Union away from the Paris–Bonn axis towards a Berlin pole, according to some views.

Admittedly this would be a development translating into the political sphere an existing economic reality (and the Union still remains first and foremost an economic union).[11] Presently, though, the overall distribution of economic power within the Union is balanced by a different distribution of military and political power.[12] With the ratification of the Maastricht Treaty, security and foreign policy issues came within the scope of the Union, which thus took an important step towards evolving from a primarily economic Union into an economic, political, and security Union (in military terms).[13] To this extent, the revision of the EU's eastern boundary would not only ratify existing economic equilibria, but also create the premises for new political and military equilibria.

It is possible, although unlikely, that all Union members including France, will accept, without opposition, the EU's eastern enlargement and possibly even Germany's sole leadership of the enlarged Union. It is, however, more likely that they will either force the abandonment of the plan, or extract a price for their acceptance of its implementation.

At this point we enter the realm of speculation, with at least four possible scenarios charting the future. The first would see the abandonment of the proposed enlargement of the Union to the East, under pressure from a coalition of the EU's Mediterranean countries led by France, and the adoption instead of the Euro-Mediterranean model for the re-drawing of the EU's eastern boundary.

The second scenario would see an attempt by France to push for the full integration of the security and foreign policy pillars into the EU, with a view to rebalancing, particularly at the military level, the power that Germany would gain at the economic and political levels through the EU's eastern enlargement.[14] This scenario would become more credible if Britain were to collaborate with France for its realisation; for instance, through the Europeanisation of their respective nuclear arsenals.[15]

The third scenario suggests a considerable increase in the price Germany would be asked to pay for the economic and political leadership of the Union in its own right. The price would be in terms of Germany agreeing to assume (or agreeing that the European Central Bank would assume) the public debts of the central banks of all the EU's member states, as was unfailingly the case in the processes of national unification during the nineteenth century. In other words, Germany would agree to scrap the convergence criteria and allow member states' participation in Stage 3 of the Economic and Monetary Union (EMU) merely on a declaration of political will to do so.[16] This scenario would satisfy the appearance of a continuing joint German and French political and joint French and British military leadership in Europe. But who would doubt the reality of Germany's economic power and its understandable desire to recoup at the political level, at least, the financial losses incurred in its acquisition of the member states' debts?

The fourth scenario would see the articulation of the Union into three fully integrated sub-regional groups: a Central-Eastern European Group led by Germany, a Northern Group led by Britain, and a Mediterranean Group led by France. The three groups would be joined together into a loose, confederal bond which would, however, be fully operational at the international level.[17]

It remains to be seen which, if any, of the above scenarios eventuates, and whether or not a version of the 'fuzzy' boundary represented by the Euro-Mediterranean Free Trade Area will in practice be adopted to the east of the current EU.

Notes

1. See K. W. Deutsch, *Nationalism and Social Communication: an Inquiry into the Foundations of Nationality* (Cambridge: M.I.T. Press, 1953), 86–106 and 166–86; K. W. Deutsch *et al., Political Community and the North Atlantic Area: International Organization in the Light of Historical Experience* (Princeton: Princeton University Press, 1957), 5 and 36; K. W. Deutsch, *The Analysis of International Relations* (Englewood Cliffs: Prentice-Hall, 1978), 241–51.
2. On this, see L. N. Lindberg, *The Political Dynamics of European Economic Integration* (Stanford: Stanford University Press, 1963); M. Camps, *Britain and the European Community, 1955–1963* (Oxford: Oxford University Press, 1964), 1–184; E. B. Haas, *The Uniting of Europe: Political, Social, and Economic Forces* (Stanford: Stanford University Press, 1958), 299–317.
3. Norway had applied to join the EC with Denmark, Ireland and the UK, but withdrew its application when a referendum resulted in rejection of membership of the EC.
4. See Christine Agius' chapter in this volume for a full discussion of the 1995 enlargement and the neutrality issue.
5. Camps, *op. cit.*, 1–124; L. N. Lindberg and S. Scheingold, *Europe's Would-Be Polity: Patterns of Change in the European Community* (Englewood Cliffs: Prentice-Hall, 1970), 220–39.
6. Commission of the European Communities, *The European Community's Relations with the Mediterranean* (Brussels, December 1994) and Commission of the European Communities, *Communication from the Commission to the Council and the European Parliament. Strengthening the Mediterranean Policy of the European Union: Proposals for Implementing Euro–Mediterranean Partnership* (Brussels, March 1995).
7. For an analysis of Islamic fundamentalism and European reactions to it, ante-dating the EU initiative, see J. Farley, 'The Mediterranean: Southern Threats to Northern Shores?', *The World Today*, 50 (2), 1994, 33–6.

8. The EEA was originally intended to be an EC–EFTA agreement. It now consists of EU and EFTA states minus Switzerland. The EEA was ratified and came into effect in 1994. See T. Blanchet *et al., The Agreement of the European Economic Area (EEA). A Guide to the Free Movement of Goods and Competition Rules* (Oxford: Clarendon Press, 1994), 1–4.

9. See the chapter by Rémy Davison in this book.

10. Commission of the European Communities, *White Paper. Preparation of the Associated Countries of Central and Eastern Europe for Integration into the Internal Market of the Union* (Brussels, May 1995).

11. D. S. Yost, 'France in the New Europe', *Foreign Affairs*, 69 (5), 1990–1, 111.

12. *Ibid.*, 116; S. P. Kramer, 'The French Question', *Washington Quarterly*, 14 (4), 1991, 84–5.

13. N. Petersen, 'The European Community and Foreign and Security Policy', in O. Nørgaard *et al., The European Community in World Politics* (London: Pinter, 1993), 9–31; J. Redmond, 'Introduction', in J. Redmond (ed.), *The External Relations of the European Community: The International Response to 1992* (New York: St. Martin's Press, 1992), 1–11. For a sceptical view, specifically concerning the Europeanisation of the 'defence pillar', see T. Taylor, 'West European Security and Defence Cooperation: Maastricht and Beyond', *International Affairs*, 70 (1), 1994, 16. For the views of a protagonist, see D. Hurd, 'Developing the Common Foreign and Security Policy', *International Relations*, 70 (3), 1994, 421–8.

14. For an early version of such policy, called 'Eurovoluntarism,' see Yost, *loc. cit.*, 123–6.

15. On joint French-British cooperation in this area, see Kramer, *loc. cit.*, 95.

16. The convergence criteria were dictated by Germany to its EU partners as an essential condition for accepting EMU. See L. Tsoukalis, *The New European Economy: The Politics and Economics of Integration* (Oxford: Oxford University Press, 1993), 205–27.

17. The futuristic literature on the EU has, to my knowledge, failed to examine in detail such a scenario. See, however, T. Pedersen, 'The Common Foreign and Security Policy and the Challenge of Enlargement', in Nørgaard, *op. cit.*, 48.

6 Balkan Boundaries: Writing History and Identity into Territory

GLENDA SLUGA

Self-determination, ethnicity and representation

In European histories of the twentieth century the practices of boundary-marking and ethno-territoriality have been most explicitly examined in connection with the peace settlements at the end of the First World War. Woodrow Wilson's principle of national self-determination transformed the late nineteenth-century association of states with ethnicity or 'national' identity from an assumption to an indispensable ingredient of social contract. Thus, the ethnic nation state was legitimated as a 'democratic' principle, and as a method of conflict resolution and geo-political stabilisation.[1]

By the beginning of the twentieth century it was increasingly common to associate 'nationhood' with ethnicity or race, which in turn were seen as expressive of the natural or essential self (often defined as inherently masculine).[2] The assumption implicit in early twentieth-century conceptions of national self-determination (whether in political, philosophical, or historical accounts) was that ethnicity linked the individual to a shared community and was expressive of an inner self. Moreover, when a state was co-extensive with 'ethnicity', then the individuals and the homologous community contained by that state were 'free'. Thus, national self-determination promised the resolution of the problem of identity and representation inherent in modern notions of democracy and citizenship.

Expressing unease about the post-war application of this new principle, the British diplomat Harold Nicolson confessed in *Peacemaking 1919* that, in the course of his involvement in the peace commissions, his 'early faith in Self-Determination as the remedy for all human ills' became 'clouded with doubts and reservations'.[3] The principle of self-determination had not, after all, guaranteed democratic processes or results. Nicolson wrote that under the pressure of the Peace negotiations, the problem of defining ethnic boundaries in the mapping of new states assumed a surreal and controversial character:

March 5, Wednesday.... Maps, plans, partitions, watersheds, canalization—all those intricate processes of thought which have become a jog-trot in my brain. The strain moral and mental is great: even the puddles in the pavements assumed for the shapes of frontiers, salients, corridors, neutralized channels, demilitarized zones, islands...

March 9, Sunday.... It is as though four architects had each designed an entirely different house, and then met round a table to arrive at an agreement, which means, of course, a compromise, in which all the designs are fused into a conglomeration which has no sense or coherence.

The disillusionment expressed by Nicolson with the democratic claims of national emancipation, and the difficulties of sustaining ethnically conceived territorial boundaries, have persisted throughout the twentieth century in the commentaries of historians, political scientists and the victims of territorial displacement. At the same time, the legitimacy of ethnicity as the key to the constitution of individual and community identities, in the present as well as the past, has endured as an efficacious means of resolving questions of political representation and the nature of democracy. One of the sources of that endurance has been an acceptance by historians of the inherently democratic impulse of national identification, and of its universalist, i.e. ungendered, character. Historical narratives which fail to problematise national identity are then utilised as points of orientation in political analyses of conflict.

This chapter offers two case studies (perhaps even historical allegories) of the way in which this century's assumptions about cultural difference and about the naturalness of 'national' identification have been translated into political boundaries, simultaneously obfuscating the problem of democratic representation. The first example concerns what in political and historical narratives has been commonly termed 'the problem of Trieste'. Currently a city on Italy's border with Slovenia, Trieste has been constructed as a problem in these narratives both because its 'ethnic identity' has been presented as complex, and because its identification in ethnic terms has been regarded as imperative. In the second example I briefly suggest the significance of my reading of the Trieste question, and of the historical specificity of national identifications of Trieste as Italian in opposition to a Balkan-Slav threat, for understanding the way in which the recent 'Balkan' wars have been, and are being, constructed in political and historical narratives.

Europe and the Balkan East—or reinventing Trieste

It was the 'Adriatic problem' which, Nicolson claimed, most fully demonstrated the inconsistencies and difficulties of the creation of a new national order in 1919. This 'problem' involved the resolution of territorial disputes between the newly created Kingdom of Serbs, Croats and Slovenes (or Yugoslavia) and the slightly older Italian state. In 1915 the 'Treaty of London' had been negotiated secretly between the British and Italian governments to obtain Italy's entry into the war. It promised to reward Italy with a coastal frontier along the Eastern shores of the Adriatic, including the city of Trieste. At the end of the war, the Treaty's lack of concern for 'ethnic' criteria of statehood contravened the principles of national self-determination: at the very least, the ethnic composition of the territory—as 'Italian' or 'Slav'—was disputed. Trieste and the surrounding region, which had been under Habsburg rule for 400 years, lay at the head of the Adriatic. Despite confusion and concern within the city, Nicolson's account suggests that the peacebrokers regarded Trieste's identity as unproblematic at this time; the 'Adriatic problem' involved particularly the city of Fiume. However, by the end of the Second World War, it was indeed the 'problem' of Trieste's ethnic identity that was being contested in the midst of the unfolding Cold War.

Before the First World War Trieste's cultural diversity, its legacy as a cosmopolitan Habsburg city, had provided a fertile matrix for the reinvention of a range of national identities, most successfully Italian, and to a lesser extent Slovene. According to Richard Bosworth, Italy's European image as a culture which was good only for sightseeing and gelati, an 'effeminate' lesser power in the early twentieth century, rankled the patriotic Italian intelligentsia, spurring among them an acceptance of Italian imperialist foreign policy and irredentism, which included the wish to incorporate the city of Trieste, as well as the Istrian and Dalmatian coastlines.[4] For Italian irredentists, reclaiming Trieste from Austrian 'occupation' was heralded as significant for completing the body of an imagined masculine national corpus, for realising Italian 'virility', and for liberating its 'Italian' population. An Italian Trieste, in their view, would also protect Italy from a Slav threat and provide a base for Italy's mission towards the East. The frontier, in this context, became, as it had in American folklore, the proving ground for the nation as a 'major' power.[5]

Socialists had generally distanced themselves from these aspirations, focusing instead on social and political reform within the framework of the Habsburg empire. However, the war and then the collapse of that empire had further polarised political choices into national choices. The 1920 Treaty of Rapallo which resulted from the peace process confirmed that, at least as far as Trieste was concerned, the Italian nation state had won the war. Following the Italian acquisition of Trieste and the Istrian peninsula, those who sought to identify themselves and Trieste as ethnically part of the Italian nation state were able to relegate the origins of its so-called 'Slav' population to the margins of the East. Rather than accept them as legitimate members of an old community they redefined them as Balkan. Italian irredentist and nationalist literature accepted only monolingual speakers of Triestine Italian as authentic Italians. Slavs were presented as uncivilised and alien peasants belonging beyond the borders of what remained of the city walls. During the eighteenth century, and into the nineteenth, these ethnically ambiguous peasants had often dominated scenic depictions of the city of Trieste, dressed romantically in folk-garb and gazing down from villages strewn on the surrounding hillsides onto the flourishing port of the Habsburg empire. Once the post-war Italian government had incorporated Trieste into the nation, the peasants peopling the pages of reinvented histories were transformed into the menacing Slav mass, too eager to enter that urban space, with all its privileges of social power and economic control. The continuing relevance of racially defined politics to the 'Adriatic' region was guaranteed during the inter-war period by officially sanctioned fascist violence against Slavs and Slav culture.

The Slav also figured in other political discourses. Throughout Western and Central Europe, the First World War and the Russian Revolution had modified perceptions of the Slav. Communism discursively overlapped with presumed Slavic cultural attributes of barbarism and backwardness. When the term 'Balkan' was juxtaposed with 'Slav' it could indicate an uncivilised inability to unite or represent a coherent identity.[6] Early in her weighty travel/ historical tome on the Yugoslavia of the inter-war years, Rebecca West confessed that, 'violence was indeed all I knew of the Balkans; all I knew of the South Slavs. I derived my knowledge from memories of my earliest interest in Liberalism'.[7] West was commenting on the metaphorical role that the Balkans had taken on in the twentieth century, as the darker side of a self-impressed liberal Europe. It was not until the closing phases of the Second World War that these cultural types were brought into play in the resolution of the question of Trieste's ethnicity.

In the early months of 1945, Trieste was a city under Nazi occupation. As the British Eighth Army fought its way up through northern Italy, one of its key objectives was the liberation of Trieste. But the liberation of Trieste was also the objective of the successful and determined local anti-fascist forces, militarily and politically organised under the umbrella of the communist 'Liberation Front' with its headquarters not in Italy but across the border, in Yugoslavia. Its internationalist slogan '*fraternita/bratstvo*' or 'brotherhood' was interpreted by both sympathetic and antagonistic locals, men and women, as specifically addressing the relations between Italians and Slovenes in the region.

The period of 'Liberation Front' government sheds light on the significance of the Yugoslav 'experiment' in the immediate post-war period for a range of groups who identified their interests with its future: working-class women, antifascists, anti-nationalists, and communists. It reveals the contradictions which informed this experiment—a self-conscious cultural anti-nationalism would be manifested within the boundaries of a new political nation, the federated Yugoslavia. Although within the logic of the new government this anomaly presented no contradiction, in practice the new principle of citizenship contradicted shared memories of the past. The theoretical application of 'brotherhood' had to deal with left over and continuing resentments, especially for those who identified themselves as Italian partially through opposition to a Balkan 'Slav' culture and the internationalism of Bolshevism, and those who associated their Slovene identity with oppression under the Italian state.

The story of the Liberation Front is also dependent on the revisions of the history of Yugoslavia. In theory the separation of the notion of 'citizenship' from 'nationality' which was the basis of Liberation Front (and Yugoslav) policy aimed to renew the relationship between Italians and non-Italians, especially Slovenes (with some separate gesturing to the place of women) on a 'democratic' basis. Yet, anti-nationalist activity and 'imaginings' were so closely identifiable with communist aims, that 'fraternity' was marked as inauthentic in comparison with the authenticity of national forms of identification. In political analyses, national identification was under threat from the ideological hegemony of Marxist-Leninist rule.

After only about six weeks of Liberation Front administration, the British–American Allied Military Government (AMG) took control in June 1945 in a military stand-off. To justify its assumption of control, the AMG referred to the need for an arbitrator between the Italians and 'Slavs'. From May 1945 until October 1954 (when Trieste was returned from Allied Military Government control to the Italian state), the political competition between the nominally 'allied' Yugoslav and British–American forces for Trieste and its surrounding regions focused on the ethnic definition of territory and boundaries. The diplomatic correspondence and AMG records from the period 1945 to 1954 reveal a progression from ambivalent interpretations of political events in Trieste to increasingly one-sided accounts which relied upon the distinctively ethnic identification of the city's inhabitants and their political interests. Throughout the period of AMG administration, its officials often disregarded local attempts at negotiation across boundaries of ethnic definition and reaffirmed that at the core of the political contest was an historic ethnic struggle.[8] While pro-Yugoslav groups interpreted any ethnic hostility in Trieste as the result of fascist manipulation and of a capitalist conspiracy to disunite the working classes by encouraging nationalism, the Allied Military Government held that anti-nationalism, or the policy of Italian and Slovene fraternity, was an ideological ploy, a devious manoeuvre to convince workers that their interests lay with communism.[9] The AMG's reluctance to hold democratic elections, promised since June 1945, was repeatedly justified by representing the relationship between Slav and Italian as so 'racially' antagonistic that such a concession would lead to widespread violence.

This Cold War reinvention of Trieste by the Allies and local nationalist groups as a site of ethnic struggle in opposition to the pro-communist attempts to legitimate 'brotherhood' and class over ethnic identity was by no means straightforward, nor the product of conscious manipulation. Not only had fascist rule taken a toll on local relations, but ethnically-defined national identity had claimed legitimacy in other European-wide contexts. The figure of the Slav whose natural homeland was the Balkans was widely used by pro-Italian historians and politicians to underscore Trieste's essential *italianità* and the integrity of ethnically-defined Italian territory. The Cold War cultural alignment between the Balkan Slavs and communism coincided with a predominant Italian historiographical (and political) tradition developed before the period of fascist government, and fostered by it, which similarly relied upon depictions of Italian national selves under threat from uncivilised, 'non-European', Balkan/ Slav others.

Even 'liberal' pro-Italian antifascists of the resistance looked suspiciously on those 'ethnically' ambiguous activists who claimed to be Italians and yet supported Tito's communist forces rather than an Italian Trieste.[10] When in early 1945 a particularly distinguished member of the pro-Italian antifascist intelligentsia, Carlo Schiffrer, encountered an Italian-speaking member of the pro-Yugoslav Liberation Front called 'Pino', he professed to have sensed that 'even [Pino] must be a Slovene who has pretended to be an Italian for the occasion' and concluded that 'the Slavs were playing on ambiguities, for them it is easy to pass off as Italian one of their own faithful bilingual units'.[11] Schiffrer's presupposition that no Italian would support what was obviously a 'Slav' cause or speak a 'Slav' language was meant to undermine the legitimacy of not only the cause, but also the sincerity of those individuals who claimed to be Italians. In Schiffrer's recollections, Italians had only one authentic identity, while Slavs/Slovenes were capable of cultural transgression and transformation because they (like women) had no essential selves.[12] Schiffrer's protestations were indeed provoked by his encounter with the incoherency of 'ethnic' identity: it was difficult to tell in this environment, he despaired, 'who is Italian and who is a Slav?'.

Despite the persistent confusion, ambiguity, and ambivalence surrounding the question of 'ethnicity' and the marking of boundaries, the definition of national difference in terms of ethnicity remained a fundamental point of reference in the ordering of the new post-war Europe and in the defence of democracy. In 1947 Geoffrey Cox, a British Intelligence Officer in the New Zealand 2nd Division of the British Eighth Army, who, before the war, had been working as a journalist in England and Europe, published an autobiographical account of his Division's journey through central and northern Italy to Trieste (in the spring of 1945).[13] It is Cox's view in *The Road To Trieste*, more than any recorded during spring 1945 itself, which has been favoured by historians of the Cold War, as it developed along the southern edge of Churchill's 'Iron Curtain'.[14]

Cox's account is replete with the certainties of ethnic hierarchies and boundaries, of their centrality to the question of the new Cold War world order, and of the constant and undesirable transgressions of boundaries. Underlying the naturalness of ethnic boundaries is a particular gender order. Cox dramatically contrasts the homeliness of Italy with the threatening unfamiliarity of 'No Man's Land', the area on the eastern side of a palpable, if invisible, Italian border. He gives contrasting accounts of the respective welcomes that his Division received in late April 1945, as it approached first an 'Italian' town, [Venezia] Mestre, about two hundred kilometres west of Trieste, and then in the area he calls 'No Man's Land'. He draws a boundary between two culturally and politically antipathetic civilisations in the most obvious yet irresistible of terms, by grounding that boundary in the norms of gender difference. When Cox is in a place he recognises as Italian, the welcome rises to a pitch of fervour:

> Here were flags and banners; men, women and girls. Above all girls. Were there ever such girls as those of Mestre on this Sunday of liberation? Brown-faced, aquiline, sunburnt, lithe girls with shining hair and with greeting and invitation in their eyes; northern Italians with blue eyes and sweeping eyebrows and high cheekbones in round faces; girls in white cool frocks with flared skirts like Americans, smiling, waving, laughing. This spectacle of a liberating army affected the women a thousand times more than the men [...] The Italian men greeted us warmly enough, with relief and with thanks, but in the eyes of the girls there was something akin to ecstasy. Some threw us kisses, some threw their arms wide as if they would embrace us all, in their exultation; others smiled quietly, and called to us 'ciao, ciao' as we moved on eastward through winding streets. [15]

In this excerpt the 'Italian' girls' desire to embrace the British Army's presence makes that presence legitimate and defines them as liberators and conquerors. The same narrative device of detailing the responses of women to the advancing Division is used by Cox to locate the British Army in the 'alien' territory of 'No Man's Land':

It may have been only that here and there a girl to whom they waved would turn aside instead of waving back, it may have been that the men shook their heads at our dog-Italian, but it was unmistakable. We felt like strangers in a strange land, as if at the Isonzo [river] we had passed some unmarked but distinct frontier. As indeed we had. We had driven from Italy into what was to become a No Man's Land between Eastern and Western Europe, and like any No Man's Land it was extremely unpleasant.[16]

For Cox, No Man's Land takes on a gender-specific significance as a threatening place where the Allied soldiers' presence is ignored by women, who decline to respond to the soldiers' attention, and where British authority is suspect. The political role of the women of 'No Man's Land', compared with that of the 'girls of Mestre', reveals them as altogether different, and the spaces they occupy suspiciously self-sufficient, sexually as well as linguistically. The women adorned in haphazard military garb are de-feminised and made the objects of sexual ridicule:

They were mostly squat peasant girls, distinguishable as we drove past the columns from the rear only by their wide hips in their battledress trousers and their hair falling on their shoulders [...] None wore makeup of any kind.[17]

This depiction of partisan women, seen in conjunction with Cox's earlier appreciation of the Italian women who welcomed his troops, is central to his attempt to imagine a cultural border that separates Italy from Yugoslavia, West from East, and democracy from communism.[18] No Man's Land marks that border as a place where the privileges of masculinity are subverted by the certainties of ethnic difference. The gender-delineated boundary in Cox's narrative underscores that 'racially'-defined cultural antagonism that was part of the Cold War. It also seeks to contain communism as a characteristic of a Slavic, Eastern, and here, Balkan world, while ideologically (and thus 'ethnically') cleansing Italy, the nation with the strongest communist movement in Europe.

In *The Road to Trieste* Cox would prefer to leave the reader with the impression that the 'ordinary soldier in the British, American and New Zealand forces' was antagonistic to the 'Yugoslavs' because of the struggle between Yugoslavia and Italy for the possession of the city, '[h]e did not mind [Cox tells us] Frenchmen bumping off Frenchmen or Italians hanging other Italians. That was their own business, and was no doubt the way they preferred to settle their political disputes'. But in Trieste, as far as the troops could see, it was 'a question of one nation running another, and this seemed in the face of it, wrong'. Nation and ethnos are conflated, yet when Cox lectures the British troops on the 'tangled racial background of the Balkans and on the way this border area had been constantly grabbed and torn from both sides', the troops instinctively retort, 'Maybe these are only Eyeties ... But that's no reason why the Jugoslavs should push them around. After all the city is more Eyetie than Jugoslav. No one can deny that.'[19]

Cox's story of the journey into No Man's Land was part of the process of defining and locating the Cold War. In 1947 United States and British foreign policies were identifying the military threat of the spread of communist influence in Europe as imminent, and the perceived boundaries between East and West were uncertain and contradictory. Cox's conception of an inevitable and proper border was often shaken by the observed political and cultural complexity of a territory and its individuals who could not be claimed or named absolutely. Cox's recognition that Maoris in the New Zealand Division had in fact developed a camaraderie with the communist 'Slav' forces seems to undermine his assertion of a 'natural' cultural antagonism. Cox explains the affinity as the result of intermarriage among Maoris and 'Slavs' who had emigrated to New Zealand. Ultimately, the 'otherness' of the Maoris means that Cox can dismiss their contact with the 'Slavs' as irrelevant.

The theme of the antagonistic relationships between the Allied soldiers and the Partisan Liberation Front has been used by historians and political commentators since the end of the Second World War to justify the Allied usurpation of 'Yugoslav'-identified partisan rule in the Trieste region. Historians have interpreted the relationships between groups involved in the war and in the period of 'liberation' within available and historically reinforced assumptions of cultural and political identification. During the decade of AMG rule, the city's political fate was never certain, and plans for the creation of a 'Free Territory' were mooted by the British Foreign Office with some local support. However, Trieste's ultimate merger with the western side of the Iron Curtain as part of Italy legitimated a conservative version of its 'Italian' history and genealogy, and relied upon the incorporation of its Slavs into a Balkan other, populating territory to the East.

Historical accounts of Trieste written against the background of the uncertainties of the post-war period both encouraged, and contested, a nostalgia for what the political theorist William E. Connolly has described as a 'coherent politics of place' and of identity.[20] In a recent article in *Slavic Review* Maria Todorova argues that a negative orientalist image of the Balkans only began to predominate in a range of public narratives in the late 19th century, but that since then it has remained 'fixed'.[21] I have attempted briefly to extend Todorova's analysis both geographically and thematically, by looking at the construction of the 'Balkans' during the Cold War as integral to the formation of Western, European, Italian, anti-communist, non-Balkan and non-Slav identities for the city of Trieste in the period after the Second World War, and to show that even at its most 'frozen' such an image is vulnerable to the anxieties which I associate above with both the concept of 'self-determination' and of the problem of political 'representation'.

At the end of the Second World War, the 'Balkan-Slav' motif also became the most readily available focus of mobilisation even for liberal and democratically-minded pro-Italian Triestines and for those strangers who arrived in Trieste as the representatives of an Anglophone democratic West. It might also be argued that the Cold War reasserted for British and American foreign policy-makers the association of nationalism with anti-communism, with the politics of democracy. In the following section I examine how the political atmosphere which has marked the end of the Cold War has confirmed prejudices about cultural and political hierarchies and their correspondence with ethno-national boundaries, rather than questioned them.

Putting the East/Balkans back into Europe

Nowhere has history been more obviously co-opted to illustrate and authorise political commentaries than in the recent case of the disintegration of Yugoslavia. As the conflict unravelled, commentators scripted their analyses, explanations and predictions on the basis of competing accounts and chronologies of the region's past, as if Yugoslavia had only one history, and that history had revolved around the problem of ethnicity. I began this chapter by expressing my interest in the ways in which ethnicity and essential cultural difference became legitimated both as principles of democratic aspiration and as the basis for the resolution of representation involved in the drawing of territorial boundaries. I want to end the chapter where I am: embroiled in the attempt to understand the conflict in ex-Yugoslavia, and in writing its histories.

In any society, disorder is often the product of a healthy pluralism, whereby a variety of interest groups are represented, and whose positions may conflict; but it is their negotiation which is the stuff of civil society. In 1980s Yugoslavia, difference and dissent was increasingly polarised around issues of political formation and political control, garnered in the corners of Ljubljana (representing liberal reform) and Belgrade (the Federal Army and the Serbian League of Communists under Slobodan Milosevic touting hardline centralisation and eventually the cause of Serbian nationalism). By the time the reformist Slovenians and Croatians declared independence, political differences had been defined in terms of national interest. The Serbian government, with controlling interests in the Federation and Army thanks to constitutional changes and coups, acted in defence of 'socialist' Yugoslavia and attempted to keep Slovenia in the fold through military intervention. Violence was resorted to rather than negotiation—and not for the first time, since the history of the relationship between Belgrade and Kosovo had already provided an informative precedent. As the attack turned on Croatia, at a moment when Milosevic and the communist party's rule was most under threat in Belgrade itself, it was the issue of protecting national minorities and the nationalist interest of Serbia within Croatia which became the defining characteristic of Belgrade's intervention. The name of the republic's army changed, just as that of the communist party had, and irregular forces recruited in Serbia took part in the struggle in the name of Serbian survival.[22]

In 1991 the philologist Svetlana Slapsak, once of the Institute of Art and Literature at Belgrade University, now a teacher at the University of Ljubljana, argued that,

> ...the war in Yugoslavia is a war of words, a war of propaganda, a war of stereotypes, in which, unfortunately, real people get killed. Only words—words called up and sent out into the public domain by intellectuals—could have destroyed the kind of multinational and multicultural society that was Yugoslavia: the process of destruction of multinational institutions could not have begun before the destruction of the balance in public discourse had been completed with the invention of collective enemies for collective national entities.[23]

Slapsak claimed the war's most bestial moments could be causally related back to documents passed on from intellectuals to their sabre-rattling henchmen, the Word, as it were, egging on the Sword to carve up multinational Yugoslavia into mutually intolerant states:

> Imaginary Chetniks and Ustasha were again and again invented until they finally 'materialised' in paramilitary units. The aim of the surrealistic movement, so important in Serbian literature, has been realised: literature has come to life.[24]

Dragan Popadic, Assistant Professor of Psychology at Belgrade University, argued in the course of the war that, as a result of a media onslaught, the Serbian population was unable and unwilling to distinguish between cultural mythology and political reality, particularly as the increasing possibility of having to accept their state's complicity as a protagonist, rather than victim, of the war provided them with a reason to distance themselves further from that reality:

> Incredible as it may seem, many people in Serbia believe that a whole series of conspiracies—uncovered by allegedly world-famous scientists and analysed in detail in books and television programmes—has been revealed in the last three or four years. Some of the most frequently mentioned conspiracies concern the

Comintern and the Vatican, Free Masons, muslims, nations which belonged to
the Austro-Hungarian empire, countries defeated in World War Two, the US as
a promoter of the 'New World Order'. Conspiracies against Serbs as 'the oldest'
or the 'holiest' nation look like explanations, but they actually serve to cover up
real events and augment the feeling of unreality.[25]

Emphasising the influence of a similar onslaught of propaganda in Croatia,
the Zagreb-based writer Slavenka Drakulic found even herself susceptible,
despite her best intentions :

Along with millions of other Croats I was pinned to the wall of nationhood—not
only by outside pressure from Serbia and the Federal Army but by national
homogenization within Croatia itself. That is what the war is doing to us, reducing
us to one dimension: the Nation.[26]

Drakulic boldly resisted the reduction of people and causes of action to
national and ethnic categories. In *Balkan Express* she recalled instead typical
'Yugoslav' lives built on bonds among individuals from all republics, bonds
generated in the intimacies of 'intermarriage' or even routine commuting
between Belgrade, Zagreb and Sarajevo. By declaring war on many of its
own inhabitants the Croatian state, nationalistic rhetoric, and the paranoia it
propagated, undermined relationships which once passed for normal. For these
beliefs Drakulic was branded by government and press 'Yugonostalgic', and
censored.

In an article published in 1993 in *Radical Philosophy*, Cornelia Sorabji,
a consultant to the European Commission mission investigating the abuse of
women in the Yugoslav war, argued that Europe was not an observer of self-
contained ethnic conflict but was complicit in the ethnic dynamic of the Bosnian
region.[27] By lending legitimacy to inflexible and historically spurious
conceptions of ethnicity, and to nationalist leaders, it contributed also to the
reconceptualisation of national identity within Bosnia-Hercegovina. She argues
that for Muslims especially, the unexpected virulence of the Croatian and
Serbian attacks, and European inaction, forced them to reconsider their ties
with what they had imagined as the supposedly cosmopolitan and tolerant
West.

From the outside, popular, journalistic and even diplomatic renderings of
the wars in Croatia and Bosnia-Herzegovina found a convenient refuge in
essentialist and trans-historical interpretations of ethnic identity in the regions
of ex-Yugoslavia, and of the nature of Yugoslavia itself—as both 'Balkan'
and 'post-communist'. This position was parodied in a 1993 human rights'
publication:

Nothing can be done about ex-Yugoslavia because no-one is in control. Politically, a few key culprits have been named, but the conflicts are fundamentally driven by ancient ethnic animosities, frozen by communism and now terribly unleashed. Militarily, the war is chaotic, and institutionally incomprehensible. These hysterical Balkans simply want to kill each other, and the world can only stand back and watch.[28]

For *Helsinki Watch* commentators, the consequences of claiming legitimacy for these interpretations were real. They allowed Europe's retreat to a non-Balkan (and thus inherently civilised) Western border, and dissipated the possibility of the international community taking an unambiguously 'moral' position against named aggressors and agents of violence. Europe's fatalistic interpretation of Bosnia's collapse paved a path, according to Sorabji, 'for Muslims to reconstrue the nature of 'Europe' in less positive terms and the meaning of their own Europeanness in more radical terms'.[29]

The recent explanation of the conflict in ex-Yugoslavia offered by a key architect of the Cold War is evidence of the possible ways in which the boundaries between Europe and the Balkans have been reinforced by commentators on the war, even those sympathetic to the plight of the Bosnians in the early stages of the conflict. George F. Kennan's new introduction to the re-publication of the 1913 Carnegie Endowment Inquiry into the early twentieth century Balkan Wars provides parallels with the war at the end of that same century— a comparison which surely the publishers had hoped their new edition would invite. Kennan, a former American statesman now at Princeton University, reliably (and unsurprisingly) retreats to the idea of the inevitability of the war in Yugoslavia propelled by the Balkan nature of Yugoslavia's inhabitants:

> ...the strongest motivating factor involved in the Balkan wars was not religion but aggressive nationalism. But that nationalism, as it manifested itself on the field of battle, drew on deeper traits of character inherited, presumably, from a distant tribal past: a tendency to view the outsider, generally, with dark suspicion, and to see the political-military opponent, in particular, as a fearful and implacable enemy to be rendered harmless only by total and unpitying destruction. And so it remains today.[30]

Kennan's depiction of the Balkans as infinitely fragmented by the essentialist almost primitive ('tribal') drive of its peoples to regard 'outsiders' with suspicion allows him to arrive at the ineluctable interpretation of inherent trans-historical antagonisms:

> ...this writer knows of no evidence that the ability of the Balkan peoples to interact peaceably with one another is any greater now than it was those eighty years ago.

Kennan provides us with just one example of the way in which the inevitability of war in areas of ex-Yugoslavia has been invoked through the iteration of 'common-sensical' theories of ethnic identity (here as 'tribal') and of nationalism specific to an area Europeans know culturally as the 'Balkans'. He may no longer be an influential diplomat, but his reflections offer some insight into the ways in which historical assumptions about ethnicity and nationalism become a way of seeing the world and delineating one's self. We can also historicise Kennan's explanation of transcendent cultural identities and hatreds. Geoffrey Cox justified what he depicted as his fellow soldiers' dislike and distrust of the 'Yugoslavs' by relying on the depiction of the 'Yugoslav communists' in Trieste as foreign, 'a strange race, speaking a strange tongue', 'men whose very facial expressions were often completely baffling, so that you could not tell when you spoke with them whether they were puzzled or thoughtful or angry or sad'. Cox also assumed that suspicion and mistrust were characteristics of that other 'tribe', the British; in explaining their dislike of Slavs he explained (and accepted) that 'foreigners' 'could arouse to the full that instinctive antagonism to the stranger which is never far below the surface of the British, whatever the Americans may feel'.[31]

The parallels in Cox and Kennan's narratives, their acceptance of the historical determining of ethnic hatreds suggest that it is not possible to extricate Europe from events in Bosnia and the 'Balkan' War, either as a political or cultural influence, or as an historical entity. The assertion that ethnic animosities fuelled the conflict in Bosnia was, during the course of the war, proffered for the consumption as much of western audiences as Bosnian ones. It was the equation of 'the right to self-determination' with the ethnically homogenous nation state and the naturalness of ethnic identities, as well as hatreds, that most directly located the war within Europe, within still extant and even mainstream European ways of seeing and imagining communities.

The Europe which has in the past propounded the principle of national self-determination sits side by side with the Europe of Maastricht. It has even been argued that Maastricht is merely the means for prolonging the political life of the European form of nation state. In an article which compares the constitutions of the ex-republics of Yugoslavia, Robert Hayden has pointed out the ways in which they emulate the European idea of the nation state, annexing the presumption of national sovereignty to territorial sovereignty. It is this vision of the nation state, increasingly on the defensive in Western Europe, which, according to Hayden, underlines an inherent contradiction. If 'ethnic-cleansing' is not to be seen as a logical conclusion of this compound concept then either the sanctity of borders, or the principle of national self-determination has to go. For Hayden the war has revealed a 'truly bitter irony...about Europe':

Far from 'turning the dream of a united Europe into a nightmare' (as the *International Herald Tribune* put the matter), the constitutional nationalism of the various formerly Yugoslav republics may simply show how much the ideals of the European Community ignore the nightmarish contradictions inherent in modern European social and political thought.[32]

Perhaps such contradictions are unavoidable. However the unproblematised delineation of ethno-national boundaries in historical narratives has only pandered to the abuse of those contradictions, rather than to their exposition. In telling the story of future conflicts, in seeking explanations in the past as well as the present, we should be aware of the preferences for understanding culture in terms of ethnicity, and democratic ambitions in terms of ethno-national sovereignty that might inform our interpretations of political problems and conflict. The inscription into history-writing of national forms of identification encourages the simultaneous writing out of the relational nature of identities, and the specific political contexts in which the 'national' is invoked. History may provide the conditions for the formation of identities, personal and group, but it also provides the evidence for the fragmenting nature of those identities. In the words of the anthropologist Brackette Williams:

> If history, even history made behind men's backs, be the siren that calls them to particular identities (personal and group) under conditions of territorial nationalism, it does so always while, at the same time, pleading the contradictory cases for dissolution and maintenance of the specificity of these identities.[33]

Notes

1. The British diplomat Harold Nicolson argued that: 'The Congress of Vienna [of 1814] allowed their councils to be dominated by the twin theories of legitimacy and the balance of power. The Conference of Paris [in 1919] was unduly obsessed by the conception of nationality contained in the formula of 'Self-Determination'. H. Nicolson, *Peacemaking 1919* (rev. edition, Methuen, 1964), xviii.
2. For an excellent discussion of *fin-de-siecle* nationalism see G. Mosse, *Nationalism and Sexuality: Respectability and Abnormal Sexuality in Modern Europe* (Howard Fertig, 1985).
3. Nicolson, *op. cit.*, 152.
4. R. Bosworth, 'Mito e linguaggio nella politica estera italiana', *Politica Estera Italiana 1860-1988* (Il Mulino, 1991), 53.
5. R. Timaeus, cited in M. Pacor, *Italiani in Balcania dal Risorgimento alla Resistenza* (Feltrinelli, 1968), 34.
6. See M. Todorova, 'The Balkans: From Discovery to Invention', *Slavic Review* 53 (2), 1994, 452–82, for a useful analysis of the Balkans in historical and political narratives.

7. R. West, *Black Lamb and Grey Falcon: A journey through Yugoslavia* (First ed., Penguin, 1982, 1940), 21. For West, however, the Slavs were a 'breed' whose men were truly masculine in contrast to the effete English male.
8. 'Secret Report No.11, 26 September 1945', Trieste Allied Information Service, War Office: 204/6400, Public Record Office, London.
9. See, for example, 'Trieste Secret Report of conditions in Trieste and the surrounding district No.6', 22 August 1945, Allied Information Service, War Office: 204/6387.
10. 'Testimonianza di Carlo Schiffrer sulle trattative fra il CLN e l'OF a Trieste dell'Aprile 1945'; *Stralcio da appunti personali*, (s.d.), Archivio del Indice Venezia Giulia: IV/311, 11, Istituto regionale per la storia del movimento di liberazione nel Friuli Venezia Giulia.
11. *Ibid.*, 4.
12. See my articles: 'Cold War Casualties: Gender, ethnicity and the writing of history' in 'Special Issue: From Margins to Centre - Gender, Ethnicity and Nationalism', *Women's Studies International Forum*, 19, 1996; 'No Man's Land: the gendered boundaries of Trieste', *Gender and History* 6 (2), 1994, 184–201.
13. Cox was a Major with GSO 2 from October 1944 to May 1945. Before then he had been Chargé d'Affaires for the New Zealand Legation to Washington (1942-4): *Documents relating to New Zealand's Participation in the Second World War 1939-1945 Vol. II* (Dept. of Internal Affairs, 1951), 410.
14. G. Cox, *The Road to Trieste* (London: 1947), 191. Extracts from *The Road to Trieste* can be found in a number of histories about the period, including Bogdan Novak's *Trieste 1941–45: The ethnic, political and ideological struggle* (University of Chicago Press, 1970); A. C. Bowman, *Zones of Strain* (Hoover Press, 1982); and R. Rabel, *Between East and West: Trieste, the United States, and the Cold War, 1941-1954* (Duke University Press, 1988).
15. Cox, *op. cit.*, 177.
16. *Ibid.*, 192.
17. *Ibid.*, 203.
18. *Ibid.*, 23 and 191.
19. *Ibid.*, 231–2.
20. W. E. Connolly, 'Democracy and Territoriality', *Millennium: Journal of International Studies*, 20 (3), 1991, 463.
21. Todorova, *loc. cit.*, 468.
22. See J. Gow, 'Military-Political Affiliations in the Yugoslav conflict', *Radio Free Europe Research Report*, 20 (1), 1992; 'One Year of War in Bosnia and Herzegovina', *Radio Free Europe Research Report*, 23 (2), 1993.
23. S. Slapsak, 'Serbian Alternatives: are there any?', *East European Reporter*, Sept./Oct., 1992, 53.
24. *Ibid.*, 54.
25. D. Popadic, 'Unreal City', *East European Reporter,* Jul/Aug, 1992, 61.
26. S. Drakulic, *Balkan Express* (Hutchinson, 1993), 51.
27. C. Sorabji, 'Ethnic War in Bosnia?', *Radical Philosophy*, 63, 1993, 35.
28. Editorial comment, *Balkan War Report*, 17 January 1993, 3.
29. C. Sorabji, *loc. cit.*, 35.
30. G. F. Kennan, 'The Balkan Crisis: 1913 and 1993', *New York Review of Books*, 15 July 1993, 6 (this is a reproduction of the Carnegie introduction). See also Todorova's more detailed reading of Kennan's introduction.
31. G. Cox, *op. cit.*, 233.
32. R. M. Hayden, 'Constitutional nationalism in the Formerly Yugoslav Republics', *Slavic Review,* Winter, 1992, 673.
33. B. Williams, *Stains on my name, war in my veins: Guyana and the Politics of Cultural Struggle* (Duke University Press, 1991), 14.

7 Europe and the 'Islamic Threat': Putting the Spectre into Perspective

JEREMY SALT

Samuel Huntington has argued, in a frequently cited article written for *Foreign Affairs*,[1] that the next stage of world history will be characterised by the clash between civilisations. 'Islamic' and 'western' civilisation are two of the eight civilisations he describes. Huntington's article attracted such attention because it appeared at a time when matters relating to culture, ethnicity and identity were moving to the top of the agenda in the United States and Europe. Of all of these questions, none seemed to be more pertinent than those relating to Islam, whether in the context of European immigration or state-to-state relations, and the implications for the outside world of political change within Muslim societies. The Huntington view, that Islamic and Western civilisations are in a state of actual or incipient conflict, only fed fears that were already gathering force. The revival of religious faith taking place across the Islamic world has created a mood of apprehension not dissimilar to European fears of Pan Islam in the late 19th century or to western fears of communism in the 1950s. These concerns are summed up in remarks made by the former Secretary-General of NATO, Willy Claes, in an interview with the *Süddeutsche Zeitung*: 'Fundamentalism is at least as dangerous as communism was. Please do not underestimate this risk. It is our duty to organise, especially with those countries facing this kind of difficulty, a dialogue.'[2]

Such views raise more questions than they answer. First, Islam cannot be reduced to a uniform religious, cultural and historical framework of ideas. It does not lend itself to simple definitions. Its history is remarkably diverse, centring on a core of beliefs common to all Muslims but otherwise subject to infinite interpretation. Islamic societies are characterised as much—if not more so—by their differences as their similarities. There is no single Islam, speaking for all Muslims in the same voice at all times, but an innumerable variety of shifting interpretations, and when Islam is presented as a threat to the West, the first task is to find out whose Islam. Mr Claes, in his statement, has provided the answer to that. It is the Islam of the fundamentalists. But not even among scholars outside Muslim societies is there agreement on what

121

constitutes fundamentalism. The most regressive and repressive Islamic state in the world, Saudi Arabia, is never spoken of in the same breath as the fundamentalists of Iran, Sudan and Algeria, or the anti-state Islamic movements in other countries. What, in fact, Mr Claes and others who employ the rhetoric of the Islamic mean by fundamentalist is those movements or states that threaten the interests of the West. Governments can be as repressive as they like, but as long as they do not interfere with the grand plans and strategies of the West, which in the late twentieth century means the United States, they will never be described as fundamentalist. Thus, in the sense in which Mr Claes uses the word, fundamentalism is a convenient label used to invalidate and discredit movements and governments which 'the West' does not like. In the devil's dictionary used by western strategists and NATO commanders there is a close parallel not just between Islamic fundamentalism and communism but between fundamentalism and the rhetoric deployed against 'radical' Arab nationalism forty years ago. Not by coincidence, many of the objectives of the 'Islamic fundamentalists' and the 'radical nationalists' are the same, and it is the determination of the Iranian government, to take one example, to adhere to an independent domestic and regional policy that lies behind its continuing vilification in the United States. The constant use of 'the West' as some kind of polar opposite to 'Islam' should also remind us of the dramatic changes which have taken place between Europe and the United States. 'The West' no longer exists in the way it was understood forty years ago, with the differences between Europe and the United States only growing since the collapse of the USSR and the impact of globalisation on national economies. Geographically, historically and diplomatically, the Europeans approach their dealings with the Muslims closest to them—Arabs and Turks—from an entirely different perspective, and in their dealings with the governments of the Middle East they are following their own interests. They have ignored the attempt of the United States to block all commercial dealings with Iran and have shown elsewhere that they have no intention of simply following the American lead. Freed from the psychology of the Cold War, they are likely to play an even more independent role in the future.

The ability to get away with generalised statements about 'fundamentalism' is greatly enhanced by public ignorance and the willingness to believe the worst of Arabs or Muslims. Although there are honourable exceptions of both newspapers (*Le Monde* for example) and individual correspondents (David Hirst of *The Guardian* and Robert Fisk of *The Independent*), there is a long pattern of misrepresentation, misreporting and sensationalism in the print media on both sides of the Atlantic. The explanation for this lies in the relationships between governments and media proprietors and the way their biases percolate downwards through the editorial rooms, so that reporters and leader writers know instinctively how far they can go without needing to be told. The result is that readers are often given the worst and most sensational aspects of 'Islamic revivalism' and nothing else—terrorist attacks in Egypt and the *fatwa* against Salman Rushdie, but almost nothing of the debates taking place in all Muslim societies about contemporary problems, and nothing of the fact that the 'Islamic terrorism' which horrifies western readers is equally horrifying to the vast majority of Muslims.

The prime concern of Muslim activists everywhere is reforming the societies in which they live. By and large they fall within the mainstream and work within the law. There are conservatives and progressives among them, and moderates and extremists. They are concerned with questions of democracy and all the day-to-day issues that would preoccupy social or political movements in any country. In Algeria, Egypt and Turkey, they have demonstrated their willingness to work for change through the ballot box, and if there is any threat to democracy in these countries it has not come from the 'fundamentalists': in Algeria and Turkey it is the military that has frustrated the outcome of elections fought fairly and squarely, while in Egypt it is not just the Islamists who believe that the elections are a charade. Neither is there anything unique about such movements appearing in the late twentiethth century. Islamic revivalism is not an aberration but part of a cyclical phenomenon: there has always been an individual or a movement to challenge the assumptions of the state or to defend the *umma* (the community of all Muslims) when it is threatened by outside forces. It should therefore surprise no-one that the conditions of the late twentieth century—the lack of basic freedoms and rights in almost every country of the Middle East, and severe economic imbalances, but even worse the wasted potential of resources—should have called forth movements demanding change.

Thus, the first concern of Muslim movements is conditions within their own societies. They do not like the disruptive effect of 'the West' on their politics, cultures and economies; but it would be a mistake to draw the conclusion that this arises from a general Islamic hostility to 'the West' or non-Muslims. Jews and Christians have their place in the *Qu'ran as ahl al kitab* (people of the book) and their place in Muslim societies as the *dhimmi* (protected groups). Their prophets and their books are venerated by Muslims. In their dealings with the outside world the attitude of Muslims has been seriously misrepresented. Although Islam is a missionary religion, aggressive warfare is condemned and forced conversion forbidden. Clear rules are laid down for the conduct of war and the restitution of peace, and the declaration of *jihad* is essentially no different from the declaration of war that any state might make, except that it is declared in the name of Islam and thus in the interests of Muslims everywhere rather than in the name of a particular state. *Jihad* itself does not mean 'holy war' but merely struggle, and basically the struggle of each individual to lead a better Muslim life: yet only its most sensational meaning is known in the West.

The whole history of Islam is a struggle for meaning. The basis of law is interpretation and of community life consensus. Not since the time of the prophet or since the last of the Shi`i imams has a single individual been able to stand as the symbol of unchallengeable authority. The real significance of Ayatullah Khumayni was overlooked. The *fatwa* issued against Salman Rushdie was merely an opinion which could have been delivered on any matter involving Muslims. It was perfectly within the right of other scholars to present a different view and indeed—outside Iran—many did. Khumayni's *fatwa* against Rushdie had such force because he was Khumayni, not merely a religious authority but a political figure of charismatic mass appeal who was seen to have delivered Iran from its oppressors. In Iran there were religious figures of greater scholarly standing than Khumayni, and if they did not challenge his view it was not necessarily because they agreed with his interpretation but because it was scarcely wise or expedient to do so. In the case of the elderly Ayatullah Shariat-Madari, who was stripped of his rank in the most humiliating way, Khumayni demonstrated how harshly he could deal with perceived rivals and enemies.

Since Khumayni's death, the Jacobin harshness of the Islamic republic has noticeably softened, with the overwhelming victory of the moderate Ayatullah Khatami to succeed Hashemi Rafsanjani as president the clearest possible indication that the Iranians want this trend to continue. In Iran as elsewhere, the struggle between the progressives and the conservatives in the legislative and executive branches of government is mirrored in the debates taking place over what is entailed in the properly fulfilled Muslim life. To some this cannot be achieved without the establishment of sharia's law; but many who are proud to call themselves Muslim—even in the most secular of Muslim societies—regard religion in the contemporary age as a matter for private belief. The battle lines move back and forth, but we need to be reminded that this debate has been taking place ever since the death of the Prophet Muhammad.

The rise of the Islamic movements in the Middle East and North Africa is clearly linked to the economic and political shortcomings of the secularised governments which have held power throughout the region since 1945. Now there is globalisation to contend with. At times of crisis, it is natural for people to cluster defensively around what they know best, and thus the Islamic resurgence can be described as a nativist reaction to a sequence of disillusioning political, ideological and economic failures stretching over a long period of time. Muslim activists are not alone in their disillusionment. But with the apparent exhaustion of secular nationalism, Islam is making the ideological running. In all countries unredressed social grievances have greatly accelerated the growth of Muslim movements. If Egypt has been in a state of incipient crisis for the last twenty years, with the government struggling to contain the threat posed not just by violent Muslim groups but also by those working successfully and perhaps more dangerously within the law, it is for reasons to do with severe economic inequities, corruption and manipulation of the political system. The Muslim movements there are working to change a system (of values as well as government) which has become dysfunctional. In Saudi Arabia, the focal point of discontent is a repressive political structure. The dissidents are not underground Marxists but religious scholars who argue that kingship is anathema to Islam, and who are being jailed or are having to flee the country for urging the Saudis to democratise the system in line with the Islamic principles of consensus (*ijma*) and consultation (*shura*).

In Algeria the people are still living with long-term consequences of colonialism. The French government has continued to support the military regime which short-circuited the democratic process in 1991 so that the Islamic Salvation Front could not come to power. French support for the military has had the result of turning France into a secondary arena of conflict, and has fuelled fears that 'collapse' in Algeria 'will result in the onslaught on southern Europe's shores of a new generation of boat people fleeing a vengeful fundamentalist regime'[3], creating a problem not just for France but also for Europe. Developments in Algeria, along with the extension of the conflict to France through aircraft hijacking and assassinations, have—at a time of general European concern over immigration and the assimilation of migrant communities—created additional problems for North Africans already living in France.

The Algerian situation is especially complicated because no Middle Eastern or North African territory was invaded more comprehensively by a European power. Invasion was followed by colonisation and French penetration of the Algerian consciousness. The paradox of 'the land of a million martyrs' is that much of the revolutionary generation which finally came to power in 1962 was thoroughly imbued with French culture, 'speaking almost exclusively in French and demanding not the world of the *Qu'ran*, the *Sunna*, or of the local holy man but the world envisioned by European thinkers—Voltaire, Rousseau, Auguste Comte. At first assimilationists, and later liberal nationalists, these men were overwhelmingly secular in outlook and they adopted to varying degrees the life-styles of Europe and hoped to rebuild Algeria in accordance with liberal models flowing from the Enlightenment and from the experiences of nineteenth-century Europe'.[4]

Even the working class leftist movement derived its inspiration from France, and only the Association of Algerian Muslim Ulama framed an anti-colonialist message that was unequivocally nativist: 'Islam is my religion, Arabic is my language and Algeria is my fatherland'. Yet it was the French-speaking elites

who succeeded to power and have held it ever since. Language has become
the supreme cultural signifier of power. As Larbi Sadiki has written 'French
is central to the whole struggle for power in Algeria'.[5] This conflict between
the Francophones and Arabisants has its roots in the colonial period. Here,
according to Sadiki, we have 'the spiritual foundation that inspires modern-
day Algeria's Islamists and feeds their visceral hatred of France and the upper
class of Francophone traditional power holders who symbolise foreign
hegemony'.[6] Another observer writes:

> ...in the eyes of the Islamic underground now fighting to destroy the Government
> in Algiers the struggle for religious and cultural emancipation has never been
> concluded. With the departure of French soldiers, Algeria found independence
> of a radical Third World stamp. Yet the vestiges of French identity lingered—
> in language, literature, newspapers, consumer products, the way the Government
> worked and the way intellectuals reasoned. To Islamists these represented proof
> that the original liberation struggle was incomplete. A pamphlet from one of the
> multiplicity of Islamic underground groups in 1994 described the Algiers French
> press—not the dailies from Paris, let it be noted, but newspapers written and
> edited in French by Algerians for Algerians—as 'abominations before the eyes
> of God.'[7]

Accordingly the struggle of the Islamists was not just against a stale and
inefficent government but against the domination of the Francophones. The
reassertion of an Algerian Arab-Islamic identity carried the Islamic Salvation
Front to the point of electoral victory, the short-circuiting of which has plunged
Algeria into one of the darkest periods of its history. The suppression of what
was regarded as a moderate Islamic movement, coming to power democratically,
has had terrible consequences—initially the murder of foreigners and Algerians
who stood as symbols of westernisation, and now the wholesale slaughter of
the Algerian people themselves, without anyone knowing who is really
responsible.

The Algerian example has been held up as a warning of what can happen
when the democratic path to government is closed off to the Islamists. The
socio-economic grievances stimulating the rise of the Islamic revivalism in
Algeria can also be seen very clearly in Turkey, another country very much
on the European mind. The deregulation of the economy by the civilian
government elected in 1983, the first since the military intervened in 1980,
has had serious social consequences. Inflation, the plunging value of the lira,
and subsistence level salaries for the bulk of the Turkish workforce have
combined to drive down living standards for most of the country's sixty million
people. Demographics are also responsible. The millions of 'in migrants'
from the east have helped to more than double the population of Turkey's

biggest cities (particularly Ankara and Istanbul) in less than a decade. These newly urbanised Turks are not only at the bottom of the socio-economic pile but bring with them the traditional culture of the Anatolian village or town, in which religion is a central value. The nexus between economic inequities, demographics and traditional values helps us to understand the striking success of the Refah (Prosperity) Party in recent years, particularly since its capture of the greater municipalities of Istanbul and Ankara in the local elections of 1994. Following the collapse of the Motherland Party–True Path Party coalition government formed in the wake of the December 1995 national elections, Refah became the senior party in a new coalition government and its leader, Necmattin Erbakan, the first Islamist Prime Minister in Turkey's history. In the only secular state in the Middle Eastern region, the electoral success of a religious party was a striking achievement. But from the beginning of 1997, the military set in motion a campaign aimed at driving Refah out of office on the grounds that 'Islamic fundamentalism' was threatening the country's secular character. By the middle of the year, Erbakan had been forced to resign. Most controversially, the party was subsequently threatened with closure by the Constitutional Court. It would not be the first time in Turkey's modern history that a political party has been closed on the orders of the Constitutional Court but it would be the first time a major political party has been shut down.

These developments are watched closely in Europe; but apprehensions about the rise of 'fundamentalism' on the southeastern edge of Europe have to be balanced against more sober realities. Unlike Muslim movements in other countries, Refah has never called for an Islamic system of government in Turkey. It would probably be more accurate to call it a Muslim rather than an Islamic party. Its success can most likely be explained with reference to the unalleviated economic hardships the overwhelming majority of Turks have been suffering for the past 15 years. Refah appeared as an alternative to secular parties of the centre-left and centre-right which were fast losing their credibility because of their failure to match impressive infrastructural growth with greater social justice. Yet it must be remembered that Refah came into government with only 21% of the vote, and, given the attachment of most Turks to secularism, an Algerian or an Iranian scenario was never likely to unfold in Turkey. The leadership of the Refah is more bourgeois than radical, and during its short time in office the party built on foundations that had already been laid with the consent of the military. It has escaped no-one's notice that in the early 1980s military figures themselves encouraged a reassertion of Muslim moral values. Refah's success at the local level has been acknowledged even by its critics, and close analysis of the political situation suggests that secularism only symbolises the struggle for power taking place between the old political class—combining the military, political parties of the centre-left and centre-right, important sectors of the bureaucracy, media proprietors and the secular intelligensia—and a different if not exactly new social movement adhering to different values, political, economic and cultural in nature, loosely connected by religion and representing the views of a significant percentage of the Turkish population.

What effect was a Refah government likely to have on Turkey's relationships with Europe? The drive towards affiliation with 'western civilisation' began in the nineteenth century and remains perhaps the most important basic marker in Turkey's development. Since 1945, the system of government and foreign relations have been oriented towards the aim of being accepted as a full partner by 'the West'. Integration into Europe has been a priority issue since the 1960s. Turkey was a founding member of the United Nations, is a member of NATO and the Council of Europe, and has been pursuing membership of the European Union (EU) since the Ankara Agreement of Association was signed in 1963. Turkey applied for full membership in 1987, and in 1991 it joined the European Free Trade Association (EFTA). Since then, Turkish governments have initialled a variety of protocols and agreements binding Turkey more closely to the EU. The customs union is the latest of such agreements; yet the goal of actual membership seems more elusive than ever, with other countries moving to the head of the queue since the break-up of the USSR.

There is a certain despair about this, a feeling that Europe is a Christian club which does not want Muslim members (a feeling fortified by the European abandonment of the Bosnians to their fate) and which tends to treat European complaints about the human rights situation in Turkey as a convenient pretext for keeping the door closed. This feeling of rejection has stimulated the Islamic trend. But for all of its inflammatory campaign rhetoric against the EU, the United States and Zionism, once in office the Refah-led government took pains to soothe American and European fears. Certainly Erbakan stressed that he intended to develop relations with the Islamic bloc; but he also confirmed that he would maintain and develop existing relations with Europe and the US, stressed the importance of privatisation and a free market economy, and handed the economic planning portfolio to his junior coalition partner, the True Path Party. 'What we want above all in Turkey is stability ... that is the one thing we have not had and may now have', one of his senior officials was quoted as saying.[8] If Erbakan entered into commercial dealings with Iran, outraging the United States government, so did European governments—and if these governments are concerned at developments in Turkey now, it is not so much because of the alleged dangers of 'fundamentalism' as because of human rights problems, the role of the military in Turkish politics, and Turkey's chronic economic problems. The Prime Minister appointed to succeed Necmettin Erbakan, Mesut Yilmaz, leader of the Motherland Party, has admitted that the state of the economy alone is a serious barrier to European integration, and that it is 'not possible' to achieve social harmony in a country where the annual inflation rate for more than a decade has hovered in the range of 100 per cent. The Turkish lira, running at 14,000 to the US dollar towards the end of 1993, had depreciated by November 1997 to more than 185,000 against the dollar. Successive governments have come into office promising to bring inflation down, but none has succeeded, and the official goal of bringing Turkey's inflation rate within the ambit of the average rate in EU countries— about two per cent—is clearly a pipedream for the foreseeable future. Fresh intervention by the military in 1997—a 'soft coup' similar to the 'coup by memorandum' in 1971 when the army forced the resignation of the government and the appointment of a new Prime Minister—has done further damage to Turkey's image in Europe by demonstrating yet again that the court of last resort in Turkish politics is not the ballot box but the Turkish General Staff. This pushes Turkey further away from EU membership. Ian O. Lesser, a senior analyst with the Rand Corporation, observes in a recent paper that

> Europe is likely to hold Turkey at arm's length through 2010 and beyond. Closer economic relations, including the full implementation of the customs union, are possible but full membership in the EU and the West European Union (WEU) will almost certainly be unattainable. Europe will continue to view Turkey as a useful barrier to instability in the south and east rather than a cultural, political and economic bridge. Cultural unease, economic and migration concerns, human rights complaints and worries about the security 'baggage' Turkish EU membership would imply all suggest that Turkey will remain in institutional limbo on Europe's periphery.

But Turkey is only one of many countries around the southern and eastern rim of the Mediterranean that present a similar range of problems. According to Lesser 'there can be little doubt that the areas on the southern periphery, from the Maghreb to Turkey's Middle Eastern borders, will be the scene of crisis and change over the next decades'. The causes of incipient or actual turmoil include economic instability, ethnicity, regime oppression and national rivalries. Hostility between Greece and Turkey over a range of issues has threatened to precipitate a conflict with serious regional and international ramifications on several occasions, posing a far greater danger to European security than internally-directed Muslim revivalism.[9]

What does the rise of Islamic movements spell for Europe? The point has been made that their priority is internal change and reform. There are absolutely no grounds for assuming intrinsic hostility to 'the West', its people or its governments. There *are* real problems, but in no sense are they the outcome of a 'clash' of civilisations. They are largely the outcome of differences over territory and resources. Islamic movements and governments are little different from the nationalist movements of four decades ago in their determination to resist external control. But whatever the flavour of governments that come to power in Muslim societies, they will need to buy and sell and deal with the outside world. In this respect, the changes made to economic policy by the Iranian government, directed towards attracting foreign investment in Iran, are very striking.

Changes in these societies obviously have spillover effects for Europe. In addition to state-to-state relations—or relations between the European Union and these states—the changes now taking place across the Muslim world expose the sizeable Muslim communities in Europe to added scrutiny. Every single incident, whether it be a terrorist bombing or the wearing of a veil to school, highlights their 'otherness' and raises not just questions of cultural difference but of ultimate loyalties. Problems of acculturation and adaptation are always difficult to resolve, and to a degree Muslims bring their problems with them—as immigrants do everywhere—but not only as Muslims. Kurds have attacked each other in Europe, and the Kurdistan Workers' Party (PKK) has carried its campaign against the Turkish government to European cities. Iranian exiles have been murdered in Paris, and France will continue to be a surrogate arena for the conflict being waged in Algeria. But what percentage of the millions of Muslims living in Europe will ever be involved in any of these activities? Their 'otherness' certainly exposes them to a degree of collective blame applied to no other group. As the director of the Institute of Race Relations in London has written, immigration has given rise to a 'Euro-culture of popular racism which stereotypes all Third World/Black immigrants as terrorists and drug-runners and all East European/White immigrants as thieves and shoplifters'.[10] These views are reinforced by pseudo-academic stereotypes which present Muslims as the 'gravediggers of the Christian civilisations they conquered', Bosnia-Herzegovina as 'the spearhead of a future Islamic thrust into Europe' and Europe itself as the object of a process of Islamisation.[11] The ability to make such statements about Bosnia at a time the Bosnian Muslims were being massacred says a great deal about the depth of the anti-Islamic sentiment that still exists in Europe. These appalling ideas, these misrepresentations of history and Islam, give credibility to the idea that there is a 'clash' of civilisations between Europe and Islam. Differences there certainly are, as there are between all civilisations and cultures; but the real problems that arise between the external world and Muslim societies are rooted—as has been noted—not in religion but in the control of territory and resources. As Chandra Muzaffer has written,

...resistance to western domination and control—and not some threat to the West as such—which is taking place in the Muslim world is a reality that is cleverly concealed from the general public.[12]

We see this very clearly in the Middle East where 'western interests' are still focused on the need to keep the Gulf in safe hands and to punish or pacify troublemakers. The Middle East is now 'safer' for 'the West' than at any time since 1945. Radical nationalism has come and gone and so has communism. Iraq is prostrate, and the PLO is negotiating with Israel. Egypt is so heavily in debt that true independence is a luxury it can no longer afford: its present state of indebtedness bears comparison to the Egypt of the khedives more than a century ago. Saudi Arabia continues to buy masses of arms from Britain and the United States which it will never use and whose only purpose can be to bind western states more closely to the survival of the Saudi regime. Serving the interests of the West in one way or another, all of these regimes are under threat from within, on the grounds of their corruption, their incompetence and their unrepresentative nature, and they are opposed not just by the 'fundamentalists' but by thoroughly secularised Muslims. Yet it is their stability that the West means when it talks of 'regional stability', in defence of which Western policymakers attack 'fundamentalism' and its principal standard bearers with such venom. It is in this context that we should understand the targeting of Iran in particular.

Increasingly, as we move into the twenty-first century, it seems that 'fundamentalism' is the ideological hammer that might eventually break the mould in which the present Middle Eastern state system has been cast. This will have ramifications for Europe but—to reiterate—Muslim movements are working first to change their own systems, and only secondarily to establish a more independent way of dealing with the West. But this, it seems, is precisely what 'the West' and principally the United States does not want.

What some Europeans seem to be resisting is the acknowledgement that Islam is now a fact of European life. The tide of immigration can be slowed down and even dried up, but unless Muslim communities are to be deprived of basic political and civil rights, European governments have no option but to integrate them into the fabric of their societies. This means making allowances for cultural difference in all sorts of ways. There will be problems of adaptation on both sides, and no doubt the racists will continue to use every opportunity to inflame public opinion against Muslim (and other) communities. However, there are now millions of Muslims who are native-born Europeans, and as time passes the similarities between them and other Europeans are likely to become greater than are the differences.[13] Nevertheless, for those on the receiving end, European racism and nationalist xenophobia is an embittering and sometimes fatal experience. North African, Middle Eastern and African immigrants are already at the bottom of the socio-economic ladder, and attempts to delegitimise their culture and present them as a people apart can only widen the gaps which the European governments say they are trying to close, and force them to fall back on their native identity. The failure of governments to deliver services is already driving them in this direction: in the urban housing projects where the Muslim migrant communities are concentrated and where 'crime, drugs and physical decay' have taken over, Islam

> has stepped in as a stabilising force ...fundamentalist groups have created socio-religious associations, teaching the Koran, Arabic and martial arts, offering summer camps for kids and providing aid to the poor.[14]

In short, cultural differences should be acknowledged only for what they are, and not as a sign that 'Islam' and 'western civilisation' are mutually antipathetic. There are cultural differences arising from the differences between Islam and other religions; there are differences between Muslim and non-Muslim states, as there are between any states; and for Muslims living in Europe there are the difficulties of acculturation and acceptance. But to subsume these problems in a 'clash of civilisations' in the irreducible sense implied by those who use the phrase would seem to seriously and dangerously misrepresent the issues involved.

Notes

1. S. Huntington, 'The Clash of Civilisations?', *Foreign Affairs*, 72 (3), 1993, 22–49. See also L. Holmes' chapter in this volume.
2. As reported by *The Age*, 4 February 1995, 8.
3. M. Sheridan, 'France haunted by spectre of past war', written for *The Independent* and reprinted in *The Age*, 29 December 1994, 13.
4. J. Ruedy, 'Continuities and Discontinuities in the Algerian Confrontation with Europe', in J. Ruedy, (ed.), *Islamism and Secularism in North Africa*, Centre for Contemporary Arab Studies (Georgetown University, 1994), 75.
5. L. Sadiki, 'The Roots of Algeria's Maelstrom', *Middle East Quarterly*, 2 (6), (1994), 22.
6. *Ibid.*, 23.
7. Sheridan, *loc. cit.*, 13.
8. Quoted in *New Europe*, 7–13 July 1996, 33.
9. 'Scenarios unclear on future picture of Turkey and Eastern Mediterranean countries,' *Turkish Daily News*, 11 November 1997, 8.
10. A. Sivandan, writing in E. Fekete and F. Webber (eds), *Inside Racist Europe* (Institute of Race Relations, 1994), v.
11. Bat Ye'or, 'The Return of Islam to Europe', *Mainstream*, February/March 1994, 16–19.
12. C. Muzaffer, 'The Clash of Cultures or Camouflaging Domination', *Asian Studies Review*, 18 (1), 1994, 9.
13. As J. S. Nielsen observes, there has been a continuous Muslim presence in Europe 'virtually since the beginning of Muslim history'. The activities of the overt racists aside, 'in the last analysis the question must be how far European society itself is prepared to adapt. It is an adaptation that is extremely difficult to contemplate, as European cultures seem to have entrenched themselves to a degree unusual in history. Monocultural and monolingual

nation states, often legitimating one religion and one legal system, grew up in the eighteenth and nineteenth centuries. Their identity, self confidence, often very *raison d'être*, was founded on superiority over others internally and externally.' Nielsen, 'Muslims in Europe in the Late Twentieth Century' in Y. Yazbeck Haddad and W. Z Haddad (eds), *Christian–Muslim Encounters* (University Press of Florida, 1995), 323–4.

14. S. Waxman, 'France and the veil', written for the *Washington Post* and reprinted in *The Age,* 11 January 1995, 16.

8 German Foreign Policy and European Security

CHRISTOPHER BARRETT

Introduction

Germany is in all senses a new European power: it is a new country, in a new Europe, with new power. The addition to the Federal Republic of Germany (FRG) of the five Eastern *Länder* has created a new country, leaving the old FRG looking very much like the temporary state its Basic Law conceived it as. For at least the life of the Berlin Wall (1961–1989), the old Germanies (with the occasional exception[1]) neatly identified their national interests, and hence their foreign policies, with the prevailing security interests of each state's alliance leadership.[2] Thus, with the end of the Cold War, the united German state faced a dual identity crisis in foreign policy. Even once membership of the North Atlantic Treaty Organisation (NATO) had been secured, Germany not only had to face the evaporation of NATO's mission along with all the other alliance members, but also the prospect of having to articulate an independent national interest within this alliance structure.

The task of developing a new foreign policy framework has been accompanied by what might be termed the 'return of history'—a way of thinking which regards the division of Europe during the Cold War as an interlude in world history, the demise of which again ushers in an old era. Under this scenario, the European continent returns to an epoch which has remained hermetically sealed, characterised by multipolarity and 'traditional European' power politics. At its most sober, this view depends on a realist ordering of international relations and predicts a more assertive role for Germany as a new power in Europe. Opposing schools of thought counsel calm, casting Germany as the model citizen of a new Europe built up on political and economic interdependencies. Bound into these strong interrelationships, Germany would find it virtually impossible to manipulate an independent foreign policy and assert new strength within Europe.

The experience of German foreign policy since unification confounds both of these predictions. Germany is widely accepted as a major force behind European integration, in particular during the Maastricht summit in 1991,

135

pressing for a Common Foreign and Security Policy (CFSP) and faster progress on Economic and Monetary Union (EMU). But Germany has not always been the model European citizen. The process of unification itself was accompanied by complaints from many of Germany's neighbours at being sidelined during negotiations. Germany drew criticism for its refusal to assume combat duties during the Gulf War of 1991, and exhibited uncharacteristic stubbornness in forcing the diplomatic recognition of Croatia and Slovenia through a reluctant European Community (EC) in late 1991.

Germany and schizophrenia

I would like to digress briefly to illustrate an important perceptional issue for analysts of German politics and society. In the minds of most foreigners, Germany appears somewhat schizophrenic, dominated by two contradictory cultural constellations: the efficiency, obedience and precision of the 'Prussian' tradition and the cheery, provincial *gemütlichkeit* of 'Bavaria'. Those who know Germany and have studied German history will recognise these as simplistic cultural stereotypes. Nevertheless, with its strong regional histories, Germany seems more prone to this type of external perception confusion than many other states.

What Germany's regional histories do for its cultural persona(e), its political history does for its profile in international politics. A similarly schizophrenic image arises of two states—one perennially trapped by dint of its geography and size into geopolitical aggression born of insecurity, and the other the star pupil of the post-war school of capitalist liberal democracy and model European.

The need for a framework

Any analysis of German foreign policy since unification requires an explicit theoretical framework which avoids this sharply drawn dichotomy of two Germanies, accommodating the conflicting experiences of German foreign policy since unification, without diagnosing schizophrenia or subterfuge. For this, I choose an approach which analyses Germany's foreign policy as the product of the interacting spheres of domestic and international politics, paying attention to the institutions and traditions of the former and the European context of the latter.

The choice of the two-level game

In his article 'Diplomacy and Domestic Politics: the logic of two-level games', Robert Putnam likens international politics to a game played between the two levels of international and domestic politics. Briefly stated, each state is represented by a 'chief negotiator', who is answerable to a domestic constituency comprised of a coalition of societal interest groups. He or she sits at a bargaining table with other chief negotiators to hammer out a tentative agreement. But this is only a partial equilibrium—the agreement must then pass to the second level at which it must be ratified by the domestic constituency.[3]

In reality, the process will not usually be sequential, as the positions of players at both levels will be hypothesised, expected, feared or hoped for by their opposite numbers. As an example, German representatives would be very foolish to enter negotiations over agricultural subsidies in the EU without a clear appreciation of France's likely bargaining preferences. Likewise, French farmers will want to have their lobbyists stationed in Paris and Brussels well in advance of the meeting, with mountains of highly perishable produce and a strong view as to the German position. The politicking begins well before the negotiations.

The eventual agreement must represent the common ground of all participating nations. To arrive at this analytically, we can define a set of agreements at the international level which will be guaranteed ratification at the domestic level (known as a 'win-set') for each of the participant countries.[4] We can then predict that the eventual agreement at the international level will be bounded by the overlap of the win-sets of each player, the size of which will be determined by the interplay of the competing domestic coalitions.

There are two important implications of this approach. First, the interaction of interests at each level will determine at which level the outcomes will *de facto* be decided. That is to say, an issue which provokes an apathetic response from domestic constituencies will tend to be determined predominantly at the international level; conversely, an issue which provokes high passions among domestic constituencies will tend to leave very little latitude for agreement at the international level.[5]

Second, the two levels are interdependent on many issues: 'On occasion...clever players will spot a move on one board that will trigger realignments on other boards, enabling them to achieve otherwise unattainable objectives'.[6] These are the 'side-payments', 'sweeteners' or 'sops', paid to marginal supporters, be they in the chief negotiator's own constituency or that of his or her opponent. An example is the concessions exempting small vehicles from emissions standards used as a side payment to secure French and Italian assent to stricter EC emissions limits in 1988.[7]

The approach is intuitively appealing to any who have read or heard accounts of processes of inter-state bargaining, but it is also compelling from a dynamic point of view, as it can incorporate the European or multilateral dimension so important to German politics since the Second World War. The European

Union context provides both the background and the limits to the practice of German foreign policy. Timothy Garton Ash has rightly pointed out that the division of Germany forced its leaders to make the division of Europe their business. The multilateral, ostentatiously European thrust of West German foreign policy was always crafted to overcome the division of Europe, that is: the division of Germany.[8]

The theoretical divides

The two-game approach has the advantage of combining what are traditionally partial equilibrium analyses of the international political process, by theorising the link between domestic agenda setting and bargaining at the international level. In this next section, I aim to establish *prima facie* appropriateness for the two-game approach by discussing the theoretical divides in international relations with reference to Germany as an international actor. This discussion aims to illuminate the shortcomings of the analyses which have accounted for the majority of opinions offered on the true complexion of German foreign policy since 1990. These have been partial approaches in that they concentrate on interactions at the international level, supposing that the domestic politics of interacting nations pass each other like ships in the night in the conduct of international politics. They tend to universalise their respective views. Germany can only be innately aggressive or benign. My argument, then, is that the international context will subject the nation state to certain pressures, on one occasion suggesting aggression, on another reticence. But the position a state adopts in its foreign policy will be modified by the domestic context.

I begin by outlining a view of European security, and Germany's place within it, which relies explicitly on a realist view of world politics—and hence a classic international-level hypothesis.

Realism and multipolarity

John Mearsheimer's article 'Back to the Future: instability in Europe after the Cold War'[9] is one of the most frequently cited works of post-Cold War security theory. It is a lucid exposition of a realist approach to the future of international relations on the European continent. Mearsheimer begins by offering an explanation of the long peace[10] after 1945, which has three elements. First, the distribution of power was bipolar, between the US and the USSR and between each of these countries' allies. Second, there was an approximate equality of military power between the opposing sides. And finally, both possessed a large arsenal of nuclear weapons.[11] Briefly stated, bipolarity is a particularly stable form of international political system: only one relationship between states, or 'dyad', is important for world security, and hence imbalances of power are easier to perceive, predict and avert.[12] Familiarity actually breeds safety: 'Bipolarity meant that the same two states remained adversaries for a long period, giving them time to learn how to manage their conflict without war'.[13] A balance of military power between the two adversaries was part of the internal dynamic which kept the system 'conflict-free', the other part being nuclear deterrence. Nuclear deterrence—or, more accurately, the doctrine of mutually assured destruction (MAD)—is described as a key contributor to a peaceful Europe. MAD ensures security by guaranteeing high costs for any aggressor; its design logic is the safeguarding of a second-strike capability for your adversary. It also has the advantage of making equality of firepower much easier—warheads must not be equal in number, they must simply be sufficient for reciprocal destruction and safe from attack.[14]

Against this theoretical background, Mearsheimer presents three scenarios for the future European security landscape. The first poses a nuclear-free Europe (i.e. Britain, France and the former USSR disarm) which would see Germany and the USSR (hereafter supplanted with 'Russia' to bring this article up to date) as the major powers, separated by the 'small, frightened' states of eastern Europe but with no nuclear deterrent and a multitude of potential conflict dyads.[15] The second scenario sees the current nuclear ownership pattern persisting and hence a nuclear-free zone in central Europe, but nuclear powers on the western and eastern flanks. This is presented as an intolerable situation for Germany, which on the one hand will want military power commensurate with its economic standing *vis-à-vis* Britain and France, and on the other will face onto an eastern Europe 'safe for conventional war' with a powerful Russia beyond. Looking eastwards, this scenario is seen to guarantee an incentive for military expansionism with attendant (hyper)nationalism and conflict.[16] The third scenario is the typical post-Cold War nightmare, namely mismanaged nuclear proliferation.

The policy recommendation stemming from these scenarios is to strive for a limited, managed nuclear proliferation which would see Germany become a nuclear power, but no other new nuclear states in Europe.[17] Only a nuclear Germany would lock in a balance of power, which could otherwise become unacceptably fluid, as it recognises the new Federal Republic as the ascending political power in the new Europe and provides it with a military bearing to suit its economic strength. In fact, Mearsheimer is pessimistic about the chances of this development as he sees a natural tendency for existing powers to resist proliferation and a concomitant tension between limiting proliferation and managing it well.[18]

'Back to the Future…' was published in 1990. We can therefore perform a preliminary evaluation of the thesis looking back from the late 1990s. This shows us that the nuclear vacuum in central Europe looks likely to remain for the foreseeable future. Mearsheimer's theory would hold that Germany would be pushing towards acquiring nuclear weapons to bring itself up to par with its West European neighbours and balance itself against the nuclear power(s) in the East. Clearly this is not the case. The consistent concerns of Germany since reunification have been to rule out acquiring nuclear weapons, to push for further European integration, establish and strengthen security institutions to safeguard a common European security and enter into 'good neighbour' treaties with the countries to the east, even working as an advocate for these countries and their membership of NATO and the European Union. Whilst it will doubtless take some time to evaluate the changes wrought by the dissolution of the Warsaw Treaty Organisation and implications for European security, Germany does not seem to be following the Mearsheimer path. I see his theoretical approach as being to blame for this, and in the following sections I offer alternative readings of the security environment.

The liberalist opposition

As even the most reluctant student of international relations will know, there is a vast (albeit disparate) body of theory opposing the realist paradigm, which can loosely be termed the liberal or neo-liberal approach to international relations. The broad thrust of the liberal approach I wish to set against the realist account theorises agency in international relations with reference to the processes by which interests of individual human beings are aggregated and translated into foreign policy positions. It offers a criticism of the realist view of the nation state as the primary actor in world politics—it is a journey to the centre of the realist billiard ball. This reformulation of agency has wide-ranging implications for our understanding of national interest. Focusing to begin with on a commercial/institutional subset of liberal critiques, I contend that there are powerful domestic interest coalitions which define the German national interest differently from the self-help prescriptions of states under anarchy. In short, I ask why Germany's domestic political actors should want to wager their economic prosperity for a more assertive foreign policy profile.

A brief survey of the German economy will help to sharpen the question: Germany's absolute economic gains from the post-war economic order in Europe have been impressive: it retains the highest export penetration of all EU countries, has won the export 'world-champions' title several times over the last ten years, and its trade in 1989 with eastern Europe (excepting the USSR) was four times that of Italy, the runner-up.[19]

The ideological centrepiece of the European Union, free trade, is also particularly important for Germany, as its economy relies on a continuous supply of cheap raw materials as well as markets for the high quality finished products these become. While Germany essentially ceded political leadership of the EU to France from the beginning, its own influence has been quiet, strong, and growing: Germany's recognised position as the major contributor to the European budget is more than offset by the large trade surpluses it enjoys, particularly when compared to the trade deficits of France, Italy and the UK.[20] In any case, the EU budget represents only one percent of EU GNP, and the structural funds, which provide the development incentive for poorer nations of the EU, comprise only 15% of the budget.[21] From this perspective, the legendary German largesse appears much more like looking after number one.

It is thus incontrovertible that there is a need to incorporate the process of domestic agenda setting within the formulation of foreign policy, as these interests are clearly implicated and could well have a significant impact on the policy position.

The sovereignty critique

Moving on to discuss further assumptions of realism, Germany is seriously misrepresented by a 'unitary rational actor' approach to policy formation, which conceives of the state as having a single set of well-defined security interests, independent of other domestic influences. Germany's political system as established by the Basic Law of 1949 and the institutional design of the allies occupying the Western zones is best described as 'decentralised federalism'—a set of domestic arrangements and institutions which distributed political power amongst parties, ministries, *Länder*, and a Federal Constitutional Court in much the same way as the allies carved up the country to disperse the power of the Third Reich.[22] The combination of these, admittedly not unique, political institutions with a culture of compromise now entrenched in German politics (right up to the logical extreme of a left/right Grand Coalition) provides the special domestic context of German foreign policy.

The institutional arrangements of decentralised federalism represent a proclivity for self-containment which virtually makes Germany less than a traditional nation state, with substantially autonomous ministries, powerful *Länder* representation via the *Bundesrat*, the prevalence of two-party coalitions in government and a strong constitutional court.[23] It is this internal structure which exposes the weakness of the argument that states manipulate a unified foreign policy in such a manner as to guarantee power gains relative to their neighbours. On many foreign policy issues, the federal government can assemble no such unified stance. The ministries can declare themselves of an independent mind on a policy issue, the *Länder* can act against the Centre, the coalition partners in Government can (and do) refuse to play along.

The 'new security' critique

Finally, realism is often criticised for an inability to theorise the processes of domestic interest aggregation and the constraints and opportunities these processes present for international bargaining. Particularly in the case of EU member states, a case can be made for the steadily increasing role of domestic factors in shaping foreign policy. A recent volume, *Identity, Migration and the New Security Agenda in Europe*, offers a fascinating recasting of the notions of sovereignty and security in the new Europe.[24] The contention is that as the countries of the EU move towards further integration, more and more state sovereignty is ceded to supranational institutions of the Union. Accordingly, many of the traditional functions of the state begin to disappear, changing the relationship between society (by which is meant clusters of political interest traditionally subordinate to the state apparatus and constituted by ethnicity, shared history, culture, religion, regional identity, etc.) and state.[25] The traditional nation state may no longer be the best guarantee of societal interest—leading to a breakdown in the society/ state nexus itself:

> One result [of integration] is that societies are more exposed. Cultural peculiarities long defended by states now come under pressure from the homogenisation and standardisation required for a single market.[26]

For the first time, the security requirements of societies become divergent in some ways from those of their state, with the result that societies feel compelled to assert themselves as foreign policy actors. The new security agenda is thus increasingly shaped by factors which threaten the 'we' identity of a society. The most striking example is of course the revival of ethnic nationalism in contemporary post-communist countries, for which the former Yugoslavia is an all-too familiar model. It should not be assumed that affluent Western European states are immune—it can be argued that the Silesian minorities within the Bavarian Christian Social Union (CSU) effectively blocked the recognition of the Oder-Neisse line as Poland's western frontier for many years. I will also argue that ethnic Croatians in Germany played some role in the recognition of Croatia and Slovenia that provoked such strong criticism of Bonn's foreign policy in late 1991.

The phenomenon of societal security has still larger relevance when one considers the impact of international capitalism in general and the European Union in particular. Maintaining a competitive edge within the international (or European) marketplace demands rapid and often highly disruptive societal adjustment to changes in scale economics and technology in the name of global competitiveness. The increasing mobility of capital across state boundaries and the increasingly free-trading world economy dramatically constrain the ability of individual states to protect uncompetitive industries. Where societal security depends on the maintenance of jobs, high incomes, traditional industries and patterns of employment, the traditional nation state apparatus can no longer deliver for its societal constituents.[27]

The outcome of this process is indeterminate at this point. What it does speak for is an increasing 'patterning' of international relations by domestic (societal) interactions. This is already evident in current European policy: the perceived threat to societal security of waves of migration from the East has already prompted new asylum laws in Germany and intensified debate within the EU generally on immigration. It is then not too large a step to see German aid payments to the East as new security policy in action.

Foreign policy analysis

The preceding analysis is an attempt to ground irreconcilable views of German foreign policy in the theoretical shortcomings of popular approaches to international relations, with the important caveat that much of it is specific to the strange creature that is the EU. It begins with a criticism of the blind spots in realist prescriptions for European security. One liberalist approach leads us to question the hold of anarchy over the environment of international relations in Europe. The sovereignty critique questions the extent to which Germany in particular can assemble and promote a unified foreign policy stance to the world. The new security critique continues in the same vein to suggest that foreign policy in any case will increasingly be patterned by domestic politics.

It is argued here that this makes a theoretical case for a two-game model which incorporates domestic politics and agenda formation as well as the international context in analysing and understanding foreign policy. As in the above analysis, this claim is made with particular reference to Germany. It remains now to test the predictions of a two-game model against some of the best-known examples of German foreign policy since unification—namely, the process of unification itself after November 1989; the unilateral recognition of Croatia and Slovenia in late 1991; and the more recent debate over military intervention in Bosnia. The aim is to explain these instances as a result of interacting domestic and international forces without resort to a stereotyped image of Germany on the world stage.

Case Study 1: German Unification—a clear set of domestic preferences

The negotiations over German unification in the wake of the breaching of the Berlin Wall were a first example of a more internationally assertive Germany. The process offered the spectacle of an independent Germany on the world stage, accompanied by the loud complaints and dire predictions of neighbours and partners alike. The analysis offered here interprets unification as a two-level game in which a strong and narrowly-focused domestic constituency captured the initiative in the bargaining process, which was then secured at the international level by means of selective bargaining and the judicious employment of side-payments.

A period of coyness (or shell-shock) followed the events of November 1989, and no formal view of the likelihood of unification was put abroad by senior Government ministers, who had clearly decided not to upset Germany's neighbours with hasty talk about unification. This lasted until 28 November, when Chancellor Helmut Kohl issued his famous ten-point plan upon an unsuspecting world, Bundestag and even foreign ministry.[28] Kohl had clearly realised that unification policy would be a major issue for the election, due within twelve months, and saw that his constituency for this election was likely to include East Germany.[29] In terms of its contents, the plan was a cautious document, providing for a loose confederation of the two states and couched in terms of a plan for 'overcoming the division of Germany and Europe'. In terms of its form, it was never likely to be uncontroversial and drew criticism from Britain and France for the lack of an 'eleventh point' addressing the fears of Germany's partners and neighbours.[30]

From this point onwards, unification proceeded with the domestic game in the vanguard, the pace and internal decisions dictated by developments in the East, with one eye on the all-German elections some time in 1990. The international aspects (alliance membership, security and trade arrangements) were negotiated in ways which would satisfy the domestic pressures; latitude was available only where the interests of domestic constituents were not clearly defined. Furthermore, the international game was characterised by very limited participation. Much of the substance was worked out in effect bilaterally with Moscow in a series of meetings, the first between Kohl and Gorbachev in February 1990. This can be seen in the fact that the major outcome of the 'two plus four' meetings, apart from German unification itself, was the Stavropol treaty between Germany and the USSR.[31] I will argue that Germany's alliance partners (particularly the EU) played the role of ratifying and accommodating the various *faits accomplis* emerging from the main game. The major exception to this was the united Germany's membership of NATO. This was secured after some extensive side-payments to the USSR in the form of troop reductions, economic aid and Germany agreeing to stay out of any NATO attack on the USSR.

The rapid political, economic and institutional collapse of the East German state, accompanied by an influx of East Germans into the FRG, forced the pace of negotiations at both levels. The East German populace was quite literally voting with its feet. If one adds to this the key issues among the West German political élite of wanting a relatively strong West German economy, a prevailing belief in the value of 'shock therapy', and the fear of developments in the USSR, there was not only no brake on the pace of unification, but also little room left for compromise at the international level.[32]

In this context, the European Community (EC) played the role of creating a framework for accommodating the unification timetable and structure so as to avoid a German *'Sonderweg'*.[33] At that time, final decision-making within the EC rested with the representatives of the member governments on the European Council. Any important decision was thus an intergovernmental bargain between national governments.[34] This convention did not seem to apply to the EC role in the process of German unification. In fact, there was particularly close coordination of most steps between the FRG government and the European Commission, particularly between Chancellor Kohl and President Delors.[35] In the final analysis, it was the Delors strategy which pushed the debate on unification through the Commission and the Council with remarkable speed, cutting off objections and delivering EC assent to unification despite complaints about the lack of consultation and the avoidance of the Polish border issue.[36] It is not hard to appreciate that if one manages to limit the number of seats at the table (from eleven to one),[37] one also limits the possibilities for dissent. The process was also forced, whether deliberately or not, by the FRG government. First, the Treaty on German Economic, Monetary and Social Union (GEMSU) was set for July 1990 after the victory of the *Allianz für Deutschland* in the East German elections, without any consultation with the EC even though it would be significantly affected.[38] Second, the decision to bring the date of German unification forward from January 1991 to the October 1990 placed an unworkable deadline on the EC's ratification procedure. This led to the Parliament, Commission and Council establishing a cooperative arrangement to approve a package of legislation to comply with unification in time.[39]

There were two processes at work here. At the international level, the number of participants was limited by the consultative arrangement with the Commission, and in the absence of a clear, unified opposition to unification at the international level, the agenda and timetable set at the domestic level by the developments in East Germany carried the negotiations. In the face of what opposition was presented (and this was not very strong), it was easy for the Germans to say: 'We would like to be able to negotiate terms with you, but our hands are tied'. Given that their hands effectively were tied, there was nothing for it but to accept this and exploit whatever bargaining strength remained. However, intractable as domestic conditions were, they were also unique. Another case offers a more complex subject for analysis.

Case study 2: Croatia & Slovenia—intervening variables

For much of 1991, German policy on Yugoslavia was firmly in line with both EC and US policy, that is, the aim was to keep Yugoslavia intact.[40] Despite this, there was a certain degree of ambivalence, at least in Europe, to the anti-recognition stance: Italy was known to be in favour of recognition of Slovenia and Croatia, and most of the EC states favoured eventual recognition, but hoped to make this part of an overall peace settlement in the Balkans.[41] It is worth sketching in the background to the conditions which made Germany a special case. Half a million Croats live in Germany, who had formed an effective lobby group at both Federal and *Länder* level after many months of the Yugoslav conflict. Millions of Germans had visited Croatia and Slovenia as tourist destinations and had enduring sympathy for their ambitions, while the governing Christian Democratic Union (CDU) had some natural affinity with these predominantly Christian republics. The FRG was also concerned to rid former East Germany of communist influence. Bonn did not want a successful campaign by the Serbian communists to embolden communists in the new *Länder*. Finally, Germany felt compelled to take a more assertive international role after criticism of its reticence during the Gulf War.[42]

All this contributed to the more rapid hardening in Germany of a general view across the continent that the Yugoslav conflict represented a threat to European security for which the Serbs were seen as primarily to blame. The coup in the USSR had made the dissolution of Yugoslavia seem inevitable and there was a fear that allowing the Serbs to profit from their aggression would encourage territorial aggression amongst other ethnic groups within eastern Europe and the Commonwealth of Independent States (CIS).[43] The *Bundestag* led the Foreign Minister in the backflip, confronting him at a meeting of the *Bundestag* Foreign Affairs Committee in July 1991: 'According to eye-witnesses, he [Genscher] went into the meeting a cautious diplomat, and came out dancing to the recognition tune'.[44]

Not long after, Germany promised to recognise Slovenia and Croatia by Christmas, and following a report by a leading legal expert, the German Cabinet voted in favour of recognition on 11 December. This was a critical move, as it solidified the German bargaining position before discussions with the EC began in earnest. Not surprisingly, this was a major shock to the EC and was followed up by some extensive German lobbying, eventually securing a change in EC policy. Even that hardened observer of German political life, *Der Spiegel*, registered some surprise at the new assertiveness this represented:

> The Brussels compromise—a delayed, but synchronised recognition—helps both the surprised EC partners, pushed into catch-up mode by the Germans, and the Kohl/Genscher government. There is nothing the Germans fear more than foreign policy isolation. To avoid this, the foreign minister has pulled off an unprecedented diplomatic campaign.[45]

The *Spiegel* account has Hans-Dietrich Genscher in a whirl of telephone conversations with his colleagues in Paris, London, Rome, Copenhagen, Vienna, Brussels and Washington, plus a number of missives directed at then UN Secretary-General Pérez de Cuéllar in an effort to rally support for the German initiative which was facing a Franco–British counter-resolution in the UN Security Council.[46] Genscher even contacted the group of Third World countries who at the time had voting rights on the Security Council. These efforts were apparently enough to push the anti-German resolution off the agenda. French support was then secured from Foreign Minister Roland Dumas with the argument that France should hardly be allowing the US (who had actively supported the Franco–British resolution) to direct European peace initiatives via the UN.[47] Germany extended recognition on 23 December, true to its word, but delayed the exchange of ambassadors until 15 January when the EC finally granted recognition.[48]

It is difficult to assemble a theoretical explanation for this event simply from the interactions at just the international or domestic level. The two-game model shows that it was a combination of the broad, if not amenable, win-sets of the other EC member-states at the international level and the hardened, tight bargaining agenda of the Germans which saw their policy carry the day. Nevertheless, this is a less than straightforward two-level game situation—there are some important intervening variables. First, without the unilateral promise by Germany to realise the agenda of its domestic constituency, artificially narrowing the German win-set, the issue could have suffered the same fate as the rest of EC policy on Yugoslavia, that is to be passed around and around, with no definitive action taken. Second, this enabled Germany to go some way towards overcoming criticism of its international reticence during the Gulf War, but importantly via diplomatic, not military activism. Germany could be seen to take some action in the crisis, but was unlikely to have to make a military contribution, due to its 'difficult' past in the region. Or, as William Horsley says:

> Germany chose to make what was described as its first active diplomatic intervention since World War Two in an area where it could not take responsibility if things went wrong. [49]

This would seem to make this an attractive issue on which to speak out—at the very least, the effect of this decision on the development of the war was always going to be indeterminate, however strong Genscher's claims were at the time.[50]

Third, the German action was being run on several different fronts, virtually encircling the realm of foreign policy in Bonn and forcing the government's hand: by early summer 1991, a number of *Länder* governments had invited Franjo Tudjman to visit as if he were a head of state,[51] and many *Bundestag* members, feeling the pressure from the Croatian lobby, were bringing that to bear in the Foreign Affairs Committee. These factors combined to short-circuit policy-making, producing a hasty action which unsettled many elsewhere in the EC. Horsley sees this as symptomatic of German foreign policy processes:

> As one FDP member of the *Bundestag's* foreign affairs committee told me informally, 'In a way our politics are too democratic: when all the parties combine to demand a certain policy, ministers have no choice but to go along.' If German 'democracy' represents no more than the sum-total of the popular mood, it is hard to imagine other countries accepting Germany as a 'reliable bridge' between eastern and western Europe.[52]

This view is suggesting that German foreign policy is too easily taken hostage by domestic interest groups, and indeed there is significant evidence in the recognition case to support this. From the analytical examples I have presented here, I will move on to discuss the implications of a two-level framework for the future of German foreign policy.

The Two-Level Game and German policy

The principal objective of this chapter is to propose an approach to the study of German foreign policy within the framework of the European Union. I have then put this approach to the admittedly not particularly searching test of its fit with an example of new German foreign policy. This section seeks to draw some general behavioural predictions which follow from the approach thus established, offering a further case study in support of the conclusions. This task must be undertaken cautiously—it is no exaggeration to say that the theoretical ground covered so lightly in the first half of this chapter is the site of considerable intellectual dispute.[53] Furthermore, generalisation from testing against two practical examples is statistical charlatanry of the highest order. All that said, I offer the following necessarily brief comments as a basis for further analysis and a structurally determined hypothesis of the future foreign policy behaviour of a unified Germany.

To highlight the influence of domestic German politics, it is worth reviewing William Horsley's analysis of what he terms the three 'fault lines' running through the realm of German foreign policy, which he believes make for unpredictable, hasty policy. First, *Länder* governments have substantial power via the *Bundesrat* and can virtually run their own foreign policy—as was the case with the invitations to Tudjman. Second, ministries enjoy substantial autonomy without any requirement for Cabinet solidarity or the announcement of important policies to the *Bundestag* before implementation.[54] Finally, there is some rivalry between the three coalition partners in Government, occasionally splitting policy along party lines. Increasingly in recent years, as a negotiated consensus at Cabinet level has become harder to achieve, political decisions have been left to the *Fraktionen* or party caucuses of the three parties in government, making the parties' parliamentary leaders as important as Cabinet Ministers.[55]

Horsley's conclusion is pessimistic—he sees these structural factors conspiring to produce clumsy, extreme policy positions as competing viewpoints struggle to lock up the agenda. I suggest instead that this stems from the fluidity of foreign policy protocols in a government which had, at the time of these initiatives, little experience in crafting independent foreign policy. In many ways, the foreign policy mantle was there for any number of players to seize. The complexity of the new security agenda requires the development of a culture of contestation and compromise amongst domestic opinion leaders which one could not have expected to appear overnight. In addition to this, it requires the development of review processes and protocols to subject competing policy options to the disciplines of long term practicality. Both the culture and the protocols misfired in the recognition case above, but did so under the pressure of virtual domestic unanimity. In the case of unification, it was barely resistible. In the recognition case it was barely resisted—I suggest because of Germany's desire to be seen to 'do something'. However, the absence of further major foreign policy controversies since the recognition issue suggests that a more appropriate foreign policy culture and appropriate protocols may be emerging. An example will help to illustrate this point.

Case Study 3: AWACs in Bosnia - Checks and Balances

The debate over the deployment of German armed forces in NATO 'out of area' missions came to a head in April 1993, with the Free Democratic Party (FDP) referring the issue of German Airborne Warning and Control (AWAC) missions over Bosnia to the Federal Constitutional Court. This was the culmination of a battle between the partners in the ruling coalition, with Helmut Kohl's CDU and their Bavarian colleagues, the CSU, of the opinion that AWACs could be sent by Cabinet decision. This position was challenged by the opposition Social Democratic Party (SPD), which refuted any military role for Germany outside United Nations peacekeeping missions. The FDP, the minor partner in the governing coalition, adopted the position of requiring a change in the Basic Law (in effect, the German constitution) to allow such missions. Failing to find satisfaction within the Cabinet, as the CDU/CSU rejected any alteration to the Basic Law, the FDP referred the issue to the Constitutional Court, claiming a violation of their rights by their larger coalition partner. In its judgement, the Court upheld the right of the Cabinet to preside over such deployment decisions, providing majority support could be secured from the Bundestag. Nevertheless, the issue highlights the inability of the Chancellor's party, which most view as 'the Government', to effect a change in policy; this is due to the opposition of its minor coalition party, which, furthermore, has the means to enforce its view as it occupies the office of Foreign Minister under a long-standing coalition deal. Helmut Kohl has bemoaned this state of affairs on more than one occasion:

> What kind of politics is it when the Chancellor makes a decision only to see it laid before the Federal Constitutional Court, with no-one sure what the outcome will be. Such a government isn't even a serious executive power—how can we justify this kind of adventurism?[56]

Structures of international politics and Germany

If the support processes in the foreign policy realm are strengthening, I believe there are grounds for revisiting Horsley's pessimistic conclusions regarding the influence of German domestic political institutions on foreign policy. Where Horsley sees successive rigidities as an inevitable result of the decentralised federalism which distributes power among ministries, *Länder* and *Fraktionen*, I would argue that once appropriate political habits have begun to develop (as I suggest the AWACs example illustrates), the need to satisfy these many and diverse groups means that the policy position worked out in the domestic German game will tend to be broader and more inclusive of dissenting views than those emanating from countries with less compromising arrangements. This broader agenda of German negotiators should increase the possibilities for agreement at the international level, at the same time offering Germany considerably less bargaining power.[57] There are many examples of this, with Germany occupying an intermediate (and mediating) position between 'wideners' and 'deepeners' in the EU and between Atlanticists and Europeanists in defence and security policy.

In addition, the structure of the game at the international level militates against German unilateralism. Germany has a long-standing and widely recognised practice of exercising foreign policy via the institutions of the EU. The political structure of the EU is therefore a major defining influence on the structure of the international game for the Federal Republic's foreign policy. As mentioned before, side-payments are crucially important to European inter-state bargaining. These ensure that bargaining strength tends to accrue to those with smaller win-sets and hence possibly less corporatist domestic arrangements.[58] Second, the EU is a managed form of bargaining insofar as the voting rules in the Councils reinforce the power of smaller states (most clearly in the case of unanimous voting on major CFSP issues) relative to the larger states such as Germany.[59] This tends to militate against an overriding German influence on the EU (and hence international politics) from the top down.

Conclusion

The concern of this chapter has been to incorporate ideas of an evolving European security agenda into the analysis of German foreign policy. The two-level framework tries to steer a course between the cynicism and idealism which arise from an imperfect understanding of the policy environment. The picture of Germany which emerges is that of a 'structurally good European'—a view relying explicitly upon a theoretical construct which aims to be pragmatic, dynamic and an accurate reflection of contemporary political practice in the region.

Notes

1. The most notable being West Germany's *Ostpolitik* beginning under the Chancellorship of Willy Brandt. However, for all that *Ostpolitik* represented a change in West German foreign policy, this was unquestionably more a change in emphasis than any kind of definitive break with the Western alliance. The West German commitment to NATO was never seriously questioned.
2. J. Sperling, 'German Security Policy and the Future European Security Order', in M. Huelshoff, A. Markovits and S. Reich (eds), *From Bundesrepublik to Deutschland: German Politics after Unification* (Ann Arbor: University of Michigan Press, 1993), 324.
3. R. Putnam, 'Diplomacy and Domestic Politics: the Logic of Two-Level Games', in P. Evans, H. Jacobson and R. Putnam (eds), *Double-edged Diplomacy: International Bargaining and Domestic Politics* (Berkeley: University of California Press, 1993), 438.
4. *Ibid.*, 439.
5. *Ibid.*, 440.

6.　*Ibid.*, 437.
7.　M. Huelshoff, 'Germany and European Integration: Understanding the Relationship', in Huelshoff *et al.*, *op. cit.*, 310.
8.　T. G. Ash, *In Europe's Name: Germany and the Divided Continent* (Vintage, 1994), 14–15.
9.　J. Mearsheimer, 'Back to the Future: Instability in Europe after the Cold War', *International Security*, 15 (1), 1990, 5-56.
10.　In this context, Mearsheimer is presumably defining 'conflict' as a direct engagement of the two superpowers, which was always averted. Conflicts peripheral to the main dyad were a constant feature of the system.
11.　*Ibid.*, 6.
12.　*Ibid.*, 14.
13.　*Ibid.*, 27.
14.　*Ibid.*, 20.
15.　*Ibid.*, 32.
16.　*Ibid.*, 36.
17.　*Ibid.*, 38.
18.　*Ibid.*, 39.
19.　A. Markovits and S. Reich, 'Should Europe fear the Germans?' in Huelshoff *et al.*, *op. cit.*, 283.
20.　*Ibid.*, 278.
21.　T. Hueglin, 'Grossdeutschland in Europe: Planned or Unplanned Effects of the German Anschluss on Hegemonic Leadership in the European Community', in W. Graf (ed.), *The Internationalisation of the German Political Economy: Evolution of a Hegemonic Project* (New York: St. Martin's Press, 1992), 292.
22.　Markovits & Reich, *loc. cit.*, 273.
23.　Huelshoff, *loc. cit.*, 308-9.
24.　O. Waever, B. Buzan, M. Kelstrup and P. LeMaitre (eds), *Identity, Migration and the New Security Agenda in Europe* (London: Pinter, 1993).
25.　*Ibid.*, 2.
26.　*Ibid.*
27.　B. Buzan, 'Societal Security, State Security and Internationalisation', in *ibid.*, 51-3.
28.　B. Lippert and R. Stevens-Ströhmann (eds), *German Unification & EC Integration: German and British Perspectives* (London: Pinter, 1993), 11.
29.　The election was due by the end of 1990. At a minimum, it was reasonable to assume that the East German populace would be a *'de facto'* voice in even an exclusively West German election. Although it is difficult to conjecture what the outcome of a West German election would have been, the subsequent popular rejection of Lafontaine's more cautious approach suggests that Kohl was wise to recognise an 'eastern constituency' as an important part of the vote, East or West.
30.　Lippert & Stevens-Ströhmann, *op. cit.*, 11.
31.　W. Smyser, 'USSR-Germany: a Link Restored', *Foreign Policy*, 84, 1991, 128.
32.　Lippert & Stevens-Ströhmann, *op. cit.*, 31.
33.　*Ibid.*
34.　A. Falke, 'An Unwelcome Enlargement? The European Community and German Unification' in M. D. Hancock and H. Welsh (eds), *German Unification* (Boulder,CO: Westview, 1994), 171.
35.　*Ibid.*, 185.
36.　*Ibid.*, 172.
37.　Or three. France and the UK were involved separately in the two-plus-four talks.
38.　Lippert & Stevens-Ströhmann, *op. cit.*, 24.
39.　*Ibid.*, 30. This reflected the internal German politics as well; only one month was allowed

for the *Bundestag* and *Bundesrat* to debate GEMSU, with the result that many of the committees formed to investigate the ramifications were disbanded.

40. H. Müller, 'German Foreign Policy after Unification', in P. Stares (ed.), *The New Germany and the New Europe* (Washington DC: Brookings Institution, 1992), 150.
41. S. Kinzer, 'Europe, Backing Germans, Accepts Yugoslav Breakup', *New York Times*, 16 January 1992, 10.
42. Müller, *loc. cit.,* 153–4.
43. *Ibid.,* 150–3.
44. W. Horsley, 'United Germany's Seven Cardinal Sins: A Critique of German Foreign Policy', *Millennium*, 21 (2), 1992, 239.
45. Ein grosser Erfolg für uns', *Der Spiegel*, 52, 1991, 18–20. Author's translation.
46. *Ibid.*
47. *Ibid.*
48. Müller, *loc. cit.*, 152.
49. Horsley, *loc. cit.*, 238.
50. And they were very strong claims indeed, as Genscher is reported in *The Guardian*: 'He maintained that recognition...had led to a 'rethink' in the leadership of the Yugoslav federal army. There were indications that the current ceasefire would continue to hold, he said', cf. A. Tomforde, 'Genscher is triumphant', *The Guardian*, 16 January 1992, 16.
51. Horsley, *loc. cit.*, 239.
52. *Ibid.*
53. For a good summary, see R. Keohane (ed.) *Neorealism and its critics* (New York: Columbia University Press, 1986).
54. *Ibid.,* 227.
55. *Ibid.,* 228.
56. 'Bis an die Schmerzgrenze', *Der Spiegel*, 15, 1993, 22. Author's translation.
57. Huelshoff, *loc. cit.*, 308.
58. *Ibid.,* 310.
59. M. Huelshoff, 'Domestic Politics and Dynamic Issue Linkage: a Reformulation of Integration Theory', *International Studies Quarterly*, 38, 1994, 269.

9 Reinventing Neutrality – the Case of Austria, Finland and Sweden and the European Union

CHRISTINE AGIUS*

Introduction

Membership of the European Union (EU) has entailed a shift in the neutral policies of Austria, Finland and Sweden. This chapter explores the accession negotiations and the breakdown of neutrality in the context of the Common Foreign and Security Policy (CFSP). The 'reworking' of neutrality is mostly regarded as a product of the end of the Cold War, and scant focus is given to the EU's role in this change in policy. The EU's conceptualisation of neutrality had the effect of 'problematising' what had hitherto been the key tenet of the security policies of these countries. This, in many ways, marginalises the contribution that neutrality can afford to a post-Cold War security environment.

The Common Foreign and Security Policy

Political integration has been part of the goal of the European Community (EC) since its inception. The founders of the European Coal and Steel Community's (ECSC) major priority was to create an organisation that would prevent a repeat of the Second World War. Amongst the plans for economic integration, which was seen to be the key to recovery and interdependent prosperity, the idea behind the Community was firmly based on the assumption that if countries (member states) were interlinked strongly enough, war would be highly improbable. This interdependence was primarily economic, but was also assumed to be political.[1]

The question of formulating a common foreign and security policy has remained a problematic issue, hitting a raw nerve with conceptions of state sovereignty. The security and defence aspects of such plans are especially sensitive. Member states were unwilling, at such an early stage in the experiment of the European Community, to pool their security and defence policies and resources under a supranational banner. Surrendering these areas of 'high politics'[2] to supranational control has been equated with a loss of sovereignty. Attempts to meld together the various foreign and security policies of the member states have generally met with failure in the past. Plans for political integration were shelved or watered-down just as soon as they were to be initiated. Examples of this are scattered throughout the EC's history—the failed plan for a European Defence Community, the Fouchet Plan, and the Tindemans Report, to name a few.[3]

It was not until the Hague Summit of 1969 that the construction of political cooperation actually began with the introduction of the European Political Cooperation (EPC) procedure. This new configuration reduced political cooperation to a form palatable to the member states, with no compromise of sovereignty. It was highly intergovernmental[4] in structure, and did not commit the member states to coordinating common decisions or actions. EPC was essentially a forum for consultation and 'harmonisation' of foreign policies. Decisions were not binding. Member states may have agreed in principle about a certain issue, but acted differently on a national level.[5] Despite being a formidable economic power, the EC lacked a parallel political power or presence. Not only were the member states unwilling to act cohesively, but the infrastructure to produce harmonised responses and united action was missing.[6] EPC was generally employed for issuing declarations and communiqués regarding international political events. The Maastricht Summit in 1991 was an attempt to rectify this problem.

The Maastricht Treaty on European Union opened up a new chapter for foreign and security policy coordination, a step away from the largely ineffective EPC. Its most important aim was to establish not only deeper political cooperation but also to return to the long-delayed goal of common security and defence. Yet the divide between supranationalism and intergovernmentalism has persisted, even with the recent revisions under the Amsterdam Treaty (1997).

During the Maastricht negotiations, idealistic or federalist-oriented initiatives advanced by the more supranationally-inclined states (such as Luxembourg, Belgium and Italy) were watered down into a plan which was more widely acceptable. Initial proposals saw the CFSP integrated into the EC structure. As national interests took hold, these plans gave way to a different, more intergovernmental rendering. It is the structure of the CFSP that is most problematic, with its 'pillar' configuration dislodging it from the supranational circle of the EC-proper.[7] This is evidenced in the decision-making structures of the CFSP, which remain on an intergovernmental basis, and the designation of the Western European Union (WEU, a separate body from the EU) as the 'defence arm' of the CFSP. This ensured that foreign policy did not escape the competences of the nation state nor encroach upon sovereignty.

The recent Amsterdam Treaty does little to redress this issue; rather, it reaffirms the role of the European Council (again, not an EU institution) as the agenda-setter. The Amsterdam Treaty does update the CFSP to include cooperation in the field of armaments, and the inclusion of the Petersburg tasks (covering humanitarian tasks, rescue tasks, peacekeeping and peacemaking, and crisis management). It also calls for the establishment of a policy planning and early warning unit, and the integration of the WEU into the EU. Yet the decision-making process remains the same, so that the hard questions of deeper cooperation remain untouched.[8] Progress towards the goal of common defence rests entirely with the member states. With no timetable prescribed for this latter eventuality, 'high politics' does not leave the control of the member states, and decision-making rests on intergovernmental foundations.

The Amsterdam Treaty does little to bridge the gap between inter-governmentalism and supranational input into CFSP decision-making. The structure of the CFSP gives licence to exclude the active participation of the Commission and the European Parliament (EP), which have been relegated to minor roles in this area. The EP's position in the CFSP remains the same— there is only a requirement to consult the EP, take its views into consideration, and for it to be regularly informed. The Commission is still to be fully associated with the work of the CFSP, which in reality means that the 'guardian of the treaties' has no right of initiative.[9]

However, the separation of the CFSP pillar from the EC-proper reveals some further discrepancies. For instance, the funding that will support CFSP actions (apart from operations that have military or defence implications) is decided by the European Parliament. This is problematic, since one institution decides action, but another controls the purse strings. The intergovernmental separation established in the Treaties sees a different set of rules and procedures existing between the various institutions.[10]

Advocates of the CFSP draw on the differences from EPC. Common positions on foreign and security matters are now legally binding. Yet it is the European Council that sets the guidelines for action. The Council of Ministers, the locus of decision-making in the EU and largely intergovernmental, determines the scope of that action. The CFSP has been constructed in such a manner as to allow little avenue for input by the more supranational institutions and the EU citizens. The aims and direction of CFSP remain vague. Article J.1 of the Treaty establishes the objectives of the CFSP, which are:

* to safeguard the common values, fundamental interests and independence of the Union;

* to strengthen the security of the Union and its Member States in all ways;

* to develop and consolidate democracy and the rule of law, and respect for human rights and fundamental freedoms.[11]

The *common values* and *fundamental interests* remain undefined by the EU. An examination of past performance in reaching common decisions places in doubt the ability of fifteen member states (or more with future enlargements) to improve on the EPC record. Questions of how a European defence force should be deployed, and under what circumstances, remain unanswered. On a practical level, the issue of an armaments agency to control and facilitate the machinery of collective security and defence remains a sensitive topic. Control over defence policies and industries have always been the domain of the nation state. Due to national control over this area, defence industries in Europe are stratified, and negotiations for achieving this objective are still proceeding. There also exists the problem of the disparity in such an industry between the member states, with a mixture of two nuclear powers, four neutral countries, and varying levels of capability and involvement in organisations such as the WEU and NATO. The absence of a coordinated armaments agency for such an ambitious project as the CFSP and European integration is a major flaw.

The precise meaning of *strengthening the security* of the EU is rather unclear in a post-Cold War Europe. The East-West conflict or ideological cleavage which characterised the bipolar system has disappeared, and along with it, an identifiable enemy. A military solution is now no longer effective against new security concerns such as immigration, drug trafficking, economic and environmental problems, to name a few. Given the proliferation of these new security concerns, it may be more difficult to find consensus on such issues between the member states. With respect to consolidating democracy, the rule of law, and humanitarian issues, once again this may cause contention, depending on the various interpretations of these objectives by the member states. It also allows the EU to proceed according to its own definition of democracy and human rights in relation to the continent and the international community.

In terms of neutrality, it appears that the inconsistencies of the CFSP may work in favour of maintaining a neutral policy as an EU member state. However, this was not proven to be the case with relation to the accession negotiations of Austria, Finland and Sweden. The question of neutrality proved to be the most difficult hurdle during the negotiations, as the EU exerted its influence on the aspiring applicants.

The neutral element and the accession negotiations

The accession negotiations that led up to the membership of Austria, Finland and Sweden saw a number of shifts in the three countries' economic policies,[12] as was to be expected with accession. However, in the course of negotiations, it was neutrality that came under the most pressure. The factors leading to the shift in this policy appear to be linked to a large degree with the issue of EU membership, backed up by justifications of the end of bipolarity.

The central concern focuses on the applicability of the *acquis communautaire*,[13] the body of rules and regulations constituting the EU that existing and acceding countries must adopt and abide by. In terms of the CFSP, it is expected that member states participate in its implementation fully, and not act as an obstacle to its development. During the accession negotiations, it was suspected that neutrality would impede plans for foreign and security policy integration. It was through use of the *acquis* that the EU was able to sway the policies of the aspiring member states. Since there is little compromise on the *acquis*, countries must adapt their foreign policies to the prescribed one set by the Union. Given the above illustration of the problems already encountered in formulating a harmonised foreign and security policy, it is curious that the EU, being a largely unformed body itself, is able to 'prescribe' a European foreign policy. This is not to suggest that the EU is solely responsible for this change in policy direction. It merely points to its role as an influential agent in this redefinition.

It is in this context that the shift in neutrality will now be examined. The neutrality of the three states in question evolved from different circumstances, particular to their specific history and relations with the international community. Briefly, Austrian neutrality came about as a condition of its post-war status and its inclusion in its State Treaty (1955). Swedish neutrality—or 'non-participation in alliances in peacetime, with a view to neutrality in the event of war'—has existed for approximately 180 years, but is not mentioned in its constitution nor enshrined in international treaties. Finnish neutrality was based largely on its proximity to and relationship with the former USSR; although the Treaty of Friendship, Cooperation and Mutual Assistance (TFCMA) was annulled in January 1992, Finland still adheres to neutrality. Neutrality in these countries has always entailed independent defence and non-participation in alliances of a military nature. Neutrality has a different foundation in each, be it legal, endogenous, or in agreement with other nations. Hence, the three cases cannot be treated in an identical manner. However, a common thread can be discerned regarding the changes in neutrality in each of these countries.

One of the common threads of neutrality between these three countries has been the political independence and identity that neutrality afforded. Until the late 1980s, membership of the EC was not an option, as it would have compromised the credibility of neutrality. Simply, 'credible neutrality' refers to a neutral country being able to convince any potential aggressors that an attack would be fruitless.[14] Strong defence is a vital aspect of credible neutrality. However, connected to this concept is a careful consideration of how the neutral country conducts its relations with other states, and membership of the EU would have jeopardised a credible neutrality policy. There was also a lack of confidence in the EC to deal with security and defence issues. This was still the duty of the state, or of established organisations such as the United Nations (UN) or the Conference on Security and Cooperation in Europe (CSCE).[15] The notion of allowing a supranational body to manage these areas was unpopular, both in government and public circles. Neutrality still enjoyed confidence as a means of dealing with defence and security issues.

This was the position of former Swedish Prime Minister Ingvar Carlsson in 1990, when he stated that '...concern for the credibility of our policy of neutrality is the reason why we are not applying for EC membership'. He also set the parameters for involvement with the EC in the same year by stating that if the EU chose an ambitious path of coordinating foreign and defence policy, then membership would be 'impossible' for Sweden.[16]

Austria also excluded membership as a national goal because of its status as a permanently neutral country. Hanspeter Neuhold notes that Austrian neutrality is deeply tied up with the nation's autonomy. Although it was 'the political price Austria had to pay to the Soviet Union for the latter's willingness to conclude the Austrian State Treaty',[17] it ensured the reinstatement of national sovereignty and allowed it to form its own national defence. Membership of the EC was not an issue in this context.

Finland did not pursue membership because of its relationship with Russia. The TFCMA (1948) with the former USSR not only ensured that Finland would remain neutral (in case of perceived threats to Russian territory via Finland), but was also influential in Finnish relations with the outside world.[18] Hence, in all three countries, neutrality was associated with notions of state sovereignty and of their role in the region. The European Free Trade Agreement (EFTA) provided access to markets, but foreign policy was determined within national boundaries.

Nonetheless, while EFTA and the European Economic Area (EEA) permitted access to EC markets and trade arrangements, there was little input into the decision-making process. Also, the 1992 Single Market project of the Community was forging ahead and the neutrals were concerned about the prospect of economic isolation. As economic interdependence grew, it seemed logical that membership should become an option, at least from a trade and economic perspective. Political parties and commerce groups began to push the issue of membership. Austria formally applied for membership in 1989, followed by Sweden in 1991 and Finland in 1992. At this stage, it was expected that neutrality could remain intact. The EU, on the other hand, suspected that neutrality would cause some problems for 'the Community's likely future development, and the wider European situation'.[19]

The reinterpretation of neutrality

It was during the accession negotiations that neutrality came under the spotlight as a 'hurdle' for the neutral states to jump. Soon enough, each applicant state began to 'learn' the mistakes of the other in the EU game: Austria learnt an early lesson when it mentioned neutrality in its application for membership, along with the firm commitment to keep it unchanged.[20] The backlash that accompanied this in the EU saw Finland and Sweden downplay neutrality as a major issue in their applications for membership. The urgency of membership was crucial from an economic point of view. This was not lost on Carlsson, although he still considered neutrality as the best way to secure 'peace, freedom and independence for our country, our democratic social order, and the right to shape our future in accordance with our own values'.[21] Finland, despite being more open to a broader interpretation for neutrality since the end of the Cold War, still preferred to maintain it due to uncertainties with the former USSR.[22] Austria tried to make amends by offering neutrality as 'an asset in a new, favourable situation of broad cooperation between East and West'.[23] Despite this, the EU was still dissatisfied. Although keen for them to accede (given that they are rich countries with good democratic traditions—perfect candidates, in fact), the EU could only conceive of neutrality as problematic for the CFSP. Concern that a 'neutral bloc' (the three, plus Ireland) would halt decision-making on foreign and security policy was one of the major issues during the accession debates.[24] As 'inclusion' became more desirable than 'exclusion', the applicant states tried to bend their foreign policies towards the preferred EU position. Gradually, between application and membership, neutrality developed 'into a different political animal'.[25]

In November 1992, the Austrian Parliament called on the government to ensure that Austria involved itself in the development of a European collective security network. This was supported by the President and the Foreign Minister, and the objectives of the CFSP were accepted in principle.[26] Austria also did not wish to appear to be problematic with regard to the CFSP, and began to relax its line of argument, announcing that it would act as an observer state in the WEU. While concern was raised in public circles, Foreign Ministry officials attempted to ease the apprehension by stating that the CFSP was a mere 'political declaration.' Chancellor Vranitzsky likened the CFSP to an idea or concept without flesh and bones.[27]

In September 1991, Carl Bildt's Moderate coalition (comprising the Liberals, the Centre Party, and the Christian Democrats) won office in Sweden from the Social Democrats. Bildt embarked on a different path with his 'New Start' package, which set out to restore economic growth, revise the welfare system and, most noticeably, negotiate membership with the EU. Bildt aligned Sweden with a European vision and made it clear that Sweden's interests were tied closely to that of the Union. In the UN, Sweden withdrew from the Group of 21 neutral and non-aligned countries and began voting more in line with European interests.[28] Bildt's speech to the Riksdag in January 1992 confirmed the 'hard core' of neutrality by his comments that: 'Sweden is not defended by anyone else...and Swedish defence is for Sweden only'.[29] However, Bildt's attempt to set Sweden on the path of 'normalisation', as Peter Lawler claims, saw a marked change in the discourse on neutrality. A less weighted term came into use, that of 'non-participation in military alliances during peacetime, with a view to neutrality during war'.[30]

Mouritzen makes an interesting point with reference to the realignment with Europe, linking the decline of the Nordic model (of which Sweden was considered the leader) with this redefinition of neutrality, claiming that the leader has 'now joined the EU class as a student'.[31] Rather than Nordic independence, Bildt was turning towards the EU as the new forum for Nordic security concerns. Bildt's coalition government established new guidelines that pledged an active contribution to foreign policy decisions made in the EU, and support of the CFSP, although participation in the WEU was at this stage still out of the question. In 1993, however, a more permissive approach was adopted, when the then Foreign Minister, Margaretha af Ugglas, announced Sweden's acceptance of a role for the WEU in peacekeeping. The realignment with Europe was not limited just to Sweden; in Austria, there was much talk about 're-entering' mainstream Europe, and Finland looked to the EU for security, given the uncertainties in the former USSR.

Finland had fewer problems given the foundation of its neutrality. With the dissolution of the TFCMA, which signified years of 'Finlandisation', membership of the EU could now be pursued, and Finland had the opportunity to have a political voice internationally. Neutrality was still being upheld. Although seeking independence, Finland had to temper this desire with uncertainty over its unstable neighbour.[32] Also, there was still a preference for established institutions deciding the course of action. Foreign Minister Pertii Paasio found the idea of the EU as director of foreign and security interests rather daunting: 'If they were decided by the Community itself, particularly in a situation of crisis, then that might pose certain difficulties for us'.[33] Yet in 1993, Finland accepted the provisions of the CFSP and 'closed the chapter' on this issue.[34]

Despite wanting to keep neutrality intact, the compromise was clear: there should be an acceptance of the goals of the CFSP. Otherwise membership was not tenable, as the *acquis* would have been compromised. The EU wanted more than a rhetorical commitment from the neutrals to prove that they were interested in developing the CFSP. The compromise that resulted was an agreement to act as observer states in the WEU upon membership. This was at first problematic, as it was seen to compromise credible neutrality. But membership was the objective, and this was recognised, even at the local level. The mayor of Vienna, Helmut Zilk, a member of the Social Democratic Party (which has strong reservations about Western security organisations) recently declared that in the long-term, 'there is no way around the WEU' and that Austrian neutrality cannot be maintained in its present sense.[35] Sweden was more obstinate and cautious about such involvement; it held grave reservations about the contents of Article Five of the WEU Treaty, which stipulates that if one member state is attacked, then others will come to its assistance. Upon membership, however, all three became observer states in the WEU. Finland was less troubled by this move given its security concerns but was still cautious about the EU playing a major role in such decisions.

Although willing to participate, the neutrals were only comfortable with the WEU limiting its scope to the Petersburg tasks for the time being. There is still a strong predilection for a wider approach to security, embracing the OSCE, the UN and the Council of Europe. At the time of membership, the issue of security was rather unclear, and there was concern that the CFSP was based on an old security agenda that did not seem to fit in with the realities of a post-Cold War Europe. The neutrals recognised that a new response to threats was required. The Finnish–Swedish Memorandum on security and defence in crisis management in April 1996 offered a conceptual framework which advocated crisis management and peacekeeping activities (the Petersburg tasks), but also requested that all states have an equal footing in decision-making and that territorial defence should remain with NATO or the nation state.[36] Sweden and Finland have since become wary of the incorporation of the WEU into the EU, and prefer intergovernmentalism in the CFSP. Independence in foreign and security matters still plays an important part. Swedish Foreign Minister Lena Hjelm-Wallén reiterated that it was the right of a nation to '... make its security policy choices and to be respected for doing so. Sweden expects others to respect its policy of non-participation in military alliances.'[37] Finland also holds a similar position, preferring independent defence. Austria, on the other hand, will be reviewing its foreign and security policy in 1998, which, incidentally, will include examination of the possibility of full membership of the WEU.

There is little doubt that the neutrals are interested in contributing to the construction of a European security environment, and this is witnessed in their contributions to peacekeeping and conflict management on the international level. In line with the wider conception of security concerns, the three new member states have signed up for the Partnership for Peace (PFP) program of NATO, and have supported the Combined Joint Task Forces, which facilitates the strengthening of a European Security and Defence Identity.

Finland and Sweden were the first traditionally neutral countries to sign the PFP Framework Document, on 9 May 1994. Finland is involved in the North Atlantic Cooperation Council (NACC), and has been an observer in semi-annual NACC ministerials. The Finns regard the PFP as a stabilising plan, which allows nations to develop cooperative security at their own pace.[38] Austria participates in the NACC's *ad hoc* group on peacekeeping. Austria also cooperates with the OSCE and the UN, in terms of peacekeeping operations, preventative diplomacy, the peaceful settlement of disputes, and crisis management.[39]

Their record in terms of contributions to UN peacekeeping forces is also impressive. Austria has made substantial contributions to peacekeeping missions in the former Yugoslavia through the NATO-led IFOR Implementation Force and the SFOR Stabilization Force, not to mention taking in refugees.[40] Sweden has contributed to UNPROFOR, IFOR, and SFOR in Bosnia. Between 1993 and 1995, Sweden contributed approximately 5000 soldiers to UNPROFOR, and has committed 3000 to the NATO-led IFOR for 1996–7 and SFOR for 1997–8. In terms of PFP, Sweden is to participate in twelve field and staff exercises in 1997—doubling its figure from 1996—and will be hosting three of these on Swedish soil. In cooperation with NATO initiatives, Sweden is also working on interoperability studies in terms of air navigation aids and communications equipment. Sweden has also contributed over 1.5 billion kronor in humanitarian and reconstruction assistance to former Yugoslavia.[41]

At the same time, these countries do not want to join a military alliance. Neutrality has kept them out of wars and has still allowed them to contribute to peace efforts and mediation, not only within Europe, but also on the international level. The EU is still uneasy about neutrality, nonetheless. This, along with these countries' membership and inclusion into 'mainstream' Europe, has seen many academics and policy-makers begin to question the utility of neutrality in a post-Cold War Europe.

There has been an emphasis on collective security and the 'inevitable' involvement with the CFSP. The debate surrounding neutrality in academic and political circles is centred upon the end of the East–West conflict as a pretext for abandoning an 'obsolete' policy. New security risks are being identified, and these risks will have to be dealt with at a European level. Along with the general willingness to write off neutrality, those advocating its demise point out that in the Austrian case, it was a condition imposed on Austria in exchange for its autonomy.[42] Also, the collapse of the USSR allowed more foreign policy options, more discussion about neutrality and the 1955 State Treaty.[43] This has been mirrored in Finland. Some former advocates of Finnish neutrality are now critical of it. Max Jakobson, former Finnish diplomat and staunch defender of neutralism in the past, does not think that neutrality can fit in with the new security environment in Europe. Neutrality is an outdated symbol.[44] In terms of the impact of the *acquis communautaire*, Finland began participating enthusiastically in the WEU and PFP, and many are interpreting this as an expression of independence from its former relationship with Russia. Finland now has a voice in international affairs, but this is under the banner of the EU. Sweden is still careful not to abandon too much of its established policy. The new position in foreign policy is reflected among members of the political elite, who explain the changes in the context of the altered political and security environment.[45] The current Social Democratic government of Göran Persson is still wary of the sensitivity of neutrality amongst the Swedes, as neutrality is tied up very strongly with Swedish identity.

It is clear that the EU has not been the only influence on this shift in foreign policy—factors such as the end of the Cold War and the collapse of the Soviet Union also play an important role. With Austria, Finland and Sweden, discussion about the end of the Cold War has been a convenient way of assisting the shift in foreign policy. The influence of the EU as an actor in this change is rarely mentioned in the debate over the changing status of neutrality. There is a growing trend to move away from neutrality, as though it were a stain on the reputations of these countries and their ability to participate as 'good Europeans'. The ability of the Union to exert influence on a third country's foreign policy via its use of the *acquis* and through the accession criteria and negotiations established requires some attention.

The European Union: an 'agent' of change?

Although the changed political and security environment has been identified as the primary source of the shift in neutrality, the impact of European integration and the EU is one variable rarely considered. In the late 1980s, McSweeney commented that neutral states were already accommodating the EC through the EFTA connection, and correctly predicted at the time that 'the increasing trend since 1945 to link international trade with security issues of a political and, even, military nature was forcing the Neutrals into a compromising position in regard to their legal or quasi-legal status of neutrality'.[46] It appears that the economic connection to the Community did indeed spill over to the political when membership was considered by the three neutrals.

It is important at this point to unpack the idea of the possibility of the EU as an influential element in this change. During the accession negotiations, the Commission exerted some influence in its 'Opinion' of the applicants. This is an important part of the process of accession, as it is the Opinion of the Commission which determines whether an applicant country can proceed towards negotiations for membership or not. Austria, being the first to enter into negotiations, bore the brunt of the criticism. The Commission regarded the maintenance of neutrality as a 'specific problem' that the EU had not previously encountered. Non-participation in military alliances and the legal nature of Austrian neutrality were obstacles to the evolution of the CFSP. Neutrality was linked to the EU's commercial policy as well, especially in terms of economic sanctions under Article 113 of the EEC Treaty. The Commission pointed out almost grudgingly that the imposition of similar sanctions would not be an issue for Austria, should they be sanctioned by the UN. By referring to Austria's preference for established international organisations deciding such measures as an 'exception', the EU cast aspersions on the credibility of Austrian neutrality. The Commission also indicated (in a footnote) that failure to comply with Article 113 infringes not only Treaty obligations, but also the free movement of goods.[47] The *acquis* would therefore be jeopardised. In the realm of decision-making, the Commission demanded 'legal certainty', or a guarantee that Austria would not impede the development of political union.

The Commission was more tolerant with Sweden and Finland. The reason for this appears to be the lack of legal basis for neutrality in these countries. What was most noticeable about the Commission's opinion of Finnish and Swedish neutrality was how it linked the changes in the former Soviet Union and in Central and Eastern Europe to the shifting consensus on neutrality. The EU regarded Finnish neutrality as a result of its geopolitical position; while accurate, this was overplayed, since it implied that it was the only basis for Finnish neutrality and ignored, for instance, Finland's contribution to mediation during the Cold War. The Commission did criticise Finland's unwillingness to enter into military alliances and its 'restrictive view' of the capabilities of the WEU.[48] Swedish neutrality was discussed in terms of its involvement in international and regional organisations. But, once again, neutrality was examined in terms of the transformations within Europe and 'problematised'. The Commission did recognise that convincing Sweden to redefine neutrality to the form it preferred would be a difficult task, and warned against Sweden's 'unwillingness and inability to fulfill the obligations arising out of the European Union's external policies in the broadest sense'.[49]

The Commission's recommendations for Austria were quite blunt. It was suggested that Austria redefine its neutral status, as the alternative was for the EU to redefine its Treaty stipulations. It was also made clear that derogations would not be acceptable. As mentioned previously, the defence that neutrality would contribute to peace and international security was inadmissible to the Commission.[50] With Sweden and Finland, the EU would seek 'specific and binding measures' to ensure that neutrality would not create an obstacle to the development of the CFSP. The Commission was less exacting, as the lack of legal base of their neutrality made it simpler to assume a reinterpretation would be easier to achieve.

The three newcomers assumed, however, that as member states they would have a voice in the Union that would enable them to safeguard their neutral status. Unlike the economic connection, now the neutrals had access to the decision-making arena. Under the CFSP, Article J.7 of the Amsterdam Treaty (formerly J.4 of the Maastricht Treaty) stipulates that the CFSP will not '...prejudice the specific character of the security and defence policy of certain Member States'. However, this clause relates specifically to a member state's obligations to NATO and other bilateral arrangements. The growing intolerance within the EU for 'opt-out' clauses, the strength of the *acquis*, and the legal implications of joint decisions and actions leave little room for escape routes. The House of Lords Select Committee on Enlargement in 1992–3 made this point rather clear, stating that there should be 'no footnotes or reservations' for the CFSP.[51] With the path set, deviation from this vision of political unity was not welcome. The 1996–7 Intergovernmental Conference (IGC) raised the possibility of a 'consensus-bar-one' rule in voting, which allows a member state to disassociate itself from a common action; but the rule does not permit the member state to prevent it, as a veto does.[52] For the time being, this rule is still being considered by the Intergovernmental Conference.

Fitting into the EU model does have implications for national sovereignty over foreign policy, and the EU's unwillingness to accommodate different approaches is problematic. Joenniemi succinctly comments that: 'The Community therefore has set the tone in the confrontation, with the neutrals pragmatically coming into line and intensifying their ties with the Community. The prevailing logic has been dictated by the EC, and it is increasingly being adopted by the neutrals'.[53] The neutrals have found themselves caught up not only in the changing security environment, but also the web of integration that is the driving force of the EU. Their ability to maintain their own position has been hampered by the methods and rules of the power brokers and the environment. Walter Carlsnaes notes that adaptation to this setting has the effect of limiting the ability of the neutrals to act independently, their roles and expectations becoming 'prescribed'.[54]

The new political and security environment has created a number of dilemmas both for the EU and its member states. Smith's conception of the emerging international order illustrates this paradox. Considering the issue of 'impact' with reference to the changes in Europe, Smith describes the problems of tension between the whole and the parts. In this context, the 'whole' refers to the European Union; the 'parts', the neutrals. The tension experienced by the two groups relates to the vision of the Union and the altered security environment, and methods of operating within it. Another salient feature is the 'learning capacity' imposed by the changes, as seen in the case of the neutrals in their path to membership of the EU, 'learning' to play the 'good European' and fitting into the mould cast. In connection with this, Smith observes the 'adaptive capacity' of state authorities, in this instance, the EU adapting through its CFSP to the new international setting. It is the 'carrying capacity', however, which raises questions of the ability of the Union to bear the burden of change and act within the altered environment.[55] If one is to examine the unwillingness of the EU to accommodate certain foreign policy perspectives, this places in doubt the ability of the EU to act as a viable 'security guarantor'. A curious paradox emerges: the EU seems to have the ability to influence other states, but its CFSP remains relatively underdeveloped, its ambition broad but largely undefined. Yet neutrality remains difficult to accommodate.

To begin to explain this situation, one may look to the integration project of the EU. Political union has been a long-standing objective and an integral part of the process of integration. The economic success of the EU has achieved the goal of post-war reconstruction, but political integration, intended to insure against war between the member states, was also connected to this ambition. The neutrals do bring a novel perspective into the formula, with their unwillingness to enter military alliances and differing approach to conflict and intervention. This, nonetheless, interferes with the 'vision' of European Union, which cannot claim to be complete without a political element.

In conclusion, the question here is not necessarily one of surrendering neutrality in exchange for EU membership—more to the point, the concern is that membership became a way to induce the neutrals to come more into line with the prevailing perceptions of security and defence held by the EU at the time, even though its own mechanisms for constituting a foreign and security policy remain incomplete. The relationship between the EU and the applicant countries can be viewed in terms of power—the EU held the final word on the acceptability of these states. The shift in neutrality touched not only the discourse of foreign policy but also the actions of the neutrals. The move from ruling out membership because of its incompatibility with neutrality to accommodating the EU position indicates this clearly. Therefore, the redefinition of neutrality needs to be considered from a perspective other than that of the end of the Cold War. This ties in with perceptions of security in a post-Cold War environment, which, despite bringing more themes onto the security agenda, still tend to focus on the dominant actors and their security interests and methods. Neutrality is often regarded, by the harshest of critics, as a policy of isolation or seen as 'free-riding'. Its inclusion in a security community is seen as disruptive, against the collective force, as witnessed during the Cold War era and the American position on the neutrals. Neutrality has mostly existed on the periphery of the security construct and, despite its playing a positive role, perceptions of neutrality have not changed over time. The EU has bought into this interpretation of neutrality, viewing it as an obstacle to security rather than a potentially helpful foreign policy option. In a post-Cold War Europe, there is still a place for neutrality, since more variables have entered the security agenda and a variety of responses are required. Neutrality does not have to be compromised in order to contribute to this.

Notes

*   I would like to thank Peter Lawler, Lucy James and Alan Atchison for their helpful comments on earlier drafts of this chapter. Any omissions or inaccuracies rest, of course, entirely with the author.

1.   The antecedent of this idea can be traced back to the writings of Altiero Spinelli and other authors of the plan for the EC. Post-war reconstruction was the primary goal, but attached to it was the long-term vision of political cooperation on a supranational level, in order to avoid the rise of nationalism in the future. See Stephen George, *Politics and Policy in the European Community* (Oxford: Oxford University Press, 1993); Derek Urwin, *The Community of Europe: A History of European Integration* (London: Longman, 1991).

2.   The term 'high politics' refers to those areas of national policy always considered to be the realm of the nation state, such as foreign and defence policy and specific levels of economic policy. These policy areas have generally been jealously guarded by the nation state and imply some level of autonomy and sovereignty.

3.   The first effort to harmonise the political agendas of the member states was in the early 1950s. The Pleven Plan, as it came to be known, envisaged a European army, to be managed by the member states. The submission prescribed an institutional structure that consisted of a Joint Defence Commission, a Council of Ministers, a Court of Justice, and an Assembly that was to act in an advisory manner. The Draft European Defence Community (EDC) Treaty was signed in 1952, but was quickly terminated. France's uneasiness at German rearmament and the idea of not having an independent military force led the French Assembly to reject the plan in 1954. In any case, the threat of the Korean War, which propelled the conception of an EDC, had diminished by this stage. The death of Stalin augmented the decision to drop the issue. The threat had receded. Ettiene Reuter, 'Foreign Affairs in the European Community', Monash University, Melbourne, 17 June 1993.

4.   The conflict between intergovernmentalism and supranationalism is one of the most divisive issues in the EU. Where 'supranationalism' refers to integration of policies and practices on a level higher than that of the nation state, 'intergovernmentalism' denotes a system of cooperation between national governments and bodies that does not infringe upon the sovereignty and autonomy of the nation state.

5.   Examples of this are constant throughout the history of the EPC procedure. In the 1980s, when sanctions were decided against Argentina following its invasion of the Falkland Islands, Denmark wanted the regulation to be implemented by national law, in order to

appear to have national control over this joint decision. When Nelson Mandela was released in 1990, Britain pre-empted the EC by announcing its intention to authorise new investments in South Africa before the matter came under debate within EPC. See B. Laffan, *Integration and Cooperation in Europe* (London: Routledge, 1992).

6.   A prime example of this is the EC's actions during the Gulf War, which prompted Belgian Foreign Minister at the time, Mark Eyskens, to comment that the EC was 'an economic giant, a political pygmy and a military larva'. The EC was able to give the impression of unity in the early stages of the conflict. It was quick to condemn Iraq and provide financial assistance to the operation; but when urged to go beyond this, there was a breakdown of cohesiveness. France refused to place its forces under US command, and attempted to secure its own peace deal with Iraq via secret diplomacy. Britain cooperated closely with the US, rather than with its European counterparts. Germany was unwilling and unable to act, under the provisions of its constitution. Belgium refused to sell ammunition to Britain. Although action taken against Iraq was not a European matter, the disarray revealed by the EC prompted criticism in the international community, particularly by the USA. These are a few of the incidents that saw the EPC process come undone. See Trevor Salmon, 'Testing Times for EPC: the Gulf and Yugoslavia 1990-1992', *International Affairs*, 68 (2), 1992.

7.   This is one of the most contentious debates surrounding the CFSP. During the Maastricht negotiations, various proposals for the CFSP were put forward. The more federally-inspired member states suggested having the Treaty structure as a 'tree', with the EC as the base, and branching off from that would be the CFSP, Justice and Home Affairs, and other policies. Instead, the intergovernmentalists won out with their version, which visualised a 'pillar' system, with the EC forming the foundation, but having the CFSP and Justice and Home Affairs as separate, but connected pillars. The difference is that the former version would have included these policy areas under the umbrella of the EC, whereas the latter makes a clear distinction between those policies that are to be supranational and those taken to be intergovernmental. See Douglas Hurd, 'Developing the CFSP', *International Affairs*, 70 (3), 1994. For an examination of the proposals during the Maastricht Summit, see F. Laursen and S. Vanhoonacker (eds), *The Intergovernmental Conference on Political Union* (Maastricht: European Institute of Public Administration, 1992).

8.   The Amsterdam Treaty's revised wording on one of the most defining clauses of the CFSP confirms the intergovernmental bias: 'The common foreign and security policy shall include all questions relating to the security of the Union, including the progressive framing of a common defence policy…which might lead to a common defence, should the European Council so decide'. This is more strongly worded than the Maastricht provision: 'The common foreign and security policy shall include all questions related to the security of the Union, including the eventual framing of a common defence policy, which might in time lead to a common defence'. See *The Draft Treaty of Amsterdam*, 17 June 1997, Article J7, Paragraph 1, and *The Maastricht Treaty on European Union*, 1992, Article J4.

9.   The Commission has been critical of the structure and voting arrangements in the CFSP. For a discussion on the position of the Commission on the CFSP, see Commission Report for the Reflection Group, *The Intergovernmental Conference 1996* (Brussels: OOPEC, 1995).

10.   *Ibid.*, p. 65. The division of competences also gives the EP a negative power in this regard. If it withholds resources, it is seen to be disruptive to the integration process. See also Article J18 of the Amsterdam Treaty.

11.   The Amsterdam Treaty kept the aims of the CFSP identical to Maastricht's stipulations.

12.   All three applicant countries had to adapt to the economic conditions of the EU. Although participation in EFTA had prepared their economies for accession, issues such as welfare provisions, environmental standards and agricultural policies had to undergo some revision.

For a detailed discussion, see Shigehisa Shibayama, 'Will the costs of greatest happiness pay off?', *Union Européenne*, 2, 1994; House of Lords, Session, First Report, Select Committee on the European Communities, *Enlargement of the Community*, 1992-3; CEC, 'The Challenge of Enlargement. Commission opinion on Austria's Application for Membership', *Bulletin of the European Communities*, Supplement 4/92; CEC, 'The Challenge of Enlargement. Commission opinion on Finland's Application for Membership', *Bulletin of the European Communities*, Supplement 6/92; CEC, 'The Challenge of Enlargement. Commission opinion on Sweden's Application for Membership', *Bulletin of the European Communities*, Supplement 5/92.

13. See Agence Europe, *European Commission Report on the Criteria and Conditions for Accession to the Community*, 1790, 3 July 1992. The prominence of the *acquis* in the accession negotiations came into force with the enlargement of Britain, Ireland and Denmark. The Hague Summit (1969) endorsed the *acquis* as the basis of accession negations. For a detailed account of EU enlargement, see Roger J. Goebel, 'The European Union grows: the constitutional impact of the accession of Austria, Finland and Sweden', *Fordham International Law Journal*, 18 (4), 1995.

14. See Bengt Sundelius, 'Changing Course: When Neutral Sweden Chose to Join the European Community' in W. Carlsnaes & S. Smith (eds), *European Foreign Policy: the EC and Changing Perspectives in Europe* (London: Sage, 1994).

15. Renamed the Organisation for Security and Cooperation in Europe (OSCE) in December 1994.

16. Quotation cited in Sundelius, *loc. cit.*, 179-80.

17. Hanspeter Neuhold, 'Security Challenges and Institutional Responses: An Austrian Perspective', *The International Spectator*, XXIX (3), 1994, 27.

18. Finland was persuaded to decline assistance from the Marshall Plan, due to Soviet concerns that it would turn to the West. Helsinki's attempts to become involved in Nordic security arrangements provoked negative reactions from Finland's eastern neighbour, which was troubled by the idea of a Scandinavian military structure linked to NATO. Finland did not join the Nordic Council, despite involvement with the drafting of its constitution. The Soviets also opposed Finland joining the Nordic Economic Cooperation project in 1970, as the latter was regarded by Moscow as dependent on the EEC. Finland was able to join EFTA in 1986 only because the former USSR's priorities regarding Finland had altered. See Efraim Karsh, 'Finland: Adaptation and Conflict', *International Affairs*, 62 (2), 1986.

19. House of Lords, *op. cit.*, 8.

20. CEC, 'Austria's Application for Membership. Commission Opinion', *SEC* (91), 1590 final, 1 August 1991, 6.

21. Ministry for Foreign Affairs, Press and Information Department, *Statement to the Riksdag by Prime Minister Ingvar Carlsson*, unofficial translation, 14 June 1991, 1.

22. There was a recognition, nevertheless, that neutrality was a condition of its relationship with Russia and '...never an end in itself but only a means of safeguarding...national existence and security' - see Ilkka Suominen, 'Finland, the EU and Russia', *The World Today*, 50 (1), 1994, 12.

23. Alois Mock, 'Austria in a changing Europe', *The World Today*, 46 (3), 1990, 37.

24. Britain, in fact, took up the issue of blocking minority votes with the 1995 enlargement, mostly out of fear that smaller states could outvote larger ones when combined. The implication of such a 'blocking minority' in foreign and security matters was not lost on other member states either. See Goebel, *loc. cit.*, 1123.

25. Nils Andrén in Pertti Joenniemi, 'Neutrality beyond the cold war', *Review of International Studies*, 19, 1993, 291.

26. See Neuhold, *loc. cit.*, 29. See also M. Sully, 'Austria: the end of an era', *The World Today*, 48 (8-9), 1992; and M. Sully, 'Austria: A Cultural Power?', *The World Today*, 50 (10), 1994, 186.

27. Lucy Walker & Nigel Dudley, 'The Austrians raise their EC game', *The European*, 8-10 February 1991.
28. Graeme D. Eddie, 'Sweden : Krona Crisis Stalls "New Start"', *The World Today*, 49 (1), 1993. Ulf Bjereld has written extensively on Sweden's voting patterns in the UN - see his 'Critic or Mediator? Sweden in World Politics, 1945-90', *Journal of Peace Research*, 32 (1), 1995; and 'Sweden's foreign policy after the end of the Cold War - from neutrality to freedom of action' in R. Lindahl and G. Sjöstedt (eds), *New Thinking in International Relations: Swedish Perspectives* (Stockholm: The Swedish Institute of International Affairs, 1995).
29. Krister Wahlbäck, 'Swedish Security in a Changing Europe', *Current Sweden*, 391, 1992, 1-2
30. Sven Svensson, 'Neutrality in question', *Sweden Report*, 3, 1991, 1; Peter Lawler, 'Scandinavian Exceptionalism and the European Union', *Journal of Common Market Studies*, 35 (4), 1997.
31. See Hans Mouritzen, 'The Nordic Model as a Foreign Policy instrument: its rise and fall', *Journal of Peace Research*, 32 (1), 1995. It is also interesting to note that there existed an expectation by the Swedish Ministry of Foreign Affairs that Nordic cooperation would continue in the EU - see Ministry of Foreign Affairs, Trade Department, *Sweden's Negotiations on Membership of the EU*, 7 April 1994, unofficial translation.
32. At a time when Finns had just begun to feel comfortable with the idea that membership would be a partial solution to their security problems, the 1993 Russian parliamentary elections saw concern grow because of Zhirinovsky's statements that Finland should be annexed as part of the Russian Federation. Not surprisingly, support for membership at this point was quite strong.
33. House of Lords, *op cit.*, 16.
34. Suominen, *loc. cit.*, 13.
35. Neuhold, *loc. cit.*, 32.
36. Clive Archer, 'Finland, Sweden, the IGC and Defence', *Briefing Paper No. 8*, International Security Information Service, January 1997; 'The IGC and the Security and Defence dimension towards an enhanced EU role in crisis management. Memorandum from Finland and Sweden', 25 April 1996; Tarja Halonen and Lena Hjelm-Wallén, 'Working for European Security outside the NATO Structure', *International Herald Tribune*, 15-16 March 1997.
37. Lena Hjelm-Wallén, *Common Security in the Post-Cold War Era - A Challenge for the Non-Aligned Nations in the EU* (Dublin: Institute of European Affairs, 1996), 3.
38. Finland has also been involved in NACC working groups, including the NACC *ad hoc* group on peacekeeping (now a PFP working group) and the NACC Pilot Study on Cross-Border Environmental Problems Emanating from Defence-Related Installations and Activities. Within the PFP framework, Finland is also interested in areas of search, rescue and humanitarian operations, and environmental protection. On this see Jaakko Blomberg, 'NATO reaches out: a view from Finland', *Recent Changes in Multilateral Security* (Seminar Papers)(Ireland: Institute of European Affairs, 1995), 2.
39. Neuhold, *loc. cit.*, 35. Austria also intensified its involvement in 1996 by finalising an Individual Partnership Programme which seeks to standardise and make interoperable some military and civilian units with those of the other PFP countries in the areas of peacekeeping, humanitarian missions, and search and rescue operations. Under this arrangement, Austria participated in ten military exercises, and has also participated in the PFP Planning and Review Process (PARP) which assesses the capacities of individual partner countries available within the framework of the PFP - see http://gov.austria-info.at/ForeignAffairs/index.html.
40. See *Jane's Defence Weekly*, 26 February 1997; http://gov.austria-info.at/ForeignAffairs/index.html.

41. See John D. Morocco, 'Sweden adapts to broader security role', *Aviation Week and Space Technology*, 8 July 1996; *Jane's Defence Weekly*, 8 January 1997; article by the Swedish Foreign Minister regarding the security changes in Europe, 14 July 1997, Ministry for Foreign Affairs Information, 'Sweden's contribution to the peace process in former Yugoslavia', *Factsheets,* 12, 1997, from http://www.ud.se/english/policy/factshts/no12.htm; Ministry for Foreign Affairs Information, 'The Euro-Atlantic Partnership Council and enhanced cooperation in the Partnership for Peace', *Factsheets*, 15, 1997, from http://www.ud.se/english/policy/factshts/no15.htm.

42. Although the political elite has moved towards a different interpretation of neutrality, Austrians still consider neutrality to be an important part of their political identity and autonomy. An exit poll conducted during the referendum for accession revealed that threats to neutrality and concerns about Austria joining a military alliance were the third most important reason for voters saying *'no'* to membership (15%). Those who were enthusiastic about the prospect of involvement in a European defence network ranked this as the fifth reason for voting 'yes' (13%). See Neuhold, *loc. cit*, 27-35.

43. The debate over the legitimacy of the Austrian State Treaty has drawn various opinions within the political parties. Generally, the FPÖ questions neutrality and wants the State Treaty abolished; the SPÖ and the Greens defend both; and the ÖVP holds the middle ground. For further discussion, see Neuhold, *ibid*.., and Wolfgang C. Müller, 'Austria', *European Journal of Political Research,* 22, 1992, 359.

44. Joenniemi, *loc. cit.*, 291.

45. Regarding the shifting policy line, a senior Swedish government official commented that: 'A radical new situation faces us with the end of the Cold War and the dismantling of the power blocs, prompting us to review our position. That is why the government has produced a new formulation of our foreign policy' - see Ian Mather, 'Sweden comes down off the fence', *The European*, 6-12 May 1994.

46. Bill McSweeney, 'The European Neutrals and the European Community', *Journal of Peace Research*, 25 (3), 1988, 206-7.

47. CEC, 'The challenge of enlargement. Commission's opinion on Austria's application for membership', *op. cit.*, 15-16.

48. CEC, 'The challenge of enlargement. Commission's opinion on Finland's application for membership', *op. cit.*, 21-3.

49. CEC, 'The challenge of enlargement. Commission's opinion on Sweden's application for membership', *op. cit.*, 18-19.

50. CEC, 'The challenge of enlargement. Commission's opinion on Austria's application for membership', *op. cit.*, 17.

51. House of Lords, *op. cit.*, 16-18.

52. European Parliament, Secretariat Working Party, Task-Force on the Intergovernmental Conference, 5, Briefing on the CFSP (Second Update), Luxembourg, 19 October 1995, 16.

53. Joenniemi, *loc. cit.*, 293.

54. Walter Carlsnaes, 'Are the EFTA Neutrals qua Neutrals Comparable?', paper presented at European Consortium for Political Research conference, Leiden, April 1993, 13.

55. Michael Smith, 'Beyond the stable state? Foreign policy challenges and opportunities in the new Europe' in Carlsnaes and Smith, *op. cit.*, 26.

Index